A Water Color Dream

A Water Color Dream
THE MANY LIVES OF
Irene Tsu

by Irene Tsu

Edited by Jim Martyka

With Special Interviews
by Pierre Patrick

BearManor Media
2020

A Water Color Dream: The Many Lives of Irene Tsu

© 2020 Irene Tsu

All rights reserved.

No portion of this publication may be reproduced, stored, and/or copied electronically (except for academic use as a source), nor transmitted in any form or by any means without the prior written permission of the publisher and/or author.

Published in the United States of America by:

BearManor Media
4700 Millenia Blvd.
Suite 175 PMB 90497
Orlando, FL 32839

bearmanormedia.com

Printed in the United States.

Editor: Jim Martyka

Typesetting and layout by John Teehan

ISBN—978-1-62933-562-9

ACKNOWLEDGMENTS

I WOULD LIKE TO THANK Aaron Rosenberg, Alfred Molina, Andrzej Bartkowiak, Arthur J. Wankel, Benjamin Ronning, Bette Midler, Betty Dorso, Bikram Choudhury, Brett Bayne, Bronislaw Kaper, Bruce Lee, Bunny Gibson, Carol Sneed, Chase Mellon, David Niven, Diahn McGrath, Dick Shawn, Don Murray, Ellen Chenoweth, Francis Albert Sinatra, Frank Chin, Frank Tashlin, Fred Ishimoto, Fred Segal, Freda Payne, Garrett Wang, George Takei, Glen Keane, Helen Chan Liu, Henry Koster, Henry Miller, Ivan Nagy, Jacqueline Dymant, Jeff Bridges, Jeffrey Z. B. Springer, Jeremy Kagan, Jim Martyka, John Ford, John Urie, John Wayne, Juliet Prowse, Kathy Garver, Ken Annakin, Linda Ho, Marie-Pierre Villemaire, Mario Machado, Michael Brisbane McCrary, Mikel Steven, Nancy Kwan, Natasha Ballesteros, Nick Hartanto, Pat Suzuki, Paul Mazursky, Peter H. S. Chan, Peter Mayer, Pierre Patrick, Razak Samad, Ric O'Barry, Robert Ito, Robert Whitney, Robert Wise, Roman Polanski, Sam Roden, Sandra Ng, Sharon Nixon Kelly, Sharon Tate, Shaun K. Chang, Stuart Hagmann, Tom Hormel, Tom Stempel, Toshiro Mifune, Vicky Samad, and Yvette Mimieux, along with Victor Z. M. Tsu, Dulcie Lin Tsu, Florence Tsu Phillips, and Yasmine Ananda Tsu.

And a very special acknowledgment to my dear friend Peter Mayer:

Peter, please watch me still. I'm taking my brush drenched in sienna, French blue, a little ocher, and perhaps a touch of hot pink, and putting down a bold stroke, moving it to form the shapes and let the water color do its own thing... I'm hoping it's a good read!

INTRODUCTION

ARTISTS WHO PAINT IN WATER COLOR are brave, adventurous, and willing to push themselves and their work as they boldly embrace the unknown. A water color artist starts with a vision, but from the moment they put that first stroke on the canvas, and with each stroke that follows, the vision will shift. Water color is a fluid art form that drips, runs, and moves. Intuition plays a great part in the execution of the water color. Through skill, time, and practice, artists are able to control the strokes better, but it will never be exact. Once the stroke is made, the artist must follow that new path and see where the next stroke will take them. Sometimes there is fear, but there is also freedom.

I have lived my life as a water color artist.

This book is my next stroke.

A Water Color Dream is a memoir of time, and faces and places. I have so many stories to share of experiences with some of the most interesting, famous, and beloved celebrities that I've met or worked with in my decades as an actress and successful entrepreneur in Hollywood. It's not that I purposely seek out famous people to connect with but for some reason it just happened; somehow the famous or talented (or both) were attracted to me as well. The experiences are true, but they may not always be in the precise chronological order. There is no past, present, or future in the Chinese language, only the experience. These recollections fuse reality and maybe just a little fantasy, blending both elements to describe the extraordinary life I have had the privilege of living.

I'll start by going through my childhood and the many challenges a young dreamer faced in growing up in the tumultuous Far East, the discipline of my father, and moving to New York, where my life as an artist really started. I'll show you how a combination of a dream, a gift, a lot of luck, hard work, and faith in the Higher Power led me to success at an early age as a dancer and eventually an actress. I'll take you through my trailblazing, barrier-breaking path as one of the pioneering Asian-American actors, and the amazing shows and films I worked on—some of the biggest and most influential—along with some of the greatest entertainers of all time: Elvis, John Wayne, Jimmy Stewart, Doris Day, Jeff Bridges, Bette Midler, and many, many more. I'll give you a look into my constant search for a father/protector figure and how it led to many interesting relationships, none bigger than my time with Frank Sinatra. I'll show you a side of Ol' Blue Eyes that most haven't seen. I'll take you on a spiritual journey to an ashram that changed my path forever. I'll also examine the other facets of my life, into marriage, a fashion business, real estate, other relationships with people of prominence, motherhood, and more, all while trying secretly to keep God at my center.

All of these memories are like the water colors I paint. I like water color painting *because* of its unpredictability. The accidental splash or movement that happens in water color can sometimes result in the best part of the painting. Yet water color is very demanding in that you have to know exactly what strokes you have to put down first and what follows. It is an expression of the playful self to embrace each happening with a fresh face and new energy. It does not always have to be a "been there, done that" portrayal. I'd rather have "maybe I've been there, but it's different every time I look back." I let the water colors do their own thing for better or for worse.

Join me as I look back on what I've painted so far, and as I prepare to take the next stroke.

☙ FILM AND TV CREDITS ❧

Over the course of my career, I have earned over eighty film and TV credits… and I continue to work today.

*Credits are taken from IMDB.com

1961 – *Flower Drum Song* – Dancer (uncredited)
1962 – *The Horizontal Lieutenant* – Oriental Spy (uncredited)
1963 – *Perry Mason* (TV Series) – Juli Eng
1963 – *Take Her, She's Mine* – Miss Wu
1963 – *Under the Yum Yum Tree* – Suzy (uncredited)
1964 – *Breaking Point* (TV Series) – Niki
1964 – *My Favorite Martian* (TV Series) – Leilani
1964 – *The Lieutenant* (TV Series) – Hoa Luu
1964 – *The New Phil Silvers Show* (TV Series) – Johnny's Mother
1965 – *How to Stuff a Wild Bikini* – Native Girl
1965 – *I Spy* (TV Series) – Girl
1965 – *John Goldfarb, Please Come Home!* – Harem Girl (uncredited)
1965 – *Mr. Novak* (TV Series) – Mexico – United Nations Assembly
1965 – *The Sword of Ali Baba* – Nalu
1965 – *The Wackiest Ship in the Army* (TV Series) – Beautiful Native Girl
1965 – *Voyage to the Bottom of the Sea* (TV Series) – Su Yin
1965–1967 – *The Man from U.N.C.L.E.* (TV Series) – Reiko / Jasmine
1966 – *7 Women* – Chinese Girl
1966 – *My Three Sons* (TV Series) – Terry Wong
1966 – *Paradise, Hawaiian Style* – Pua
1966 – *Women of the Prehistoric Planet* – Linda
1967 – *Caprice* – Su Ling
1967 – *Island of the Lost* – Judy Hawiiani
1967 – *Laredo* (TV Series) – Jem Sing
1967 – *Off to See the Wizard* (TV Series) – Judy Hawiiani
1967 – *The Wild Wild West* (TV Series) – Reiko O'Hara

1968 – *Insight* (TV Series)
1968 – *The Green Berets* – Lin
1970 – *Family Affair* (TV Series) – Ming Lee
1970 – *The Name of the Game* (TV Series) – Miss Takashima
1971 – *Cade's County* (TV Series) – Mimi Drake
1971 – *Sarge* (TV Series) – Akiko
1972 – *Cannon* (TV Series) – Lavonne Rowan
1972 – *Mission: Impossible* (TV Series) – Penyo
1972 – *Stand Up and Be Counted* – (uncredited)
1972 – *The Smith Family* (TV Series) – Nancy
1973 – *Hawaii Five-O* (TV Series) – Alia
1973 – *Owen Marshall, Counselor at Law* (TV Series) – Miss Shirado
1973 – *The New Perry Mason* (TV Series) – Nhi Khanh
1974 – *Airport 1975* – Carol
1974 – *Ironside* (TV Series) – Laurie Li
1974 – *Judge Dee and the Monastery Murders* (TV Movie) – Celestial Image
1974 – *Three the Hard Way* – Empress
1975 – *Deadly Hero*
1975 – *Paper Tiger* – Talah
1976 – *Damien's Island* – Momi
1976 – *Hot Potato* – Detective Sgt. Pam Varaje
1977 – *Future Cop* (TV Series regular) – Dr. Tingley
1977 – *The Rockford Files* (TV Series) – Daphne Ishawahara
1977 – *Wonder Woman* (TV Series) – Mei Ling
1978 – *The Yin and the Yang of Mr. Go* – Tah-Ling
1980 – *Father Damien: The Leper Priest* (TV Movie)
1983 – *Ryan's Four* (TV Series)
1984 – *A Touch of Scandal* (TV Movie) – Woman in Restaurant
1985 – *Airwolf* (TV Series) – Carol Oshiro
1986 – *Down and Out in Beverly Hills* – Sheila Waltzberg
1986 – *Trapper John, M.D.* (TV Series) – Dr. Julie Lok
1987 – *Steele Justice* – Xua Chan
1988 – *Noble House* (TV Mini-Series)
1990 – *A Girl to Kill For* – The Counselor
1992 – *Unbecoming Age* – R.J.
1993 – *Mr. Jones* – Mrs. Chang
1993 – *Snapdragon* – Hua

1994 – *Compromising Situations* (TV Series) – Li Miau
1996 – *Baywatch Nights* (TV Series) – Lili
1996 – *Comrades: Almost a Love Story* – Aunt Rosie
1996 – *Widow's Kiss* (TV Movie) – Dr. Joyce Sabata
1997 – *Tell Me No Secrets* (TV Movie) – Mrs. Ching
1997–2001 – *Star Trek: Voyager* (TV Series) – Mary Kim / Kim's Mother
2000 – *The Michael Richards Show* (TV Series) – Woman #3
2000 – *Unauthorized: The Mary Kay Letourneau Story* (The judge-TV Movie)
2002 – *Golden Chicken* – Kam's Aunt (as Irene Tsui)
2003 – *Lost at Home* (TV Series) – Brenda
2003 – *The Division* (TV Series) – Madame Lin
2004 – *Strong Medicine* (TV Series) – Mrs. Fong
2005 – *CSI: NY* (TV Series) – Madam Tuki Song
2006 – *The Heart Specialist* – Mrs. Olson
2007 – *Alibi* – Chu Fan
2009 – *Cold Case* (TV Series) – Da Chun Lu
2011 – *Fred 2: Night of the Living Fred* (TV Movie) – Mrs. Rhee
2011 – *Law & Order: LA* (TV Series) – Christina Yu
2012 – *Sleeping Dogs* (Video Game) – Mrs. Chu (voice)
2019 – *Caregiver* (Short Subject) – Mrs. Sugita
2019 – *Over the Moon* (Animation) – Grandma

CHAPTER 1

WHEN I WAS BORN, I had huge bulging eyes and dark skin. I didn't look like any of my cousins who had porcelain skin and almond eyes. My relatives would come by to look at me. They would glance at me, then at my mother again, then at me, then her again, and laughingly whisper, "Oh you adopted her." Mom just laughed, giving me the biggest head-to-toe hug. I could feel her love coursing through my little body. I was happy.

It was a dentist that was engaged to one of my aunts who brought me into the world. Mom said when the "doctor" brought me to her bedside, my big eyes were wide open, looking all around the room. Even though she was told infants can't see, she knew I could. She knew I was going to see the world. I was already getting started.

This teasing about my eyes went on for some years, whenever relatives visited. I have a lot of relatives as my mother was one of six sisters. I was lovingly called "Eyeballs Tsu, Little Coal Balls." I was a curiosity. My mother never objected, was never upset. She just laughed along with her sisters and aunties.

The home where we are born is often physically ingrained in us. After more than sixty years I can still recall the stairway in the 6th District house off Avenue Joffre in the French Concession of Shanghai. The staircase had carved banister posts shaped like an "S." The banister top was built from beautifully buffed mahogany which made for a really awesome curved slide. It was my favorite place to play. I was a monkey child who would climb up on my tiptoes, swing my leg over, and hug the banister with my belly and little arms, sliding for the ride of my life. My mom would be screaming from the next room, "Get down right now, Shao (Little) Wei Wu!" My belly would still be tingling from the brush with the mahogany. I loved it!

Then came one afternoon I wanted to try something new. I slid my body (or was it my head?) through the banister shaft. I quickly realized that I was stuck. I couldn't loosen myself from the grip. I screamed and cried. Mother came running to me and pushed and pulled to get my head out of the shaft. The more she tried, the more I was stuck. As I kept kicking and screaming, she called the rest of the family to figure out what to do. It was quickly decided that a carpenter had to be summoned to saw a section from the shaft and release the screaming three-year-old. Moments later I had stopped screaming and my body went limp from exhaustion. Mom held me for comfort and my limp little body miraculously slipped through the shaft quite easily to the other side. "Hallelujah!" everyone cried in unison.

"Hallelujah!" sounds the same in Chinese.

Another thing I remember about growing up is the trolley. There was a long green one and a double-decked red one. On its back it had a fishing pole with a wheel that touched wires overhead that sparked and made popping sounds. I called the green single-decker trolleys "baba cars" which meant "daddy cars" and the red double decker ones "popo cars" or "grandmother cars." I pointed to them every time they hissed by on their steel wheels, smooth as a boat on an endless track, among the bobbing and bumping cars and bicycles, along the big boulevard past our gated compound.

My father named me "Wei Ho." Ho (or Wu) means "peace." "Wei" is a character taken from our family book. All girls in my generation have Wei in their first names. My sister is named Wei Shin. Shin is for "prosperity." My father also chose my English name "Irene," which also means "peace." He showed it to me in a huge dictionary he kept on his bookshelf. However, mother said that Irene was also a Greek queen who murdered her husband and married her son.

Apparently, she was not so peaceful.

I remember one day when I was older and we were living in our New York apartment. My aunts had been visiting all afternoon and again, and they were talking about how I looked different than my siblings. In the evening, when we were finally left alone and the house was quiet, I blurted out to my mother, "Mom, was I really adopted?"

"You silly girl, of course not!"

Then my mother told me she was near thirty when I was born. That was *ancient* in those days. She'd been married already for so long and no children...tongues were wagging! But Dad was adamant about not having any children until he could provide for his future son's college education. Dad was prepping for a big career with the Chiang Kai-shek government. Working for the newly built railroads in Kunming, China was the most prestigious job for a young man returning from university in the U.S.

"Excuses, excuses," Mother thought. "I cannot endure the well-meaning, but teasing relatives and nosy neighbors any longer. I'm going to have a baby one way or the other." Mom's sister, Dr. Ling Lin Da, lived next door. We called her Dr. Linda. She told Mom that the sperm contained in a condom was still alive and stayed alive for about a day under certain conditions. If Mom could collect the sperm and bring them over to her house next door, she would gladly introduce my father's sperm to my mother's egg. My father's sperm was put into a turkey baster and Dr. Linda emptied the baster into my mother… and I was conceived.

I was a turkey baster baby. That baster was my Big Bang.

That was pretty brazen of her to disobey her husband's wishes and have a kid on her own, so to speak, back in the forties. She used him as a sperm donor. Where was the wifely respect for the man's wishes? He wanted his first child to be a son. The fact that she had a baby without his consent and that the baby was a girl explains the strained relationship and strange stability of the arranged marriage they had for over sixty years.

After she told me this, she grasped my wimpy shoulders, gently shook me, and gave me the biggest hug. Her happy story of how I came into this world made my heart feel so wide. The corner of my mouth turned up, and I smiled the biggest smile.

"I love you, Mom."

"And I love you, Shao Wei, from here to eternity."

Then another big hug.

This love would last me a lifetime and more.

CHAPTER 2

IN THE 1930S, before WWII, the Japanese invaded China, swept aside all Chinese opposition—Generalissimo Chiang Kai-shek's Nationalist forces in the south and Mao Tse-tung's Communists in the northwest—and took vicious control of the nine northern districts of Qingdao. Ling Tsuan Hua (Lin Xiao), my mom's father and my grandfather, had been an admiral in Chiang Kai-shek's service at the naval base on the south side. The Russians, British, Japanese, and Germans had fought each other and Chiang Kai-shek for control of Qingdao and all the seas of western China south to Taiwan and Hong Kong.

The Japanese occupiers made the Chinese admiral the head of the Provisional Government. Grandpa Lin was stuck between a rock and a hard place. Grandpa did the only thing he could to ensure the safety of the civilians and the city of Qingdao. He cooperated to keep the Japanese from imposing control on the Chinese population by massacre and other atrocities. That same year, 1932, the Japanese used Nanjing like the Germans used Guernica, to test new weapons and tactics. He didn't want the Japanese to do the same thing to Qingdao. Yes, a Chinese admiral with no navy worked with the Japanese occupation. And of course his politically ambitious wife, my Grandma Ling Li Hua, thought it would be an advantageous move for his political future. She was certain that, after the war, Chiang would reward his honorable soldier for such self-sacrifice.

Chiang kicked out the Japanese after the war, with the aid of the Americans, but the Communists were marching down from the north. The civil war between Generalissimo Chiang and Mao's Communists that had been overshadowed by the war against the Japanese now overwhelmed China.

My grandfather on my father's side, a high-ranking member of the Chiang party, warned my mother's father, Admiral Lin, that he would be the first one to be executed when Generalissimo Chiang arrived victoriously backed by the U.S. He was right. Grandfather Lin was executed by Chiang in Qingdao for treason. Grandpa Lin was a victim on both sides; he was Judas for the Japanese and Generalissimo Chiang's scapegoat. Grandpa Lin was a soldier while Grandfather Tsu was a politician.

Grandma Lin raised all seven of her children after the tragic death of her husband. My mom and her two sisters were given German names by their governess. They named my mom Dulcie and her sisters, Linde and Lida. Grandpa Lin's December 26th birthday was celebrated every year until Grandma passed away in 1990 at age one hundred in Washington D.C. She even received a congratulatory letter from President George Bush Sr. I have seen a photo of her riding side-saddled with my grandaunt and others at the turn of the century. They were called the "Fight Till Your Death Brigade" women revolutionaries. They were the real woman warriors!

Chiang was married to the beautiful and Wellesley College-educated Soong Mei Ling. They said she loved power. I remember that it was His and Her power. Her oldest sister Soong Ailing was married to H. H. Kung, the Generalissimo's crooked financier. They say she loved money. The middle sister, Soong Ching Ling, was married to Dr. Sun Yat-sen, the founder of the Republic of China. They say she loved China.

The Generalissimo's love of power and money did a great thing for the other side of my family by paying off their war bonds. He made one of my granduncles filthy rich. That's why we called him Uncle Richissimo! That granduncle was the laughing stock in town for years because he would buy war bonds by the barrel at a penny on the dollar. They would be stacked up to his ceiling. People visiting would always be uncomfortable. "I like the smell of the paper," he was famous for saying. Out of the blue, the good Christian Chiang Kai-shek cast money on the bondholders and my granduncle was instantly rich. He never left China after the Communists took over. They didn't persecute him, but put him to work teaching Chinese chess—of which he was a *master*—from city to city. So yes, he loved the smell of paper… and the clacking of the tiles.

When the Communists were taking over China, my father arranged to have his family, along with Hou Po (his mother), leave China aboard a large ship out of Shanghai bound for Taiwan.

I have very little recollection of Taipei except that the whole place stank because it had open sewers on either side of the streets. We lived in a Japanese house built on stilts. They built them that way so the house wouldn't sit in the wet, stinky water. However, there were large creatures living on the walls. They were huge lizards lurking above our beds while we were sleeping or our dining table while we were eating. They were waiting for little leftover morsels. Sometimes they would fall, and the maid would beat them with a broom to chase them away. These lizards would also sometimes lose their tails and the maid would curse when that happened. I would scream, "Mom, Mom…" but she never came because she was always too busy caring for my sister Florence. The maid would hush me up, saying, "Be quiet or the lizard's tail will wriggle into your ears tonight." I cried and cried, and I would try to stay awake as long as I could so the tail would not get into my ears.

What a terrible lie to tell a child!

Luckily, we were only there for a short time before my father decided to move us to Hong Kong. He remained in Taiwan to serve the Chiang government. Whether it was for money, or for his rumored other family that was whispered about when we children were not within ear shot, we were always one country away from Dad.

He always said it was for safety reasons.

Hong Kong was very much a British Crown colony at the time and rather international, sophisticated, and physically stunning. School in Hong Kong began with a faulty start. The first couple of grades I spent in a Confucius school where we had to line up to get beaten on our palms every day after school. Mom would ask how come I was always so late walking home. I told her one or two of the boys would get twenty or even thirty whacks with a wooden ruler on their palms and the girls maybe got five to ten. Our palms would burn like fire for a long, long time. Mom took me out of that sadistic school and enrolled me in Heep Yunn, a private prep school.

All the prep schools in Hong Kong were private and boys and girls were separated. I went to a parochial school that emphasized more Chinese instead of all English like Mary Knoll or King George V. It was a great school. I loved my teachers, and I did well. We had great outings and I made a lifelong best friend in Helen Chan. We were both Girl Guides (scouts). Two days a week we would wait on a little hill next to the school building for a vendor to come by with freshly baked French rolls, crunchy on the outside and soft white inside. French rolls never tasted that good again.

There was one bad thing about Heep Yunn: our uniforms. In the summer, we wore one- piece, thigh-length outfits that were white on top and blue on the bottom. It would look like a white blouse with buttons down the middle and attached to blue culottes below. Now can you wrap your head around how we had to get out of them to go to the bathroom? We either had to unbutton the top and the waistband and wriggle out of the whole thing, let it hang around our ankles, or try to squeeze our butt out of one side of the culottes. No easy matter. Sometimes we would see girls with toilet paper hanging out from their tangled culottes walking around school. Winter was no better, as we had to wear "cheongsam," a form-fitting Chinese dress with a side zipper and frog buttons to the neck. Again, when going to bathroom, we'd either have to unbutton and unzip everything or wriggle our butt out from the side slits.

Yves Saint Laurent would have loved it!

It was also at this school that I would get my first real experience with religion. Unbeknownst to me, my mom had signed me up to be baptized. One day my teacher said I was to report to the chaplain to have my baptism in the Episcopalian church (Church of England). I was taken to a room behind the chapel. They undressed me and dunked my whole body into the freezing water in a stone vessel that looked like a coffin. The chaplain mumbled a series of words. My teeth were still chattering when they asked me what my Christian name was, so they could enter it into some big book. I didn't comprehend any of what they were saying. The only name that came into my head was "Mary."

So, Mary it was!

Mom and Grandma were devout Methodists or Baptists, so Sunday school, Christmas, and Easter were big days growing up and I loved it. I never let on to anyone, but faith remained the core of my being as I wandered through my Hollywood years. I didn't really have a dad present in my life, but I had my manager Fred, Jesus, and miles of intuition that I think must have helped my underdeveloped teenage frontal lobe make some big decisions on my own. As you'll soon see, I had to grow up in a hurry.

Thank you Jeezzus!

CHAPTER 3

WHEN I WAS EITHER EIGHT or nine years old, I saw a poster at a bus stop for the movie *The Red Shoes*. It was hypnotic! I tried to pose in front of our mirror, arching my back like a ballerina, head tilting to one side, eyes gazing downward in sensual abandonment. Then there were the red satin toe shoes! Not even the ladies down the corner had red nail polish quite so potent and seductive. I would visualize my little feet in those red satin shoes. How they would arch like the ballerinas, my toes squeezing into the points. Then I would magically be able to glide with swift little steps across the stage. I stared at the poster whenever we passed the bus stop until I projected myself into it.

I wanted to be a ballerina!

Luckily I had an aunt who *was* a ballerina. Ballet was acceptable in our family because it was set to classical music, a class art form. I would beg Mom to take me to Auntie Alice's house on weekends so she could show me a few steps. I'd come home, stand in front of the mirror, and I'd practice and practice and practice. Plie, port de bras, or bras bas. Finally I asked Mom if she would take me to a ballet school in Tsim Sha Tsui. I pleaded that it wasn't that far and if she took me there I could take a bus home.

And that's what we did! This little ballerina took a bus home two nights a week. I lived for my ballet classes (plus a little more training with my auntie on weekends). During my last semester at Heep Yunn, I choreographed a whole ballet number for a graduation production. I chose the music and cast three of my schoolmates. Mom made the costumes and my teacher Mrs. Dragon applied the makeup because she always had *a lot* of makeup.

You can do anything when you're young because you don't know what fear is. The study of ballet was a turning point in my young life. I may not have realized it then, but I loved expressing myself through my body with a single-minded focus. It is no accident that later in life I found hatha yoga to be my lifelong pursuit because it lets you experience the union of body, mind, and spirit. It is also that same creative impulse that drives an actor, musician, or athlete. It's sublime.

When I was eleven, my ballet teacher enrolled me in a big contest put on once every four years by the Sadler's Wells Royal Ballet from England. At the time, I didn't know how I did, as I was way too nervous. I was just glad it was over. Three or four weeks later I found out that I was the only one chosen to be in their program out of all of contestants from the Commonwealth in Southeast Asia.

Next stop… London!

Then my father came in from Taiwan and had a meeting with the Sadler's Wells people in a high-rise office in Hong Kong.

"You have to realize that for your daughter, it's like going into a convent," they told him. "She is going to eat what we feed her, sleep when we tell her. She will have rehearsals five to six hours a day plus her regular school. Also, and this has really nothing to do with her ability, but she has to measure up to the weight and proportions that we require for the Royal Ballet."

At eleven, it was very hard to tell what I would look like at sixteen. Furthermore, they said, "There is no guarantee that she'll be a prima ballerina or in the corps de ballet. In which case she'll be like an indentured servant to the Royal Ballet for about seven years to pay them back."

Father looked at me with my scared dark face and my big round eyes. "This scrawny little stick will never look like a ballerina," he proclaimed.

I was crushed. They wanted me but my own father rejected me on the spot. I hung on to my mom's fingers and bit my lips to stop the tears. My mother didn't say one word on our bus ride home. She too was heartbroken. She explained to me later that it was not entirely my father's fault. It was not possible for me to go to London because we had already applied to go to America, and it had taken us seven years waiting for the Refugee Relief Act to clear us. We were finally granted to enter the U.S. as political refugees. All that meant to me was that I wasn't going to Sadler's Wells. It was my first major heartbreak. For years after, even when I was in Hollywood and working in films, I would wonder what my life would be like if I had gone to London.

My mother told me once she had wanted to be a dancer, but she was born in the wrong time. She was even a little jealous of my ballet lessons,

I think. She took up ballroom dancing and was great at the fox trot, waltz, and even tango. She had a young, tall dance partner who had the face of her father. His name was David.

I wished David was my father.

Speaking of my father, he was highly respected for his intellect, charm, and sense of humor. Dad was of average Chinese height. He was five foot eight or nine, and very handsome. He was either idolized, envied, or despised by his compatriots. He was a brilliant, conflicted man. Mom said he was an abused child, that his dad would be so cruel that he would lock him in a tiny closet for hours when he was still little. His uncle couldn't even stand his own brother's abuse of the child and said one day, "Your son is brilliant and I'm going to send him to university in America!"

So, he did. My father graduated with high honors from Jiao Tong University in Shanghai and received his master's degree in Economics from the University of Illinois in 1936. Later on, he was the controller at the Council for United States Aid in Taipei for many years.

When my father visited us in Hong Kong, he would take me to afternoon tea at the Peninsula Hotel, Hong Kong Jockey Club, or The Repulse Bay Hotel so I could see which side of the plate the forks, knives, and spoons were set, how the napkins were folded, and how you spread the napkin on your lap. He said, "Just watch me. You pick up whatever I pick up." I would watch how to pick up the spoon to stir the tea, how he laid his fork down, how he would pick up the teacup. I was a good mimic. Maybe that's how I started acting; I just copied.

He would never trust the water in China. He only drank boiled water. And the knives and everything in the restaurant would have to be cleaned. He would ask for an orange and he would peel it, cleaning his knife and fork with the inside of it. "Because the inside of an orange has never been exposed to the outside." Of course, he also always lavished me with gifts when he visited us in Hong Kong. I must've had half a dozen watches by the time I was ten years old.

I really didn't know how to use a watch.

Beyond these experiences, I don't remember much about my relationship with my father as a child. Let's just say I did not know my father at all. We never really spoke to each other. Even if he did want to say something to me, he usually spoke through my mother. He never lived in the same household with us, and there were very few dinners together or any outings except the times he took me to the clubs for tea.

He also did not speak much at family gatherings. He was a silent man who kept everything to himself. He was emotionally damaged from childhood, a sad fact I learned about later. I'll never forget once when we were in his room. My parents were sitting on the edge of the bed and I was on the floor just observing a rare moment of watching the both of them together. I gently touched his shoes to be a little closer to him, then reached out to touch his arm or shoulder. Out of nowhere he pushed me away hard, sending me halfway across the room, where I hit my head on the opposite wall. I let out a wail and was picked up by Mom and my nanny as he banished me to the kitchen. I couldn't understand at all why I was punished. Mom told me later that it was because I had touched his shoes, and they were dirty. He was a germophobe. But how was I to know? I was like six or seven.

I spent all of my early life trying to win his love and approval, wondering if I could ever measure up. I craved his attention and the love he could not give. I remember when my sister and I were grown up and my sister was already a lawyer. She actually thought we should disown our father, if there was in fact such a way we could do it. We also secretly wished that Mom would divorce Dad and marry another suiter, which there always were. She was attractive and a wonderful dancer and painter. We thought she deserved so much more, but, alas, it was only our fantasy. She loved this brilliant, strange, abused man!

Not letting me go to London hurt badly but it was just another little tear to the heart of a little girl who never knew her dad. I survived and thrived.

Especially when we got to America!

CHAPTER 4

It must have been close to midnight in February of 1957 at the wharf in Tsim Sha Tsui, Kowloon when the S.S. President Wilson pulled away from the dock. My mom, sister, and I were still clinging onto the railing of the ocean liner as I craned my neck to catch the last glimpse of my best girlfriend from fifth grade who had been standing on the dock for almost four hours. The ship let out several huge bellows like some giant sleeping dragon ready to leap into the night. It was at once both horrifying and exciting.

It was the most anticipated night of my young life. I was sad and terrified to leave my best friend, my school, my teachers, my home, my street, my ballet teacher, my girl guides, everything with which I was familiar. But still, I was excited to go to America! The three of us stumbled forward in semi-darkness into the dark and chilly night to look for our cabins. We went down many staircases and endless hallways before Mom matched the cabin number to a scrap of paper she was clutching in her hand. It was small and had a bunkbed and a single bed. Mom thought I should be on the top bunk and my sister below because it would be safer as she was still small and may fall out of bed. Mighty fine; the top was my choice anyway!

Immediately after (semi) unpacking I dashed out the door. I couldn't wait to explore the new world of an ocean liner for the next twenty-eight days. It might as well be a lifetime! I tried to remember every staircase, whether they had shiny brass railings or just equally beautiful mahogany banisters, and the carpet colors and patterns in every hallway, and the fancy landings with chandeliers. I must have climbed five or six stories, though some I could not get through. I remember going up to where there were doors that were too heavy for my twelve-year-old arms to open. I stood on my tippy toes to see the darkness outside and listen to the roar of the pitch-black ocean beyond. I could feel the slow rolling movement that made my legs kind of wobbly and suddenly I felt kind of sleepy. In an instant I felt unsafe and scared, and I started scrambling down the stairs to find our room. As fast as my feet could move, I was flying down those stairs, hallways, and landings. Not really knowing where I was going, I started feeling dizzy and lost. Then I heard my mom yelling out my name, "Wei Wu Wei Wu ah…"

"Mom, Mommy, I'm here, over here!"

She kept repeating my name and I kept walking closer to her voice until we ran into each other and she grabbed me and held me tight.

The passage from Hong Kong to Yokohama was rough, and my mom spent the first five days in bed. She would go to the bathroom and then back to bed. I, on the other hand, would go up the stairs to the shuffleboard deck and lounges where grownups were talking about serious things or complaining about something.

Why can't they just have fun?

Maybe ten days later I worked up enough nerve—or maybe my curiosity finally got the better of me—and I went all the way up to the top deck. The moon was full and bright. I heard guitar music and a guy singing with some intermittent laughter.

Oh my, they are having so much fun, I so wish I could be next to them.

Every night I would sneak up there and get a little closer. Surely, they would not mind me there. I was twelve already, almost a teen. I did get close enough to see the guy singing. He was so handsome. He was perhaps seventeen or eighteen and had dark wavy hair like a photo I saw in a magazine in the hair salon where my mom had me get a hair bend every six months or so (my great fear was that they would not have black bobby pins in America so I begged everyone to get me black bobby pins to take with me!). The singer wore a shirt with sleeves rolled up and jeans. His face would be etched into my memory forever. I saw him for the last time on that trip when we were coming down the gangplank in San Francisco. I looked at him so intently and willed that I would see him again when I was big.

And I did! I met him again in Hollywood many years later. His name was Mario Machado and he became a sportscaster. We even became friends and I asked if he came to America on the President Wilson. He said he did but that he never saw me. Underage and awkward girls are invisible to guys!

The most magical moment—next to the handsome singer—was when the ship was approaching the Golden Gate Bridge. I thought we would never make it under the bridge; it seemed way too low for our big ship. As we came closer and closer, I was clutching tight to the coins my mom gave me to throw under the bridge when we sailed past for good luck. It was said if you do so, you will return to the City of the Gold Mountain.

Sure enough, I came back less than five years later, but that's a story for another chapter…

After a five-day train ride from San Francisco we arrived at the Grand Central Terminal in Manhattan. It was definitely a grand place, but I was not the least bit interested. I was lovesick for the singer who never knew I existed. We were greeted by the son of my mother's friend who was traveling with her two kids on the same ship. We changed trains and headed straight upstate to Larchmont, New York where my distant Aunt Rose lived. It was decided amongst the family that we were to live with her as she was all alone and had a big house in Larchmont.

Aunt Rose was no ordinary woman. She was in fact the wife of the former vice president to Chiang Kai-shek. It was not for long because Mao was already marching down from the north and Chiang was retreating to Taiwan. She must have been in her sixties or seventies but stood tall and had a great carriage, short, steel-grey hair, and the ability to speak good English. Of course, she too graduated from Wellesley along with the Soon sisters, one of whom was married to Chiang. She lived a military life. She got up at six every morning, cleaned up, went for a half hour walk and sat down to breakfast at exactly at 7 a.m. She took diner at 6:30 p.m. after watching the news. She would watch some other programs, then lights out and she would go to her bedroom. On Saturday nights we were allowed to watch some musical shows with entertainers like Perry Como or George Gobel.

Mom enrolled me in Mamaroneck Junior High School and Florence, my sister, in elementary school. The first Americans I met in school were the nicest and friendliest people. America in the late fifties—at least in Mamaroneck—was sprawling and clean, not congested like Hong Kong. There were no poor people, beggars, or pickpockets on street corners. Americans were generally sweet and nice to foreigners. They went out of their way to help me, like walking me to the next classroom or to the bus stop. They wrote nice things for me in my yearbook: "Welcome to America! I hope you will succeed! I wish you a real good time…and eat a lot of fries! You are beautiful! Don't worry about English 101." They all went out of their way to help me even though I could hardly tell them apart. The girls were either Carol something or Betty something. Americans all looked alike to me!

They also all wore bras which made me beg Mother to buy one for me.

"Shao Wei, what for? You don't have anything to put into a bra."

"Mom, please, I just need the straps so they will show on my back. How can I face the lunch counter with no straps showing through my blouse another day? I know they are all laughing at me." I feigned a bit of tears and got my bra straps the very next day!

Less than a year later we moved to Manhattan so Mom could start looking for a job. We moved into a thirteen-room apartment with Master Wong, a famous artist whose specialty was painting goldfish, who was also my mother's professor in China. He was now teaching at the Art Institute in Manhattan. Looking back, it was amazing seeing him practice every day and to be surrounded by his work. He also had paintings and screens from some of the most famous Chinese painters, which he had saved, around his house. They had been smuggled out of China when the artists went in hiding, some in South America and some elsewhere, and he didn't want their work to be confiscated by the Communists. The museum-caliber pieces were of Zhang Daqian, known for his brilliant landscapes (called mountain and water paintings), and one of Xu Beihong, famous for his paintings of horses. The most impressive piece might have been the bold and powerful black-inked lotus of Qi Baishi painted on a five-sectional gold screen with black lacquer frame. There were quite a few times my mother would yell at me for roller skating around the house, almost crashing into the gold screen which was used as somewhat of a room divider. It was way too surreal!

Thinking about it today, it's hard to fathom that these world-class works of art were actually hanging about on the seventh floor of a rather dilapidated old apartment building at 157th Street and Riverside Drive in Manhattan. I wonder what their fate was after we moved or after Master Wong passed.

The move to Manhattan also meant another school for me. This time it was George Washington High School in Upper Westside Manhattan. It was an enormous school with all kinds of different looking people. The girls wore big hoop skirts and had pennies in their loafers. Some smoked cigarettes and "made out" with boys behind the stairs. I made no friends. It was like *Grease!*

It was also where I would first be introduced to dancing on stage.

CHAPTER 5

Mrs. Levis was born in Shanghai, China. She taught modern dance at George Washington High School. She had studied with Martha Graham and Florence Humphrey. The spritely woman walked about in a long black skirt and scoop-necked, long-sleeved leotard with black ballet slippers, and had her gray hair held back by her steel-rimmed glasses in a knot by the nape of her long neck. She approached me one day and asked if I would like to be in her new production of *Finian's Rainbow*, to which I replied, "I don't speak English very well."

"You don't have to speak. The character is a deaf mute. She speaks with her feet."

I looked down at my feet and up at her and said, "Oh, okay."

The next afternoon I watched the rehearsal in the dark auditorium and felt strangely comfortable. As I watched the lead character Susan's feet glide across the stage, I tried to emulate her every move and felt my feet twitch and turn on the dark concrete floor beneath my seat. Quite frankly, I was exhausted after watching her number. Several afternoons a week I watched the rehearsals and my teacher would show me some of the numbers to practice on my own. Mrs. Levis would sign me out of my classes when necessary and I had this feeling that I was somehow unique and special, not trapped in the mundane shuffling from classroom to classroom.

I was happy and surprised that my years of ballet lessons were recognized by my prestigious instructor and I started thinking maybe I could develop them into a professional career. It also showed me that dance was universal and not bound by traditional racial boundaries. This was really the first moment I had crossed over, though unintentionally. It would happen again much later in my acting career. Although I never had a chance to go on, it definitely gave me the feeling that I could be a dancer!

While in Manhattan, I continued ballet classes at Carnegie Hall whenever I could after school. I took up jazz (like what they did in *West Side Story*) in the hopes that more dancing parts would come along. Sure enough, the more I worked on my dancing, the more opportunities arose. An actual paying dance job appeared one summer through my boyfriend's sister, who was a glamorous model type. The show was with the touring Keigo Imperial Japanese Dancers for four weeks. They needed two replacement girls in Quebec in a hurry after two dancers dropped out after a tour in Mexico City.

I was elated! I was truly going to be a professional dancer! They were in such a need they even took my Korean girlfriend who didn't dance much. I convinced my mother to buy me a white hat box and matching train case. I put my name in Gold Dymo on the front and was taken to the airport. It was my first plane trip anywhere!

We were to open in a nightclub in Quebec. As soon as we arrived, we went straight into rehearsal, learning two jazz numbers and two traditional Japanese numbers which was no easy feat. Especially having to wear the heavy wigs (katsula) harpooned to our head with chopsticks, and shuffling about in the Japanese platform sandals (zories). My katsula fell off my head a couple of times in rehearsal. I laughed hysterically to the displeasure of Bill, the choreographer, who commanded that I hold on to my head while in those numbers. That just led to more giggles.

Everything was so new to me as a fourteen-year-old, from sweeping off an entire table of cocktails with my kimono bottom to hurrying out of the nightclub every night, bowing and whispering, "No speak Engrish." God forbid the customers learn that I was really only fourteen and my Korean girlfriend was sixteen! I befriended the drummer who painted me a beautiful picture of Southern California where he had a home with a white picket fence and trees with avocados. He said he would invite me there and marry me. I had some very warm dreams of Southern California until my roommate said that he was gay and lived with Ishi, the wardrobe mister. My roommate herself was a klutz who would constantly lose her contacts and had the habit of leaving them in water glasses, which I almost drank a few times.

Beyond learning how to dance Japanese, I also learned that men always said they loved you and that women could be hazardous.

Once the trip was done, I went back to school, starting the tenth grade. School would never be the same again…

Not long after I returned, Mother went down to Washington D.C. with my sister to enroll her into grade school because the school in our neighborhood was getting seedy. Florence had a schoolmate that killed herself while they were reading Sylvia Plath.

They were only gone for a weekend, but while they were gone one night, I was asleep in my twin bed facing the wall in my room across from Mom's. All of a sudden, I felt a warm body pressing into my back. Before I could scream, he had his hand across my mouth and whispered, "Shh, don't be scared, you silly girl. It's only me, your big brother Paul. I've been dying to hold you for so long."

Paul was a medical student from Singapore whom my grandma had adopted. Not legally, but there were always some young students hanging around our house to freeload because Grandma lost both of her sons and always wanted some male energy around instead of just the six daughters. She liked young men.

And Paul liked me.

He continued to press into my behind. He lowered my pajama bottoms and pushed his way into me. *Oh my God, is this how it's done?* It kind of hurt, but it was not altogether unbearable. During it, I saw (or sensed) that the old professor was peeping through the crack in my door. The doors never closed completely in those old apartment buildings; they have too many coats of paint.

When it was done, I jumped out of bed and dashed into the bathroom across the hall. I grabbed Mom's handheld mirror to examine myself. I must look different now, I thought. My mother will surely know when she comes back. My face is all strange now. And what am I to do with Old Master Wong? He surely saw me in my bed with Paul. He'll tell Mom!

Later in the day, I snuck into his room and looked through his diary which he wrote in every single day of his life. Sure enough, it was right there, written on the last entry. I agonized on what to do. I snuck back into his room the next day and carefully cut out that page in his book. I have never done anything like that in my whole young life and I felt terrible.

I moved to the little maid's room next to the kitchen to be far away from Mom and old Master Wong. I had a little privacy. I listened to the radio and read fashion magazines. I would pinch my nose with hair clips and put a little Scotch Tape on my eyelids to make myself more western looking, like in the fashion magazines. I'd do my hair in different ways, and I snacked on saltine crackers. I knew that I would not go to NYU or City College like my cousins. They went there not so much to get an education but to find a husband. By their second year they would find a boyfriend, the third year they would be dating, fourth year engaged, and then they'd get married upon graduation. Their mothers would give them a big wedding with all the relatives and red envelopes full of money. Of course, they would all be virgins.

I felt different than my cousins. I didn't want to go to college to meet a husband. I'm not sure exactly what I wanted but I knew what I *didn't* want. I thought I could perhaps be an artist, but my mom thought that I would starve. "What about an architect?" I asked. Dad told Mom, "Who would hire a Chinese woman architect? It's a man's job."

I was already a professional dancer. To my family that was a bit unusual and risqué. But I had already dreamed myself into a different universe. I wasn't sure what it was or how to get to that new universe, but I was going nonetheless.

Sooner than I thought.

CHAPTER 6

I WAS IN LINE AT P.J. CLARKE'S with some friends from school. It was a popular place for burgers but there would always be a big line. A man standing in front of us in the line unexpectedly turned around and stared at me. Then he asked if I was Tahitian?

What? Tahitian?

"Do you *speak* Tahitian?"

"What? No."

"Well, we are looking for a Tahitian to do a commercial. Here's my card. Would you like to come to my office tomorrow?"

I took his card and passed it around to all my friends. They looked and were impressed that he was a real agent. "He's even on Madison Avenue. Maybe you should go see him."

After school my friends and I hopped on the subway and went to his office. It was indeed a real agent's office. He even had a secretary and lots of photos and posters on his wall. He asked me for a photo, but I only had one from the park that my mom's friend took. It was okay, as I was in shorts and my dancer legs looked good. He gave me some pages with lines and sketches. He said it was a storyboard for Wish-Bone "Tahitian Isle" salad dressing.

"Learn the lines and sound Tahitian and come back here tomorrow."

"Okay, thank you, Mr. Agent."

I got to thinking when I got home and talked to my friends again. I knew that Tahitians spoke French, and I had two years of high school French. I decided I would say the lines with a poor French accent… which came out kind of Islandish. Whatever, I didn't know what else to do.

The next afternoon I came out of the 9th Avenue audition office and I could barely walk. I had never been so nervous. I forgot how it went and ever how I made it home, and I never said a word to my mom. Maybe it was the day after when Mr. Agent called my house to say that I got the part! As it turned out, the high school French was actually a lucky charm. Funny enough, it later got me my first speaking part in a big feature film!

I went back to the 9th Avenue studio a couple of days later and there were lots of other people there; other actors, I presumed. There was a big storyboard with drawings and dialogue on it. The other actors spoke a few lines and I was told to say something about the new Tahitian Isle salad dressing in my "made up Islandish." I smiled and pointed to the salad dressing on the display, then other actors spoke and that was it. I have no idea how long I was there or who I even spoke to. I was told that I could go home, and that they would talk to my agent if necessary. I never spoke to the agent again and I can't even remember what I got paid, if anything.

The Wish-Bone commercial was hardly the launch of my acting career, but it did make me curious. I was beginning to wonder if this was where my new universe was going to be. I was still at George Washington High School, but I was thinking of bigger things.

One day I heard they were auditioning some replacement parts for the road company of *The World of Suzie Wong*. My heart raced! I borrowed a cheongsam dress from my fashionable aunt and high heels from my boyfriend's glamorous sister and showed up backstage of the Broadhurst Theater across from the St. James Theatre where *Flower Drum Song* was playing. Imagine two Asian-themed hit Broadway plays at the same time! The year was 1960.

The stage manager asked me to come back the next afternoon to watch the show and to pay attention to the part of Fefe. He even gave me a script, not that I knew how to read it or understand it. But I was a fast study and a good mimic. I copied every word and move the actress did on stage. When she laughed, when she crossed her leg, when she swung her hair back. It was just like how I mimicked the dance moves of Susan in the school play or even with my father picking up the proper cutlery at the Peninsula Hotel.

Okay, I can do it.

I came back a couple of days later and won the part! The next step was my mother had to go to producer David Merrick's office to sign my contract because I was only fifteen. My mom did not read that much English, and she signed on the dotted line and sealed my fate in fifteen minutes so that she could get back to work in a china factory where she painted vases and fruit bowls.

I enrolled in Quintano's School for Young Professionals where lots of kid actors were taking classes, like Patty Duke, who was in *The Miracle Worker* on Broadway, and some of the kids from *The Sound of Music*. I even saw a textbook with Sal Mineo's name on it. My mother was told that it would be the appropriate school for kids on tour with shows because they offered correspondence courses that we could study on the road.

What a joke!

The road company experience is a novel in itself. I remember traveling by train and every few days we were in a different city. A beautiful Eurasian girl from Hong Kong named Nancy Kwan was to play Suzie in the show. When I met the future trailblazing star, we exchanged a few words in Cantonese and realized that we both took ballet from a famous teacher from Hong Kong, but at different times. Still it was comforting to have someone from your hometown. Nancy left a month or two later to star in the movie version of *The World of Suzy Wong*, which would help launch her career.

In some cities the Asian cast was not allowed to stay in the same hotel where the Caucasian cast stayed. Most of us were young and didn't understand racism, nor did we care. Afternoons were rehearsals and we did the show every night. There would always be men in every town who flocked to the stage door to bring us flowers, and to try to wine and dine us. No one really checked my ID or even asked my age. The two stage managers had their hands full trying to control almost a dozen young girls running wild on the road. In reality, most of the guys in the cast were gay except for three straight men and they had their pick of the girls in the cast... even though all three were married. They would be all lovey-dovey until their wives showed up every few weeks or so. For a teenager like me, it was all very funny. On the road is where I learned that all grownups lied.

I didn't want to grow up.

All was going rather smoothly until the week we hit Las Vegas and I was invited on a talk show of a local television station. The host asked me how old I was, and I was stuck for an answer. I was desperately trying to come up with the right answer and I blurted out eighteen which I thought was safe.

No. Wrong.

I had to be twenty-one.

The sheriff threatened to close down the show and the New York office heard about it. They sent lawyers down to negotiate. I believe even

Jerry Miyazaki, who played Suzie, was barely seventeen. They agreed to let the show run, but I couldn't walk through the casino and had to be escorted out the back and driven back to the hotel in a sheriff's car. He would stay in my room and watch me do my correspondence homework until my roommate came home. My roommate would come back and try to seduce the sheriff. He was kind of scared of her.

When he left, she would sneak me out to some casino downtown where they would have no idea who or how old I was. I watched her gamble sometimes. I played a little, too, and she would sit by some tipsy old man on a blackjack table, pretending to play some small hands next to him. Flirting continually, she would say every other hand that she lost, and he would push more chips in front of her. She was pushing most of those chips into her humongous straw basket she used for a purse. She told me to go back to the motel, and she came back some hours later and emptied out the whole basket on her side of the bed. I awoke to the clacking of the chips, a few flying over my head. She'd grab a handful and say, "Here, here, take it!" She was howling. "I could have made more but the old guy passed out at the table. Damn! I'll go back another night. That's my lucky table! I tip all the dealers, and they love me."

Despite her taking advantage of drunk men, my roommate had a golden heart and she taught me a thing or two. I had to grow up in a hurry!

One surprising thing that happened while I was on the road was the appearance of my father. I didn't know that we were even living in the same country. It turned out that my father came to America to reunite with my mother. No one told me anything, now that I was in my new universe. He came to see me in Chicago, I believe, though it could have been another city. They all blurred together. Of course, he was quite horrified at the kind of lifestyle I was living. This was unthinkable, to be dropping out of high school to be on the road with this theatrical troupe.

"It's like walking the streets," he exclaimed to my mother.

Luckily, my roommate happened to be a wonderful cook. She prepared a great dinner for my dad and nearly charmed his pants off. By the end of the evening, all he could do was smile and nod. Later mother would ask me, "Who is this Linda Ho…Linda Ho Ho?" which meant "Linda Goody Goody."

Still, it wasn't enough. My dad wasn't happy with me. At that point, he decided to cut me off. He said to my mother, "She'll starve, and sooner or later she'll come home."

I think that gave me the drive.

I had no place to go back to. I was truly on my own and I was just fifteen.

Was it Confucius or my father who said, "Never let your child a soldier or an actor be!"

CHAPTER 7

THE TOUR ENDED WITH EVERYONE scrambling to pick up their lives from before, like someone coming out of prison. Most of us had no idea what we were going to do. It was not so easy for Asians to pick up another show.

I actually did go back home to New York for a short while to see my mom, but she was so busy working and didn't really have much time for me. She couldn't really understand my new universe either. My father barely knew I was home… we would pass each other in the hallway and I would scrape my shoulder on the wall to avoid touching him.

Lucky for me, I heard about the audition for the film version of *Flower Drum Song* starring Nancy Kwan, produced by Ross Hunter Productions at Universal Studios in Hollywood. I went to the audition for the choreographer Hermes Pan, whom I thought was Fred Astaire. They did indeed have a huge resemblance and I found out later that Hermes choreographed for Fred for years. I got a dancer part and was told by Ray Stark, Nancy's producer/manager, that I would travel to Los Angeles for the filming and that Nancy had asked me to be her roommate and companion. Wow! Did Nancy know that she had to room with a sixteen-year-old? Still, it seemed like a good idea that hometown girls should stick together in strange old Hollywood.

I was indeed born under a lucky turkey baster!

I got to go back to my new universe.   Even though it was a great opportunity for me, my father was still disappointed. He had other ideas for me.

"We should take Shao Wei to my fortune teller!"

He said this just prior to my leaving for Hollywood to start work in *Flower Drum Song*. He knew this very reputable fortune teller from his days in Taiwan who now lived in Brooklyn. He said he wanted to know what was in the plans for me. My father was considerably worried as he realized I was seriously pursuing my "craziness" showbiz dream.

Going to the Brooklyn fortune teller was scary as we entered this dark staircase to a dilapidated brownstone in Brooklyn. He was of an undistinguishable age and had a mole or two on his face with long hair growing out from them. My father introduced me and ordered me to make a full 360-degree turn and then face him. I looked to my mom for a little confidence, but it was so dimly lit in the room that I could hardly see her expression. He spoke and my father asked some questions for maybe fifteen minutes or so. I really couldn't make out what he had to say.

Later at home, Mom and Dad told me the fortune teller had said I would have success but it would be sporadic and not continuous, that I would be a jack of all trades and master of none, and that I was restlessly creative. My father looked disinterested or disappointed and never brought up the subject again.

Over the course of my career, I remembered the fortune teller's observations from time to time, but continued to pursue my "crazy" dreams with no reservation nor remorse. What my mother had instilled in me from an early age was much more deeply ingrained into my psyche. "Never depend on a man. Always rely on yourself. Don't think just because you are married you can rely on your husband, only on yourself."

Okay, Mom.

Still, I secretly craved to rely on *someone*, a higher power than myself, which is something I would continually seek.

Excited does not even begin to describe the feeling of going to Los Angeles. I was mostly numb, not knowing what to expect whatsoever and just going with the flow. The flow of the water color is like that; one never knows how and when it will change let alone how it will end. I knew that I had a place to live with Nancy and that I got to ride to Universal in a limo every morning with the star. I got lunch and came home in a limo and slept in the same bed with Nancy. It sounds kind of strange now but back then it seemed quite normal. It was the biggest bed I have ever seen. I think it was called a California King. Whoever heard of something like that back then? We had telephones in white and beige and even red, I told Mom, though I don't know whether she believed me. And I got *paid* for all this adventure!

We started rehearsals and Nancy was amazing. Not only did she act, dance, and sing (though the singing was later dubbed by one of Mickey

Rooney's ex-wives), she made it seem so easy. She was truly a natural born entertainer. Where did she even learn all of that in a parochial school in Hong Kong?!

The days would also include makeup tests and wardrobe fittings with the famed Irene Sharaff who would custom dye silk fabrics for our costumes with matching shoes. One day Irene invited me to dinner. I thought she liked me because we had the same name. I was really excited until I realized I was the only one of the dancers she invited. I instinctively quickly made up an excuse and declined. I was later told that Irene was a lesbian and an Academy Award-winning costume designer.

An entire Grant Avenue was built on the Universal set and we rehearsed dance numbers with Hermes's assistant Gino Malerba of Milan. He was overwhelming with his machismo and it was impossible to put up too much of a fight when he came over to our apartment and pushed me down on the mattress, kissing me all over. Luckily, I was saved when Nancy came trouncing home.

Flower Drum Song also gave me my first encounter with a director in Henry Koster, the famous German-born artist who directed the first CinemaScope film *The Robe* with Richard Burton, *Harvey* with Jimmy Stewart, *Dèsirèe* with Marlon Brando, *The Virgin Queen* with Bette Davis, and so many more.

Mr. Koster called on three dancers to sing one line of a song while stepping down one step and putting our open hands next to our faces. "Look to one side of the camera," he said. "Any side but not *at* the camera."

Got it! Sounds simple enough. We all nodded. Then the assistant director silenced the set and called out: "Roll sound." Mr. Koster then called out: "Action."

We stepped down in unison. "Chop Suey… living here…"

"Cut, cut!" yelled the director looking straight at me. "You are looking into the camera! You can look at either side but not into the camera." Fairly calmly he explained this, looking directly at me. I'm not sure he knew my name then.

"Oh me? I'm…I'm so sorry."

"Okay, let's do it again. No looking into the camera, okay?"

"Okay," I uttered.

They rolled sound again and Mr. Koster yelled: "Action!"

Step down, hands up next to face. "Chop Suey… living here…"

"CUT! CUT!" the director yelled. "No looking into the camera PLEASE!"

I was so humiliated. I couldn't believe I did it again.

"I'm so… so sorry."

"Okay Irene." Now he knew my name. "Take a couple of deep breaths and let's go again."

The third time was not exactly right, either. I think I looked into the camera for a second and then looked to the side, so there were two more takes. I was so embarrassed and really thought that I would be fired. For hours I was preparing how to handle myself in this horrible situation. Would I burst into tears or start screaming and run out of the room? Knowing how much I wanted to act mature, I would probably apologize profusely, then go home and cry my eyes out for three days. I prayed and prayed, and no one came to fire me. No one mentioned anything. I was thinking my problem was that up until this film, I'd only been photographed by a still camera and I had to look straight into the camera. The photographer would tell me to smile, look this way, tilt my head that way…

I decided I would try to hide from Mr. Koster. There are always lots of people on the set, so I'd be invisible. And that's what I mostly did.

Not long after the shoot, I went back to New York and I was absolutely bored.

I would go down to Chinatown on weekends with some Chinese kids from my Upper Westside neighborhood. We would hang out at Lucky's, an old and dingy curio shop, because the owner Kenny Gee was so sweet. He'd give us snacks and let us read magazines and just hang out. He would always be in the back of the store running some poker or pai gow games. We didn't know any better. We liked him and call him "Smiley" because he was always smiling.

One day he asked me, "Do you want to go to San Francisco for the Miss Chinatown contest? I really need to have one more girl to represent New York. Please? They pay for your airfare, hotel, food, everything, and they'll even make you a cheongsam dress and matching high heels."

"Really? I don't know, I should ask my mom. I'm not even seventeen."

"No worries. Any girl my shop sponsors, no one ask questions. You'll have a great time and get plenty of gifts and jewelry."

I called him back the following week and agreed. Of course, I was thinking about this guy who played the conga drums in San Francisco, whom I met during *Suzie Wong*. He was in one of the few nightclubs I could get into back then and we had a little fling.

After I went, I never had the chance to thank him or even saw Smiley again because I heard he took a rap for some mobster he was involved with and ended up in a prison in the Bronx.

The pageant took place at the humongous Masonic Temple in downtown San Francisco after days of rehearsals, dress fittings, and rounds of lunch and dinner at family associations. By the time the actual contest came I was exhausted and couldn't remember anything I was supposed to do. Each girl had to walk around the enormous stage smiling and stopping at designated spots. I just remember my cheeks started twitching and then the smile was frozen on my face. It was the scariest thing I had experienced so far in my young life because hundreds of eyes were watching me and judging me like a prized stallion. I wished I could just fly away, like Peter Pan.

But it got better when it came to the question-and-answer section of the program.

"Who was your favorite person in Chinese history?"

"Hua Mulan," I blurted out triumphantly. I got rounds of applause when I did modern dance in orange tights and a black fringe top for my talent portion. There were eleven judges, and eight were Americans. They said I won because the American judges liked me. There were many pretty Chinese girls, but they thought I was "sexy." But I know I won because my lucky number was fifteen and I drew my lucky number.

Wow, I was so happy! I thanked God, then called Mom. They said they had just heard it. For once I think my dad was actually a little proud. In the weeks that followed, life was like a fairy tale, and I did fly around town like Peter Pan. But it made meeting up with Conga guy very difficult.

Here's an excerpt from *The San Francisco Examiner*:

Miss Chinatown U.S.A. Irene Tsu – *The smile of the East in the West…dimensions tell the rest: she's 5'5" tall and 36-23-36. She likes jazz, digs beatniks, hates formality and beauty contests. For Irene looks out on the world with a sly amusement born of high intelligence and sophistication of the type seldom found in an 18-year old just out of a private New York High School."*

Really?

I was not yet seventeen, but I kept quiet because I was afraid I would be disqualified. I wasn't the first or the last aspiring artist to lie about my age. Twenty-one is that magical number that every young girl or guy aspired to be!

After I won, life became a bit of a whirlwind for a while. Beyond all the gifts I received, including three solid 24k gold medallions from family associations, I was also given a trip around the world as a goodwill ambassador.

I was chaperoned to Hong Kong by a most handsome Chinese Pan Am passenger supervisor, Mr. Shen from San Francisco. We stopped in Taiwan for two days and he made the driver stop at the cemetery where my Hou Po (Dad's mother) was buried. She had suffered a fatal heart attack at the U.S. embassy. She was going to come and live with Mom, my sister, and me in the U.S. Visiting her grave turned out to be a huge emotional experience. I remember giving some money to the guard and asking him to direct me to Hou Po's grave. He pointed in one direction and I couldn't stop running as tears were rolling down my face uncontrollably. I wasn't sure where to stop but somehow, like I was pulled by a magnet, I came to stand right in front of the headstone. I read the carved names of Mom and Dad and when it came to my name and my sister's, I started wailing and my whole body shook with every sob. After some time, I moved my legs toward the bus and was consoled by Shen. We bonded and became close friends our whole lives until he passed away a few years ago after playing eighteen holes of golf and eating a big lunch. He loved and lived life to the fullest!

In Hong Kong, I was interviewed and captured by a young American who ran a newspaper called *The Far East American,* among all the other big Hong Kong papers. They did articles on me, sort of "local girl does good" kind of stuff. The young American was Michael Brisbane McCrary, the son of Tex McCrary. His grandfather was Brisbane, who was the chief editor/publisher of the *San Francisco Examiner,* which was owned by the Hearst Corp. He was shocked I spoke Chinese as all the other Miss Chinatowns he had interviewed did not. He was mesmerized and introduced me to Chinese street food. We are still friends today.

And would you believe, it was his half-brother Chase Mellon (yes, like the two banks) who arranged the blind date for me to meet my future husband, Ivan Nagy? Again, another story for later.

Life is bizarre!

It was about to get even more so.

CHAPTER 8

After my tour of Asia as Miss Chinatown U.S.A was over in Hong Kong, I met up with my ex-roommate Nancy "movie star" Kwan who was visiting her family there. She convinced me to re-route my itinerary to go back to the U.S. via Rome.

Rome? Why not? I can just go around the world on Pan Am 1 forever!

Nancy of course had plans to meet up with her then beau Maximilian Schell, and I had no clue what I was to do.

As it happened, Gino di Milano turned out to be a decent friend and got me a part on *Cleopatra* as one of Elizabeth Taylor's handmaidens. Who can complain as it was Cinecitta with Elizabeth Taylor and Richard Burton? The handmaidens all got a close look at Burton and Taylor. They were so beautiful and electric that it was hard to know which one to look at… but it was Burton's voice that hypnotized you. Was he even speaking English? Not American for sure, but who cared? I think Elizabeth must have fallen under his spell like the rest of us.

I was assigned a dressing room at Cinecitta with another very tall, statuesque model type from Amsterdam. Or was it Sweden? I'm not sure, but she had some sort of accent. Most of the handmaidens were selected from different countries and were of different ethnicities. After getting our makeup done in the classic Egyptian eyes style, we'd go to our dressing rooms to get into our costume, which consisted of two panels of gossamer with embroidery. The costumes were definitely expensive and intricate; they looked like Egyptian paintings. My dressing roommate and I would wait around butt naked because it was hot and stuffy, and we didn't want to ruin the rather delicate costumes. They probably cost more than our wages for the entire shoot! She would tell me that I should definitely go to Paris and be in the Folies Bergere because I had the perfect breasts for the show. It was where Josephine Baker got famous. The Madame would take me in a heartbeat, she said. She explained that the French liked smallish, perky breasts, unlike the Americans who are into the bigger the better. I never made it to Paris as I was missing L.A. way too much… and I wanted to keep my breasts to myself.

With *Cleopatra*, a film within a film was in the making right in front of our eyes. Most scenes took days to shoot. All the handmaidens had to have our hands and feet painted gold and had to shuffle quickly backwards exiting a room where Cleopatra was sitting. One long day was finally coming to a wrap when they discovered on the monitor that one extra had walked across the set with a Timex watch on his wrist that wasn't covered by his toga.

"Ma fan corro… que cacco!"

Swearing in Italian always sounds mighty fine to foreign ears.

Back to places and: "Silencio, roll sound… action!"

Every Thursday, everyone would line up to pick up their checks. People just walked off the street to collect; no one knew or cared. When I went back to Fox later, the studio was like a ghost town. As has been documented, *Cleopatra* had bankrupted Darryl F. Zanuck's 20th Century Fox Studio.

But for me, working on the film was just one of many interesting experiences. I made some Chinese student friends while in Rome studying at the conservatory at the Chinese ambassador's home where he entertained us sometimes. Dating was non-existent. There were only three kinds of women in Italy then: the donna (wife), the mistress, and the puttana (the whore). I didn't quite fit in with any, so I ate and got chubby. But the Italian men liked chubby, I soon found out.

Three or four months later I got back to my real world. I had moved to Los Angeles to fully pursue my crazy dreams, but now I had no money and no job in sight, not even a car. Plus, now I was chubby! That started my whole obsessive "starving myself for beauty" syndrome.

As everyone knows, film and photos put weight on you, even up to ten or twelve pounds. It became about trying to be thinner to look better on film. If you see real life actors and models, they are inevitably thinner and smaller. This was especially true back in the sixties and seventies. Some absolutely ruined their health with uppers and downers, some had to be hospitalized regularly. Nowadays, actors—both male and female—get buff rather than emaciated. It never got out of control for me, but I definitely did fall into that trap during my career.

Around the same time, I got my first speaking line in a movie, and the first of many experiences working with a true Hollywood legend. Sure, I had just worked with Elizabeth Taylor, but I'm talking about actually working *with* a legend in a scene!

Back while I was working on *Flower Drum Song*, the director, Mr. Koster, walked over to me during a break and asked if I spoke French. "Well, I actually had almost two years of French in junior high and high school," I quickly blurted out.

"I'm preparing my next picture with Jimmy on the lot. I would like for you to come by my office at lunchtime tomorrow or the day after and I will show you the script," Koster said. "Yes, of course."

"I'll let you know what day." He smiled, shook my hand, and walked away. I was a little bewildered. Jimmy? Jimmy who? After lunch I asked around and found out that it was Jimmy Stewart and it was a movie with Sandra Dee called *Take Her, She's Mine*.

I went to his office and he explained the story to me; that Jimmy goes to Paris to look for his daughter (played by Sandra) and in a bar he encounters a young French hooker who helps him find a number to a hotel. Then later, she claims he was her husband before the police drag her off to jail.

Oh shit, I have to do all of that?! And in French?!

He showed me the script and handed me the copy explaining that the French lines had not been written yet, but we'd improvise something.

"Say something to me in French."

I opened my mouth and blabbered whatever French I could muster up.

"Good! Not to worry, we'll have the dialogue coach to help you. We are not going to shoot for a couple of months, so you'll have time."

That's it? He wants me for the part?

I didn't even have an agent or knew if I was even getting paid. I think my mom had to sign a contract. I also didn't realize that I crossed over into my first SAG job, not playing a part written for a Chinese/Asian. A few months later, after I got back to Los Angeles, we filmed.

Wardrobe was an indigo cheongsam with side slits up my butt, high slide-on heels, and a dreadful wig with a big flower, both of which barely sat on my head. I improvised the French that I knew and didn't get real help from the dialogue coach or anyone. Then came rehearsal on the day of the shoot.

I rehearsed with Jimmy in the rather dilapidated bar/café. A worn, long bar with some old stools was more or less in the middle of the set, and to the right side wall was this old black coin phone atop of a small shelf where there was an overrun ash tray and a worn phone book dangling on a chain. It was a seedy bar in a probably seedier French neighborhood. The scene started with Jimmy's character Frank walking into the bar looking rather haggard, probably from walking all over Paris in search of his daughter. He staggered in and looked around. The bar was rather empty, and I thought, "Wonderful, a customer at last." I walked over to greet him, all smiles and batting my eyelashes. Mr. Koster said to flirt with him, but Jimmy's character was not interested; he asked to use the phone. I took him to the phone and helped him find the number of a hotel where his daughter was supposed to be staying. He spoke to me in English and I responded in French, but we seemed to understand each other (the universal language of *need*). I helped him dial and he got on the phone speaking "Jimmy French." I left to go to the bar to hustle a drink for him, but all of a sudden some big commotion was going on near the door, and the cops came charging in. I knew they were here to arrest prostitutes. Koster told me to make a bee line and jump on Jimmy's back and wrap my legs around him. Even though I was yelling in French that he was my husband, the cops tore me off his back. Easier said than done.

Let's not forget I was wearing four-inch slide-on heels, and as I ran they came off a couple of times. When that happened, we had to cut and do another take. Then I wasn't jumping high enough on Jimmy's back, so another take, and another. Don't forget he must have been six foot two and very, very slim, and I was a chubby teenager. Then came the French cops to drag me off his back. More takes. It must have been thirty takes until Koster was satisfied. I was a little sore, but Jimmy's back must have been *real* sore after that scene.

But he never complained. He offered great suggestions to make the scene better, smoother, and less likely for mishaps. He suggested that they put some kind of tape under the soles of my shoes to help me from slipping and falling and he offered to stoop down, or sometimes bend forward more so I could make my jump easier and safer. He never once complained but always tried to be helpful. He even asked for more takes despite fatigue. I realized then and there that I was working with a true Hollywood legend and a great man who had a lot of integrity. He was so kind to cast and crew alike.

Jimmy and I didn't speak much between takes as he was very focused on the job at hand: having this chubby China girl jumping on his back, kicking and screaming. He did ask where I was from and I told him New York. I think it kind of threw him off as he was probably thinking Thailand, China, or maybe even San Jose.

It was a tremendous experience, and all of a sudden, I realized something.

I was an actor!

My only dream growing up was to be a ballerina. I was becoming an actor by accident. I found that it wasn't so hard, at least not for me. They would say that I am a natural. Maybe so. Later I did go to all kinds of acting classes and studied "method acting" to the point that I couldn't even walk and talk at the same time. It was awful and it killed acting for me for a while. I mean I always did good work by instinct mostly and I had to unlearn everything and only keep the part that worked for me.

One thing I did learn is that for actors who have experienced success in Hollywood, once it starts, it often comes very fast. That's exactly what happened for me.

After *Take Her, She's Mine* I was told I best get an agent. There were only two offices that handled Asian actors: Fred Ishimoto and Bessie Loo. Fred had a small office in an old building on Sunset Strip next to the larger more established Paul Kohner Agency. With the few stills that I had, I walked into his small office with a large desk and some actor's photos on the wall.

He was a fairly tall Japanese man of an indeterminable age and he had the sweetest smile. He was easy to talk to and I didn't feel intimidated or pressured. We talked about our backgrounds for quite a while, and he never asked me to sign any contracts or anything. He said he was born in the U.S. and spent some time in Montana or somewhere in the internment camp where they kept the Japanese Americans during WWII. There wasn't the least bit of anger or bitterness about it. He said he met his wife there, and that they let him study journalism, and how he learned to play baseball. This was his unique characteristic: always looking on the bright side of things. In the movie biz, one really needs a large dose of that. I left his office gaining not just an agent but a friend, protector, and a dad, someone who would be all those things to me for quite a long time. He would drive me to interviews and arrange rides for me as well. Sometimes I would come back from interviews all stressed, "Freddie, I did terrible. They didn't like me."

"At your worst, you are still better than anyone else." He would smile that sweetest smile and say, "You know it's Mary (his wife), Maya (his daughter), and you."

He was my protector, my champion, and someone I could always rely on to bring a positive outlook to life. I would find that I would need that (and him) quite often as my career in film and television began to rapidly take off!

CHAPTER 9

TO BE HONEST, I'm not even sure how this all happened. All I know is that one minute I was dreaming of being an actress in Hollywood and the next minute, I was one.

So it goes for a water color artist.

As I mentioned earlier, I have over eighty credits to my name and that's not including all my commercials. There are definitely some stories I want to share.

I was in a commercial in the late sixties that filmed at the Ponderosa where they also shot *Bonanza*. I had only been on a few sets at that point. I was there shooting a Chevrolet commercial and Michael Landon was there. He walked by and started flirting with me right away. Sure enough, he soon invited me into his dressing room. I wasn't sure if I was supposed to refuse or accept. I didn't want to upset him, so I went into his dressing room and he just lay there on his couch flirting with me. I could see that he was not wearing any underwear beneath his fit-like-a-glove trousers. He was so attractive I could hardly speak.

When they called me to the set, I hastily left but I would think about him for a long, long time after. I managed to meet him again on another set, but he had already left his wife and fallen in love with another woman. Friends would ask me who I've met in Hollywood that I think was the hottest guy. I would say Michael Landon. "Honestly? Little Joe? Irene you've got to be kidding. We thought you would say Marlon Brando or Paul Newman or something."

Nope, Michael Landon.

My biggest campaign was for Hawaiian Punch. I got a call from my agent to go meet famous photographer Cal Bernstein who needed around ten girls to shoot the print ads. As usual, I was tardy. I couldn't find the place and got lost, arriving about a half hour late. When I got there, he was just about wrapped, but they still needed one more girl, so he shot a lot of photos with me. They must have liked me because they chose three different photos of me to use for the campaign. I looked like a different girl in each one. I was "Leilani" from Fiji, "Malia" from Bora Bora, and "Kailani" from Kauai. It was a complete fluke!

Later I went to meet Mr. Atherton, the head of the agency bearing his name. He liked me so much I ended up doing all their national print ads, posters, and industrial promotional films at the John Urie Studio. I became the Hawaiian Punch Girl! That's something that would always help me in my career. I can photograph very differently and can have many looks, which meant I could cross over into different parts.

It was around this time I started to work in guest roles in a number of TV shows as well, including *The Man from U.N.C.L.E.* with Robert Vaughn and David McCallum. I did two episodes, but I never spoke to either of them off set. Robert would be totally immersed in a paperback. He would read them nonstop in his trailer while his girlfriend kept track of him on the phone, practically hourly. McCallum was very specific as an actor. In a scene with the three of us, he would instruct me to speak precisely when he was picking up or reaching for a certain chess piece. I really had to pay attention. He was not a happy camper because I think most people knew his wife Jill Ireland was having an affair with Charles Bronson. They divorced and Jill later married Charles.

The only real kick I got working on that show was when the respected British actor Herbert Lom was watching me one day doing a close-up shot with only the script supervisor. He told me after, "Wonderful, young lady, wonderful. And so were your feet. Did you know your feet and toes were twisting, turning, and emoting the entire time? Amazing…"

Only a British actor observes such detail!

I did an episode of *My Three Sons,* which was one of many during my "slave girl/ picture bride" era. TV writers kept pounding on the Chinese proverb that if someone saved your life, your life belonged to them. You willingly become their slave to pay back your debt. It did make for very comical settings and was well written with big TV stars like Fred MacMurray and Don Grady. I had really good parts and it helped me a great deal to develop my craft. The big thing that stuck out from this shoot was once on set, I overheard the AD saying that I was a New York actress. I was treated with respect, like I was a *serious actress!*

This phase also included *Laredo,* where I got to work with some real hunky cowboys such as Neville Brand, Peter Brown, and Bill Smith. Bill and I were fond of each other. Maybe it was because I was his slave girl in the show, which is every man's fantasy, right? He had this gallantry about him, like how he would always be looking out for me on the set. He knew I was green, and he would give me little tips of what to do. He always ate a can of tuna for lunch and worked out at lunch time just like Michael Landon. I wondered if that was the super hunks' lunch time regiment.

Bill was kind of washed up a decade or so later and would call me and beg me to let him come over and visit. One night he called, and he sounded drunk or drugged out or both. When he finally showed up at my door several hours later, he looked and smelled awful. I gave it to him straight.

"Bill, what's going on? Look at you, you're a mess. How could you even work in this condition? I've always admired you so much. A Rhodes Scholar, a good actor… what in the hell are you doing to yourself? You have to check into rehab right now and clean up. I don't ever want to see you like this again. Ever!"

I don't know why or how these words came out of my mouth. A few years passed and I was at Cedars-Sinai Medical Center in L.A. from a serious car accident, and my ankle was shattered. Somehow Bill found out and he called to thank me for that night at my house when I yelled at him. He said whatever I said that night completely turned him around. He cleaned up his act and now lived with a loving woman. He had not touched drugs and alcohol for several years. He came to visit a few days later with flowers and held my hand to give me his healthy energy.

During this time, I also shot an episode of *I Spy* with Robert Culp and Bill Cosby. Lucky for me, nothing happened. I guess I wasn't Bill's type.

Around the same period, I also co-starred in an episode of *Family Affair* starring the great Brian Keith, Sebastian Cabot, Johnny Whitaker (as the orphaned boy), and Kathy Garver (as the older sibling). It was a unique TV show in that it wasn't really a comedy; it was very well written and had serious social commentary about people and their complex lives. I played the picture bride who was sent over to marry actor Benson Fong's character on the show. Ironically enough, he played my grandfather in an episode of *My Three Sons* we were in together. In our *Family Affair* episode, he actually rejected me so he could continue living his swinging bachelor lifestyle. Kathy Garver's character introduced me to a handsome young American who my character dated like a true American teenager. While I remember that experience fondly, it is sad to see the tragic circumstances that followed the cast after the show ended, including suicide, drug overdose, and other unfortunate accidents that took some of the show's stars at an early age.

One of the most interesting films I did was *How to Stuff a Wild Bikini* with Annette Funicello and Frankie Avalon, as well as the legendary Buster Keaton. I honestly didn't know who Buster Keaton was at the time, that he was such a huge silent film star. I only knew he was one of the most bizarre-looking people I had even seen, with his crazy bug eyes. I didn't have much interaction with him as his wife was always no more than five feet away from him, keeping watch. She was always just out of sight of the camera.

Still, the scene I have with Buster Keaton is one of my favorite film scenes of myself. I was such a kid! I had all the childlike expressions, pouting and giddy. Then the surprise came at makeup one morning. I was handed some pages and was told by the assistant director that I had to learn a song, a duet with Frankie!

"Not to worry, you have time. We won't get to it till about 10:30 or 11."

It took me a moment or two to digest this. *Oh my God, this is terrible!* Absolutely no one told me I had to sing. Singing is not my forte. In fact, I don't sing at all. After makeup I took a look at the song sheet and went blank. Sensing my nerves, the AD came over to explain things to me and calm me down.

"Sweetheart, you don't even have to learn the lines. You can sing anything, any song that you know. But you have to sing it out loud, not just mouthing. We have to see your vocal cords and your facial muscles move. We'll loop in the sound later. Sing 'Happy Birthday,' sing anything, but sing it out loud."

Okay, of course no song came to my mind except "Happy Birthday," so that would have to do. I can hardly remember the takes. I just remember that I was sitting on the sandy beach under some fake palm trees waiting for Frankie to come to the set. I was playing with the sand to calm myself, digging my hand into it, scooping up handfuls and letting it run through my fingers back into the beach. I only stopped when some prop guy came running toward me yelling.

"Don't dig your hands in the sand, it's only about five or six inches deep. You are going to expose the cardboard beneath. We've been here since five this morning to get it looking just right. Stop it, okay, kid?" He smiled and walked away gingerly.

Much later, when I saw the scene, it was several close-ups of Frankie and I singing to each other in a romantic moment on a South Seas island beach under some palm trees and it looked mighty fine. I'm still astounded at the magic of film.

There was also *7 Women* with John Ford. I had a small part with one scene. However, I had to go to rehearsal every afternoon, led by John Ford with all of us actors and the script supervisor. We would sit around this large table where he served tea. I was sitting next to Anne Bancroft, a replacement for Patricia Neal who had suffered a heart attack. Ford was of the same school as John Wayne. He would be chewing tobacco throughout the day like some of us chewed gum, even when he was sipping his tea. It was often difficult to understand him.

He was apparently talking to me one tea time, but I didn't hear. He yelled out my name and asked me a question to which I didn't have an answer. He was upset and mumbled something to me and turned away. I was so scared, I just sat there. All of a sudden, someone grabbed my hand under the table and gave it a big squeeze. It was Anne. She glanced at me and whispered, "You see, I'm scared too. My hands are sweating."

Anne was such a marvelous actor, a truly giving person. And she was funny! Sometimes in the dressing room in the morning she would be telling jokes. One time she said, "Mel is making me go to this party at six. I won't even have time to take a shower, so I guess I'll just have to take a PTA bath…pussy, titties, and armpits." She chuckled and everyone laughed so hard. I could see why she was married to Mel Brooks. She was down to earth and had a great sense of humor.

The day when they were getting ready to shoot my scene, Ford came over to give me a little direction, gesturing to Mike Mazurki, who was in the scene with me.

"This evil warlord there just killed your family, burnt down your village, and now he's going to take you away and fuck you."

Oh my God! I have never heard anyone talk to me like that, let alone give me directions like that! I gaped at Ford, who wore an eye patch, in absolute astonishment. Without another word he walked away. I guess he got what he wanted. I was terrified! As it turned out, Mike was a real sweet guy.

Of course, like all other Hollywood actors and actresses, I had one or two movies I *didn't* get as well. One that I remember the most was *The Sand Pebbles*.

Fred, my manager, had been keeping tabs on the development of *The Sand Pebbles* as it was to be directed by the Academy Award-winning director Robert Wise and to star Steve McQueen and Richard Attenborough. It was about a U.S. gunboat that went down the Yangtze River in 1920s China. More importantly, it had a great part for a young Chinese girl… a female lead.

I was called in to meet Robert at Fox studio and he liked me right away. He said he would call for me in about two to three months after he finished his location scouting in Asia and set up a screen test for me. I'm not even sure if that's common protocol. However, true to his word, he called and had a screen test set up with actor Simon Oakland. I was so green I didn't realize the screen test for a huge movie like that would require a contract to Fox. I was just worried sick about the screen test. The day came and we shot on a real set with extras and actors. We rehearsed and shot it a few times and Robert seemed pleased.

I was a wreck. It seemed like an eternity when I finally was called into Robert's office to meet with him. He motioned for me to sit down, let out a sigh, and said, "This is terrible what I'm going to tell you. You were my choice and still are, but I'm outvoted by our studio head Darryl Zanuck. He has promised the part to his mistress. I'm so, so sorry."

He then leaned forward and whispered, "She is too old."

He waited a long while till I was able to get up from the chair. I uttered, "Thank you, thank you, goodbye." I don't remember how I got back to my car or got home. I couldn't even call Fred. My young heart was so shattered for a long, long time.

The mistress went by the name Marayat Rollet-Andriane, who later wrote and produced a very erotic film based on her life called *Emmanuelle*. I saw it and loved it. She had talent.

Along with all the amazing people I met on projects, I also met some just by being a part of the industry. One of the most amazing is composer Bronislaw Kaper, a true Renaissance Man. I always joke that he was also my first Uber driver. He was at MGM for thirty-five years, and did the scores for *Green Dolphin Street*, *The Red Badge of Courage*, *Gigi*, and *Mutiny on the Bounty*. Fred told me I could always get a lift home to Beverly Hills from Broni if I needed one… and I often did. I was working on *7 Women* at MGM, so after work I walked over to his office to get a ride back. I didn't drive as I had no car, of course.

Broni's home was the old Carmen Miranda house in Beverly Hills. I would go swimming there almost every afternoon while he would have tea with his friends. Among them were great musicians like Itzhak Perlman, Isaac Stern, Daniel Barenboim, Johnny Green, Zubin Mehta, and so many others. He was also very involved with the Young Musicians Foundation. I didn't speak much to any of them. I just jumped in the pool, swam, and ate babka.

One day I went to swim as usual and heard the most incredible and heavenly piano music from the living room, so I tiptoed into the house to take a peep at what was going on. I saw the most unusual sight in the living room: two grand pianos were set up end to end. Broni was playing on one, and on the other was an elderly man with white hair. I thought he looked sort of like Einstein.

I stood in the shadows for an immeasurable amount of time. I was transfixed by this live piano concert. I then tiptoed into the kitchen to find something to drink and ran smack into the German maid Katherina who immediately put her finger to her mouth to hush me. "You shouldn't come in here! He's rehearsing with Arthur Rubinstein for his Los Angeles concert."

"Oh, I'm so sorry, I didn't know."

I had heard of him of course but had never met him let alone hear him play right there fifteen feet in front of me. That's the kind of fortune that I fall into!

Broni was very sweet and supportive of me. I remember much later when I got fired from Bikram Yoga because of a run-in with Bikram's brother, I was so distressed. I wouldn't know what life would be like without yoga, so I came to the pool, jumped in, and started doing laps. I don't know how many laps I did until I got tired and held on to the rail to catch my breath. I looked up and there was Broni standing over me.

"You want to tell me what's going on?"

"I got fired from yoga school."

"That's terrible. Get out of the water. Come and have some tea and babka and we'll talk about it."

He would take me to all the symphonies at the Dorothy Chandler Pavilion where I learned to appreciate classical music. I was somehow rewarded with another father mentor.

On a rather bizarre note, Broni's wife died believing the Nazis still occupied Europe and kept every scrap of newspaper and letters she carried with her from Poland. Her room upstairs in the home was kept just as it was. He forbade anyone to touch her personal properties. Roman Polanski, a fellow Polish man, did the film *The Pianist* inspired by Broni's life.

I also had the fortune to meet acclaimed writer Henry Miller. It was through Broni that I met "Henry San," as he liked to be called then because of his Japanese saloon singer wife Hoki Tokuda. We would take

Henry San to lunch or dinner every few weeks or so. Broni would give him or buy him clothing. He would be looking rather shabby at times, yet had a vanity for clothes. It's hard to imagine one of the literary giants of our time would be penniless for clothing.

We became friends and I would go to his house—a rather rundown ranch home in Huntington Palisades—every couple of weeks. He was spritely and moved well for an eighty-year old. I had a great time playing ping pong with him and listening to him telling stories. I would ask him if he had taken any trips lately and he'd say, "I take teeny tiny airlines in my head. I go everywhere I want… hahaha!"

He did go to Japan in person with his wife to publish an art book. He painted Picasso-esque. He also would tell me that he was in love with the Chinese actress Lisa Lu and wanted to take her out on a date, but so far had only succeeded in having her over for tea twice at his home. He wondered what his next step might be, and he asked what I thought.

What do you tell a lovesick eighty-year old?

I wrote a paper for my UCLA English class titled "Henry Miller, Ping Pong and I," and I had the propensity to show it to him. He told me that he didn't think it was written in English. I was really ashamed and promised myself never to write again. Knowing my inadequacies, I would take English writing and English literature from time to time. I felt enormously lacking in a formal education and secretly envied those who had one instead of the bizarre vaudevillian life I led as a teenager.

It was freedom with a price. There was something to be said about the security of being in a college atmosphere, to be able to make mistakes, to have a family, to be with people my own age. Mine was a life of deprivation in the ordinary and extravagance in the extraordinary. Did I really have a choice?

Years later, I had a small dinner party one night and invited Henry San to my Benedict Canyon house. He called in the afternoon and asked if he could bring a date. "Of course, Henry, bring whoever you want." He said he knew this great gal, an actress who just lived down the street, Di-ahn Williams. "Great," I said. "Of course, I'd love to meet her."

When they came through the door, I saw this statuesque, beautiful, red-headed actress who greeted me with such warmth. I liked her immediately. She then proceeded to walk into my somewhat ill-equipped kitchen and ask what she could do to help. She was so absolutely down to earth and sweet that I was blown away. It's so seldom seen in this self-centered industry. We became instant friends.

A few months later I asked if she could help me throw a surprise birthday party for Ivan, my boyfriend at the time. She suggested her home down the street and told me that her incredible cook would prepare Hungarian goulash for a twenty-two person sit-down dinner. I gave her my list of guests and she also put together some of her friends: the Smothers Brothers, Robert Towne, Julie Payne, and Jack Nicholson. Jack was going to bring Michelle Phillips. Unbeknownst to us, he switched dates at the last minute and showed up with Dennis Hopper.

It was a huge success. To this day we are still the closest of friends though she lives in New York. She got her law degree in her fifties and is still practicing strong. I am delighted to say that I have a permanent guest room in her Fifth Avenue condo looking over the Metropolitan Museum of Art.

There are still times I look back in awe of the famous people I've met… and I was soon going to meet a big one!

CHAPTER 10

OF EVERYONE I'VE MET in my time, there are few if any that were like Elvis Presley.

I worked with him on the movie *Paradise, Hawaiian Style*. Of course I was an Elvis fan, as everybody was, but if I'm being honest, I was not one of those crazy, obsessed fans. I was actually more into the Beatles and the other big rock bands of the time. But of course, I was very excited to work with him.

I remember being very nervous because I had to go to a screen test to get the part. I was working with an acting coach to try and be as prepared as possible and he did nothing to make me feel relaxed and confident. Just the opposite, in fact, as he actually came on to me a couple hours before my screen test.

I did get the part and once again I was cast to be a Polynesian in the film. I was to be one of the female interests for Elvis. How lucky can a little Chinese ballerina get? I must have been a Polynesian princess in my past life.

I arrived in Honolulu and checked into the Ilikai Hotel on a summer day. The filming of my main scenes took place at the Polynesian Cultural Center on the leeward side of Oahu about forty-five minutes from Waikiki. My first day on set, I was nervous and uncomfortable with the heat. Plus, there was a bit of a wardrobe crisis.

Handling the costumes for this production was the famed designer Edith Head. I was fortunate to work with Edith twice in my career; on this film and later on in *Airport 1975*. I clearly remember thinking how unique she looked, this skinny little woman with her iconic big, black glasses. Like all other great artists, she was very intense and highly energetic. She was always standing and walking around, directing her team on what to do. I remember being amazed at not only her vision, but how quickly she and her seamstresses could work when it came to altering anything I was wearing.

Unfortunately, her initial design did cause quite the crisis because, after multiple fittings back in L.A., my costume was deemed unacceptable by the Hollywood censors. They were powerful then. Her design was a bra top with a sarong that sat on my hip bones, exposing my belly button. It was typical Polynesian garb except it was made of the finest silk matte jersey with Hawaiian-inspired print. The board insisted that the sarong had to be lifted up three inches or so to cover the belly button or they would have to put a cotton ball and makeup in my belly button.

No, that would make me look like a freak of nature. Let's scrap that one!

I never understood the female belly button issue in films in the late sixties and seventies. I would deal with the same issue during the filming of my Chevron Island commercials a little later. For the commercial they would have to strategically tape the plastic lei onto my belly button to avoid it being seen. What a nightmare! How is it that in other parts of the world there was belly dancing celebrating the female belly, but here you couldn't even *show* it?

When I arrived, I was nervous. I barely ate lunch but did show up to greet our producer Hal B. Wallis and director Michael Moore, as well as some of the cast and crew to break the unfamiliarity of the first day shoot for me. I really just wanted to lay down in my trailer for a bit. After exchanging some pleasantries, I walked to the trailer and found that the air conditioning was not functioning. I was ready to pass out.

Not wanting to disturb anyone at lunch, I started walking to the nearby Queen's Hut building hoping to find a cool place to lie down. I walked with my head down, careful not to step on a rock or something when all of a sudden I heard a commanding voice saying, "Stop young lady, you can't come this way." I stopped and looked up to find an outstretched hand three inches from my chest. I discovered it belonged to one of Elvis' buds.

"Sorry, the AC was not working in my trailer and I have to lie down. I'm about to pass out."

"Wait here, sweetie, I have to check with Elvis."

Holy shit, what on earth is happening?!

He came right back, introduced himself, and then he told me to follow him. Next thing I knew I was taken into the cool Queen's Hut and led to a massage table. "Young lady, make yourself comfortable, you can lie down here." I believe he brought me a large towel of sorts and covered me up.

"Thank you so much," I said as I quickly drifted off.

When I came to, I smelled a strong scent of baby powder and milk. I opened my eyes… and there was Elvis just twelve inches from my face applying a cold compress on my forehead! For an instant I thought I was hallucinating. No words came to my lips, but I think I did manage somewhat of a smile. When in doubt, smile. That's my motto.

"How are you feeling?" came that familiar Elvis voice. I smiled a little again.

"I guess the heat got to me…and I had a little wardrobe crisis."

"You don't need wardrobe, baby." I guess he called every woman "baby." "You want something to eat or drink? I'll have them fix you whatever you want. Oh, hey baby, we are in Polynesia, so probably no Southern fried chicken, okay?"

He chuckled and left the room. I shut my eyes and burnt every detail of his face and his smell into my mind. Wow! I never met anyone that looked like Elvis. He was just so beautiful.   I had something to drink and walked out to the main room where half a dozen of his boys were sitting about, as well as The Colonel, who was always holding court. The guys were goofing around like circus monkeys to entertain him and Elvis. The mood darkened when they saw me, and I couldn't wait to get out of there.

"The AC in your trailer is working now, so good luck, young lady," said one of the guys. I said thank you and turned to Elvis and waved aloha with my lovely hula hands. We smiled and parted. He was truly a Southern gentleman.

I collapsed onto my trailer bed and dreamed about Johnson baby powder and milk.

I didn't see Elvis again until we were shooting our first scene. There were no rehearsals of any sort, just like working with Frank Sinatra or John Wayne.

Bummer.

I came to the set and went to the spot where my stand-in had been waiting in front of a helicopter. Elvis appeared out of the blue along with two assistants, one holding a comb and the other what looked like a glass of water. The director told me to enter from off-screen with outstretched arms to greet Elvis while saying something like, "Aloha Nui Rick, so good to see you. Does this mean you're going to stay in the islands for a while?" He said he was starting a helicopter service with his buddy Danny, played by handsome Japanese/Hawaiian actor Jimmy Shigeta. Elvis then asked Pua (me) to help send him customers. "You scratch my back and I'll scratch yours..." or some equally corny dialogue.

This was yet another Elvis musical movie that The Colonel devised to sell the King's records. Thinking back, it's really sad that Elvis was exploited like a slot machine. He had so many people who used him and threw him away in his younger years. He was so young and yet so worn out.

Even though it was a relatively short scene, it took quite a few takes as it involved perfect timing and lots of extras. Elvis graciously entertained the extras in between some takes and asked how I was feeling. I felt great now that I was standing next to him! I was excited but I always came off aloof for whatever reason. I guess it was just my East Coast demeanor or perhaps my ballet dancer nature. How embarrassing!

The next set up was a big one. In other films, it would probably take an entire day or even two. Elvis and I were to ride a canoe manned by a couple of natives and paddle down the entire winding river, probably about a half-mile long with natives dancing and singing along the banks. Elvis was belting out one of the big songs of the film. "Drums of the Island...you're beating in my heart...you are with me wherever I go..."

Since we never rehearsed and I'd never even heard of the song, I didn't know what to expect. The song was played over the very loud speakers with Elvis lip-syncing to his own tracks. No one told me anything, not even what to do or where to look, so I just looked around, waved like a pageant queen, smiled, and looked at Elvis adoringly once in a while. However, we never synchronized our looks, so our two heads would be turning in opposite directions most of the time. It was so awkward! They were shooting with three cameras, so they were doing the master shot, medium shot, and the close-ups all at the same time. We did do a second take only because they didn't like some of the native actions in the background. Then we hopped off the canoe as we were greeted by a little girl of about six years old. Elvis hoisted her up to the stage as I looked on. It was quite the family portrait!

There were of course other days of waiting around while other scenes were being shot or delays and changes due to weather or other unforeseen circumstances. That's how it is on location; days of waiting, get ready to get ready, sometimes they get to you, sometimes they don't. You are in this state of perpetual suspended animation. Some actors form friendships with crew members, some try to bury themselves in books or try to check in with family members. There was no texting or cell phones, so communication was limited. One had to try to relax as much as possible and still be focused on the job. Run dialogue and remain in character. But with this particular job there was really nothing much for me to prepare. I just had to hang out and be available.

The Polynesian Cultural Center was located next to a giant Mormon temple. Perhaps the Mormons built it as a replica of the Polynesian villages, their people, and lifestyles. It was more of a Polynesian Disneyland though I was told a lot of the people who worked there were actual natives from those villages. I tried to fit in and asked them to teach me some phrases and dance moves. I tried to learn as much as I could about their arts and crafts, their music and dances. I was especially fascinated by the Samoan fire throwers and the power of the Polynesian physiques. From my experience, they are a happy, childlike people. No wonder the artist Paul Gauguin never wanted to move back to stinky old Paris with its corseted women with rotting teeth. The Polynesian way of life can be intoxicating for the Anglos, for a while anyway. I was told their children are raised by the whole village regardless of who their parents were. That was just one of the amazing things I learned about this incredible culture.

Some days, when neither Elvis nor I were filming and The Colonel was not around, I would just chit chat with him in his trailer. He was seriously into martial arts then and we talked about different kinds of martial arts. I casually knew Bruce Lee though he was not yet known in Hollywood. Some days we would talk about faith. He was raised a Southern Baptist while I was raised Episcopalian with a grandma that started two Mandarin-speaking churches on the East Coast. We had an affinity for Christ. Despite the attraction, he drifted away from any basic sexual instincts of a red-blooded American idol. Though I was told some other co-stars did have a taste of Johnson's baby powder!

On one of our last times talking, I was leaving his trailer when he grabbed my hand and whispered, "Keep the light burning." He winked and gave me that crooked smile.

When filming ended all the co-stars were given an entire box of signed photos, posters, albums, and 45s. Such generosity wasted on an unconscious teenager. A number of years later, the whole box got wet during one of my moves and I just threw it away. My mom really got mad at me. She loved Elvis. Mom called again when dear Elvis died at the age of forty-two… so senselessly, so tragic. She wanted me to attend the memorial in Graceland and, as usual, I was working on some TV show or film, so I didn't go. Though in 2018, I was invited to Graceland to attend the fortieth anniversary of his passing. It was my first time at Graceland, and there were fans from all over the world there. I met some of his cousins and ex-girlfriends and thought about my brief time with the King.

Actually, in the seventies, my husband and I went to Vegas to catch his show. I called up Joe Esposito, the King's right-hand man and a free ringside table was offered to us. Such loyalty and grace! We were moved by the show, but sadly we also witnessed the King's very visible physical decline. He looked twenty to thirty pounds heavier then when we were filming. He was sweating profusely and really struggling with his performance. He was obviously not well and just going through the motions of his act. It was shocking and sad for us to witness. Just a short seven or so years prior he was in great form and seemed happy. I thought for sure they would pull him off the road and let him go into rehab for as long as he needed.

But no, he couldn't stop. The Colonel wanted that last nickel from the slot machine and maybe Elvis didn't know how to say no by then. It's a macabre dog-eat-dog food chain. Elvis's light stopped burning and he lost his way home. All he wanted was to be loved tender…

I actually saw the film at a matinee in a theatre on Hollywood Boulevard. My friend and I sat right behind a middle-aged couple looking like they were from out of the area. When my scene came on, the wife turned to the husband and said, "What is she…some sort of native?"

Most Americans had no clue about anything from that region, not even where Vietnam or Saigon or Phnom Penh was when we entered the incomprehensible war.

"A Fijian or from Tonga… my buddy was in the Navy."

"Oh."

CHAPTER 11

IN THE MID-SIXTIES, I kept working, working, and working in both film and TV as my career continued to take off. Looking back, I consider myself to have been a "bread and butter actor."

In that time, I shot the film *Island of the Lost*. It was an otherwise unremarkable shoot on the beaches of Miami, though we had to deal with chiggers! Getting bitten by chiggers was no laughing matter as those bugs would burrow under your skin and live there. We were covered from head to toe every morning with repellent, but I am unfortunately extremely allergic to bites. I slept in the bathtub a few nights because the itching was so severe that my skin was raw from scratching and I couldn't get a wink of sleep.

And then came the accident.

After lunch one day, we picked up filming a scene that had me swimming in choppy waters. "Irene, you will be in the water and I'm going to give a signal for the grips to turn on the motor of their power boats," the director said. "You are to swim from screen left to right through the turbulent waters. It'll look great! Go get ready."

When it came time to shoot, I got in the water and the last thing I heard from the director's bull horn was, "Irene duck down, get the top of your hair wet, then start swimming toward the power boats. Mark (my co-star) will be right behind you."

I ducked, I swam, and within seconds I felt something strike my foot. It was one of the motor blades. I let out a scream and instinctively Mark grabbed my arm and pulled me back. Two stunt men dove in and got me out of the water. I was in a lot of pain as they rushed me shaking and crying all the way to the hospital. When I opened my eyes there, I saw a woman standing over me. I had heard growing up from my family members in the medical field not to ever let anyone in the emergency room operate on you if you possibly can. Remembering that, I demanded a surgeon. I yelled at the woman, "Don't touch me, I want a doctor, a surgeon!"

"I *am* your doctor, your surgeon," she replied. "I want to tell you that you are very, very lucky because the blade of the propeller missed your main tendon by about half an inch, so the deep cut was almost entirely in your heel. You will go into surgery shortly, after a few more tests."

I was numb and dumb, no words coming out of my mouth. I closed my eyes and secretly said my prayers. I knew I was still lucky, and that God had been watching over me.

I didn't sue the producer, Ivan Tors, even though I did have a case. He had hired a nonunion local crew who didn't even bother to put cages on their outboard motors. They didn't even know that they were supposed to! Everyone said this would've never happened if we were shooting back in L.A. We had to re-stage some scenes for me to sit on rocks instead of standing. I had to use crutches for some weeks, but I did heal and all was eventually forgotten, like it was just a bad dream.

I do remember some laughs from the shoot, like eating Chinese Cubano food and getting so stoned with actress Sheila Wells and her Cubano friend driving around the loop in downtown Key Biscayne. We didn't remember how many times we drove around the loop and we couldn't seem to get out of it. We laughed so hard. We thought we'd be stuck in the loop forever. Our friends would have to bring us food and water and we'd have to figure out a way to go pee… such goofiness. Well, that's one of the best things about being actors back in the sixties; let other people be serious!

I was also in *Caprice* with Doris Day. This film came as a consolation prize for me at Fox because I lost the great part in *The Sand Pebbles* to the mistress. I was still under contract to Fox because of the screen test and was given a two-bedroom dressing apartment larger than most L.A. apartments today.

Caprice was a spy spoof starring Doris Day and Richard Harris, conceived by Frank Tashlin as "the spy who came in from the cold cream." Tashlin, sadly, is almost obscure now but if you looked him up, you'd see that he was a fabulously talented animator, cartoonist, children's writer, illustrator, screenwriter, and film director. He was brought to Hollywood by Disney to work on so many cartoons that he couldn't even remember them all. He had directed most of the Jerry Lewis films and the wonderful *Will Success Spoil Rock Hunter?* with Tony Randall and Jayne Mansfield.

I went to meet with Tashlin and had no idea what an accomplished artist he was, but we immediately had a good rapport. I told him I grew up with an artist mother and watched her paint water colors and that we had world class paintings in our apartment in New York City. Shortly after, he invited me to his home and said that I could paint there. He had the most impressive, large, architectural home in Beverly Hills. It was built as a guest house to an estate less than a third of a mile away. The home had a huge swimming pool and a tennis court with rows of seats for viewing guests. Honestly, I've never seen such a setting! Tashlin had an easel set up for me with water color and brushes in front of the pool and he was also working on an acrylic at his easel. He said that he had been painting anything and everything for the past three months and only stopped to eat and jump into the pool once in a while to clean himself off. When I met him, he was so depressed that his wife, an aspiring opera singer, had left him. He simply could not afford all those extravagant singing coaches and the money needed to promote her career any longer. He was from humble origins in New Jersey and was notoriously thrifty. I actually painted my very first water color there with a little instruction from the famous artist. He declared that I was a natural and encouraged me to continue to paint, and I did for a while. That first water color still hangs on my wall today, and it still brings me joy when friends comment.

"Who did this?"

"Me. It's my first water color."

"Wow… it's wonderful!"

A Frank Tashlin gift to me.

I jumped at the opportunity to play Ray Walston's secretary/companion in the film. It was another crossover part for me as it was not written for a Chinese or even an Asian actress. Though I didn't realize it at the time, this was a big moment, not just in my career, but also for Asian actresses. At that time, most of us could only get work in Asian roles, so to get a part that was more culturally open or that would normally go to a white actress was a big deal. I certainly didn't seek to cross over intentionally as I was just focusing on working as much as I could. But I realize now that it is significant, and I'm thrilled that I was able to do that quite a few times in my career.

Doris Day was my mom's icon! Her favorite song was "Que Sera Sera." I grew up listening to the enchanting voice of Day. I had the song played at Mom's memorial as I knew she would really have loved it. With *Caprice,* again I realized I had the great luck of working with another Hollywood legend. Day was a unique energy on the set, exuding that famous smile and a voice like none other. She was also sweet. I loved all her movies. When we would ride together back to makeup or wherever, she would close her eyes and be absolutely still and silent. There she would turn into a whole other person.

I guess it would be exhausting to be Doris Day every day.

There was quite lot of physical humor in the Tashlin film, maybe because of his background working with Jerry Lewis. We shot a scene on the swimming pool deck of my character's boss's house. Like a good, hard-working secretary, I'm sunbathing by the pool and chatting with my boyfriend on the phone, while Miss Day is standing on her tippy toes under the slatted deck trying to cut a piece of my dangling hair. Of course, my darling Great Dane "Tiny" senses some danger and gets all agitated. Grumbling, I jump up and run to Tiny to calm him down. Then back to sunbathing, then back to calming Tiny minutes later. Poor Miss Day was practically dangling off the deck to snip a piece of my waterproof hair. It was an important story point as she really needed to find out the secret formula in my hair.

In another scene, I got to work closely with Michael J. Pollard, who had just come off of the hit *Bonnie and Clyde*. I remember Tashlin and casting complained that Michael's agent had wanted five thousand dollars for the one scene, but boy am I glad they got him. He *made* the scene. In the film, he played my boyfriend, and in this scene, Michael and I went to the movies. While cuddling and eating popcorn, Miss Day sneaks up on us, once again trying to snip a piece of my hair. However, she snipped a piece of Michael's hair instead. Michael thought perhaps she was trying to get cozy with him. He then moves his hand up her thigh which makes her squirm and she tries to extricate herself from his mauling. I, of course, think she's coming on to my boyfriend and I clobber her with my purse. We three cause quite the scene at the theater with people shushing us and popcorn flying!

I not only had crossed over into a non-Asian specific part in this film, but I was way ahead of my time in that I had two boyfriends… and waterproof hair too!

Speaking of waterproof hair, there was another scene where I was called upon to dive into a pool. This time we shot at Tashlin's Olympic-sized pool. They shot the rehearsal, and when I hit the water the bottom part of my bikini slipped down to show part of my bottom. I said to Tashlin, "I've got to hold on to the bottom of my bikini for the next take. I'll just use one hand."

"No, that's going to look ridiculous," Tashlin said. "We won't use the clip if it does fall down, okay?"

So I dove in and the bottom came down again. And, of course, they used that take and it caused a sensation with the censors. *Time* magazine ran an article with me in a bikini and right below was a butt-naked picture of an English actor in *Ulysses*. It said, "Why was it okay for him but taboo for her?"

There was no female empowerment then!

CHAPTER 12

AROUND THIS TIME, I got a call from the same John Urie of Hawaiian Punch that there was a commercial casting a Tahitian Polynesian dancer.

"And you're a dancer," he said.

"Not really," I said. "I mean, I am a dancer but not a Tahitian dancer."

"Well, go watch *South Pacific*, get a record with Polynesian music, and practice!" he replied.

I had one day to learn and practice Tahitian dancing. I got there for the audition and they had already been casting people all day long. I think I was one of the last ones to audition. I saw real Tahitian dancers that came from these Tahitian revues, like the Seven Seas on Hollywood Boulevard and even from Las Vegas. These girls had maracas and coconuts and everything.

Holy crap, I'm never going to be able to do this!

I had been there since two in the afternoon, so when I was called, I was told to do a little dancing and talking. I will never forget what I had to say.

"Hele my iki mokoo ayna oh Chevron!" which means, "Come to Chevron Island, under the Standard sign."

A week later, my manager Fred called and said, "You know what, you got the job! You are going to be on national TV for Standard Oil of America."

I was so excited I jumped up and down.

It was a Chevron campaign for the Standard Oil of America Eastern seaboard which was headquartered in Louisville, Kentucky. They flew me there once to meet the chairman at one of the most impressive office buildings that I've ever been to. It was like going to Buckingham Palace. It was immense. It took me half a day to get up to his office from the car park. The chairman's huge desk must have been a hundred feet from the door. He was a rather short man who resembled Harry Truman and had a name that sounded like Mr. Gasoline.

I swear it sounded like Gasoline!

I was too afraid to ask the Chevron representative who escorted me around town what his real name was. I do remember he said Montgomery Clift was his brother. Is he kidding? Montgomery Clift's brother is working in Louisville for Mr. Gasoline? I don't think so.

One of our directors was Stuart Hagmann, who went on to direct *The Strawberry Statement*—which won a Jury Prize Award at the Cannes Film Festival in 1970—as well as many TV shows. Stuart had taken us out into the desert pretending it was some Hawaiian island. They propped up half dead palm trees and painted extras with brown body paint to look Polynesian. They had not figured on a sandstorm for two days. I was too busy trying to get sand out of my... everywhere back in the trailer when the rigs started to pull out. They almost left me there! I think they had to scrap the whole thing.

Another time they built a whole island on a float and old tires out in San Pedro harbor. That was another bad idea because it must have been December and it was a night shoot. It was freezing and of course, once again, I was hardly wearing anything. Everybody would be huddled in huge coats or anything they could find. One of the gaffers or the grip handed me a flask. We were just getting drunk waiting for the helicopter to swoop down over as they were trying to get a shot of the island. It was a complicated shot that had to be timed just right. When the lights came up, I was supposed to be dancing on top of a gas pump. I was just trying to stop from freezing and concentrating on not falling down. "Okay, get ready, the helicopter is flying over... get ready... now!" The lights would come on and I'd hear, "Coming this way" bellowing over the walkie talkie's bullhorn. They would then prop me up onto the pump. It was amazing I didn't fall off the damned thing. I would start dancing and then the helicopter would zoom by.

There were so many takes!

"Okay, timing was off."

"Don't move!"

"Please don't stop dancing."

"Not sure we got it that time."

"Okay, one more."

"Nope, once more around."

"Okay, I think we got it that time."

Please God!

After we shot, I did PR tours all along the Eastern seaboard, visiting gas stations, doing interviews, and getting pictures taken. I only got into a little mischief in New Orleans. I was picked up from the airport by another representative and dropped off at the hotel. He offered to take me to dinner, but I really just felt like getting into a bath and being alone.

But not for long.

I was tired and bored and couldn't sleep so I slipped down to the lobby looking for some je ne sais quoi. Very soon, some young man came over to talk to me. After some small chitchat I found out that he went to LSU and had to go back to school in the morning. Tonight, though, he wanted to take me for a ride around town and maybe have some drinks. Four hours and six bars later I was still in the car, now with three drunk guys that I'd never seen before. I barely knew the first guy's name. Let's say I barely escaped what could have been a very bad experience. I'd never done anything like that before. I'd never had the college experience. I was their age, but I had been working as an adult since I was fifteen.

The campaign was a huge success and it won all the advertising awards in *Progressive Age* and *Advertising Times*. After about a year of it running, the oil company decided that they wanted to go national with this "Chevron Island" campaign. By this time, I had started filming *The Green Berets* and on the couple of weeks off I would be shooting the national Chevron Island commercials, which in itself was like a TV series because the budget was so huge. We shot in Hawaii and the Caribbean, every place the ad executives in New York wanted to go. We stayed in nice hotels and catered sushi for lunch (most people didn't even know about sushi in 1969). They gave me my own makeup man and wardrobe guy.

Yeah, but what wardrobe? I was barefoot, I wore a grass skirt, a lei down over my belly button, two coconuts, and a flower behind my ear. But all that takes a lot of work. It all had to be fireproofed and the skirts weighed about fifteen pounds.

The whole thing was a whirlwind and I was soon seen everywhere!

Speaking of *The Green Berets,* that film gave me yet another chance to work alongside a Hollywood icon: The Duke himself, John Wayne.

I was called to Warner Brothers to meet with Michael Wayne, the Duke's very handsome older son who was producing *The Green Berets*, based on the Vietnam War novel by Robin Moore. They really wanted me for the female lead of the Vietnamese singer who was used as bait to capture the Viet Cong general. There was a little problem with this, not only because I didn't sing... but I was not Vietnamese! There were big objections from the Vietnamese military and Wayne needed the military, so they compromised and used the Vietnamese singing star only for one singing scene. I became the top model and bait.

Wouldn't you know, in the movie she sang a French song, "La Vie on Rose." I'm never far from something French!

I was on location with John Wayne and company where the 83rd battalion was based in Fort Benning, Georgia. It was serious stuff. The real Green Berets were training there before they got shipped off to the real war in Vietnam. I remember seeing huge parking lots full of used cars, except this was not a regular used car lot. These cars belonged to soldiers who would never return, and you could actually buy these cars at a great price if you wanted. Some of our stunt people bought them and shipped them back to Los Angeles.

The weird reality of war!

My first meeting with John Wayne was in a limo as we were being driven out to the set. He greeted me and we said our hellos. He invited me for a drink after the shoot and I said I didn't drink. What an idiot I was! Also, what an insult to the Duke. He didn't take it too kindly and referred to me as the little hippie chick after that. It didn't help matters that one day in the limo I opened an envelope from my friends from L.A. and a few neatly rolled joints actually fell out onto my lap.

Filming of *The Green Berets* went slowly as the sets were big and on different locations. Most actors would have to be shuttled from set to set and different crews worked on different sets. Asian extras were not easy to find so they would have to come from neighboring states, or we would get them out of the Army. Imagine the soldier preparing to be shipped out to Vietnam and he ends up in a movie playing a Viet Cong. Acres of brushes were sprayed green to resemble the jungles of Vietnam as weather in Georgia got colder. All this was technically difficult in 1968.

The studio sent in an old pro, Mervyn LeRoy, as the supervising director, though Wayne was still technically the director. LeRoy was a small, cigar-puffing, velvet slipper man, looking like he just stepped out of the Polo Lounge into the war zone. He mainly took drinks with Wayne and David Janssen. LeRoy stayed just long enough to collect his money, then goodbye Vietnam!

Other dignitaries who came to visit were the famed director John Ford who discovered Wayne, Robin Moore, and his publisher, the handsome Peter Mayer, who would be smoking and talking and doing things nonstop. We became good friends.

As a side note, Peter later ran Penguin Group and published Salman Rushdie's controversial book *The Satanic Verses*. The Ayatollah wanted Rushdie dead and Peter's life was threatened but he took a hard stand not to go into hiding. The Ayatollah apparently didn't know how hard it was to catch this Peter Rabbit. He just moved too fast. We would attempt to meet at random book fairs or my filming locations between his tennis, breakfast, lunch meetings, horseback riding, and dinners and we'd often miss each other altogether. I visited him a year before his passing at his SoHo office of Overlook Press and he encouraged me to write my book, even offering some advice on what interests readers, what is important, and so on. He had a phobia for Los Angeles and the movie crowd, but they would fly him out to L.A. to pick his brain for the next bestseller when he was with Penguin. I sent him some early drafts of my story and went back to see him in August of 2018. Three days later, he passed away as quickly as he lived.

But back to the Duke. Wayne would be in a scene while he was also directing. Several big actors like Brando tried it but it's never easy. Tempers flared. One scene I remembered well… actor Luke Askew was supposed to walk up to a mound and deliver his lines to Wayne as George Takei and I looked on. Well, Wayne did not like the way Luke delivered the lines time after time. Wayne would show him how to read the lines as he walked it for him as well. "Here, you take three steps… one, two, three… put your weight on your right leg and say your line, turn, take another step and say…"

I've never seen anything like it! I later saw in a documentary on Federico Fellini that he directed all his actors like this, and that they would have to repeat after him word for word, move for move. You never would have guessed that the Duke directed just like Fellini!

Most nights after filming, I went to have supper at Janssen's or Wayne's or whoever had a chef. They would make the best fried chicken I've ever tasted (the black ladies told me the secret is the sweet milk). Other nights we would go to one of the two restaurants near base.

One night, George Takei and I decided to go to an Italian(ish) restaurant. The large restaurant was dimly lit and quite empty as we sat down in one of the booths. I was looking through the menu as George was telling me, "Don't get fancy, Irene. Just stick to the spaghetti with meatballs." No sooner had George spoken those words, when I heard this big intimidating voice over my head. "You should be so lucky to be even allowed in here."

I didn't know how to react. I saw George clutching his knife and fork. His face turned red, green, and white. I was scared. Something bad was going to happen in that instant and I couldn't speak or move.

Then I heard a booming, cheery voice coming from the entrance. "Hey there, mind if I sit with you guys?"

In came Mike Henry, one of our actors and a famous football player. His six-foot-four, two hundred and fifty pounds of muscles and smiles came walking over to our table. My shoulders dropped about three inches. George also eased up his grip on the dinnerware and relaxed his facial muscles some. The guy behind us who made the comment just sank down into the booth never to be heard from again. It was my first direct encounter with racial discrimination, and wow, it felt like nothing else. It made your hair stand on end, numb and rigid all at the same time. That was how it was in 1968 in Fort Benning, Georgia.

I also remember the suave, sexy-voiced Janssen sitting around Fort Benning getting loaded all the time. He seriously stayed drunk the entire shoot. He didn't have a whole lot to do as the war correspondent. He was called on the set every few days to do a few lines. He was utterly bored, so I asked, "Why did you accept the part?"

"Wayne called me and offered me the part, so of course I had to say yes. Everyone says yes to the Duke."

Every chance he got, he would fly out on some private jet to L.A. or Vegas to see a girlfriend or two. He invited me to come along a few times, but I always said no. I was too afraid to leave the set without proper release from production, which I knew they would never grant. It's a good thing because we really didn't have a whole lot to say to each other. However, he persisted when the film was wrapped in Fort Benning. "You've got to meet me in Atlanta. The owner of the Braves invited me. It'll just be for one night and you'll have your own suite. Sweetheart, you really shouldn't be hanging out with the stuntmen. You're a star now."

I'd never heard it put that way! Still, I said no to Atlanta and thank you to David.

At one point while I was filming *The Green Berets,* I got a call from my manager Fred with exciting news about the Chevron Island national campaign.

"Will you come in to tape your voice?" After asking why, Fred explained, "Because Madison Avenue found a girl to be the Chevron Island Girl for the commercial, but they did not like her voice. They wanted you to dub this girl's voice. Irene, would you come in and do the lines?"

"What?" I couldn't quite understand.

"That voice has gotta go," Fred almost yelled into the phone

I, of course, said okay. I was working all week, so I flew in over the weekend. I got to L.A. at like 6 p.m. and went straight to the recording studio. We started recording at nine. I could see why they had to dub her, as her English was very strange. It was not that she had a huge accent. It was her emphasis of the words; her enunciation was all wrong for the American ear. I tried to sync to her Tahitian lips the best I could.

I was in English 1F for foreigners less than a dozen years ago and now I was practically an English coach!

To be working in both the Chevron commercials and *The Green Berets* at the same time was a very surreal experience. John Wayne told me he was on *The Tonight Show Starring Johnny Carson* promoting *The Green Berets* and Carson asked who was the female lead in the film. Wayne mentioned my name and said I was the one on TV dancing on top of the gas pump and inviting people to "Come to Chevron Island." Johnny and the audience recognized the commercial immediately, but that segment was not broadcast because Shell Oil was the show's sponsor.

Bummer!

As an interesting side note, in recent years I've received residual checks from the TV series *Mad Men*. It just said for "Beautiful Girls." I vaguely recall that one of my agents made a deal with *Mad Men* for they referred to my commercials or my likeness in the show. What a hoot!

As exciting as it was shooting that campaign, what was more exciting was who it led me to, through a little bit of luck and timing, and the great adventure I was about to embark on with one of the biggest entertainers of all time… Francis Albert Sinatra.

CHAPTER 13

I WOULD START AN UNEXPECTED ROMANCE with the Chairman of the Board that would last for more than two romantic, adventurous, and most interesting years. In that time, I experienced much more than an up-close-and-personal look at what it was like to live with both the privileges and burden of superstar celebrity status. I also saw a man who loved the spotlight, but also yearned for the freedom of privacy with a desire to equally enjoy both the bigger and smaller things in life. I also saw a man notorious for being bold and brazen with a devil-may-care attitude at his sweetest, most caring, and most intimate. I saw the other side of the fantasy and it was eye-opening and yes, very, very exciting.

I first met Frank Sinatra when I was in Miami filming a Chevron Island commercial. I was staying with my friend and (at the time) dolphin trainer Ric O'Barry in Coconut Grove. For whatever reason, the advertising company I was working for said it was bad for my image to be hanging out with him. When I was with him, I often found myself in the company of rock stars such as Crosby, Stills & Nash and folk artists like Fred Neil, who was known mostly for his songwriting on songs like "Everybody's Talkin'" used in *Midnight Cowboy*. O'Barry would, of course, eventually become an avid activist against keeping dolphins in captivity, form a world-wide nonprofit organization "Dolphin Project," and conceive the Oscar-winning documentary *The Cove*. Back when I was staying with him, he was still training dolphins for the hit TV show *Flipper* and literally sleeping out on the rafters next to his beloved creatures. But I didn't care; he looked like Jean-Paul Belmondo!

My incredible manager Fred was always looking out for me and tried to get me away from "Flipper." He thought I should look up Aaron Rosenberg who produced *Caprice* along with Marty Melcher, who was

Doris Day's husband. He said Aaron would call me in a few days to have lunch. He said it would be a good thing to do for my career connection and that Aaron was such a nice man, so I agreed. Sure enough, Aaron called and invited me to lunch at the legendary Fontainebleau restaurant the following day.

Oh my heavens, that was a fancy place that I'd only heard about. I never expected to be able to experience actually eating there! I would later learn that this was one of Frank's spots. I showed up for lunch not knowing who else was going to be there or what to expect. I found the large table where Aaron and six or seven friends were already seated. He sat me down at the only vacant chair, which happened to be directly across from Frank Sinatra. He was in Florida shooting the film *Tony Rome*. Needless to say, I was more than a little surprised to see him. I, of course, knew who he was because *everybody* knew who he was. I was almost too shocked to have any first impressions of him. Of course, he was good-looking, and he had that essence that most famous people have, that there's just something unique, different, and special about him. But what I most remember is the expression on his face. He seemed a bit agitated. I would learn over time that was sort of a natural state for Frank.

I also remember that he didn't seem the least bit interested in me, which actually made me relieved!

I was introduced around the table and sat down to basically stare at my plate. I don't remember what I ate and what was said but I know that I did not look up very much. I was in a state of shock to be this close to Frank and I was afraid I would be caught staring. Still, I keenly listened to that unique, sexy, baritone voice. Some people embody one or two elements, like fire and air, or water and earth. With Frank, he is all the elements at once. Even at that first meeting, he frightened and thrilled me, and I knew I would never meet anyone else like him. Frank had that kind of effect on people. He was just so extremely intense, explosive, and of course, sexually attractive at the same time. It was hard and mesmerizing to look into those bright blue eyes, which I think I only did once or twice in that first meeting.

I do remember that at one point an older woman came up behind him and touched him on his shoulder to ask for an autograph. She spoke with an intimacy that made it sound like she knew him. Without warning, he swung at her and almost knocked the poor lady down. His security guards immediately dove in to usher her away. I was told later when a similar incident occurred that Frank hated being touched in public due to his early career years when he would be mauled by fans. He was fascinating and dangerous, like a jaguar. Not wanting to overstay my welcome, and feeling slightly intimidated, I quietly removed myself from the restaurant shortly after they took the plates away. I thought that chance meeting would make for an interesting story. Little did I know that this was just the beginning…

Several weeks later, back in L.A., I was with a friend at the Candy Store, a very hip and private club on Rodeo Drive. It was crowded as usual and the line to the ladies' room was insane. I soon realized the reason why. At the corner booth, adjacent the ladies' room, was Frank and some of his friends. When I came out, I saw he was sitting with actor Harry Guardino, with whom I had done some TV work. Harry saw me and yelled out, urging me to come over to the table. He introduced me and I met Ol' Blue Eyes again. This time he seemed less edgy and more relaxed… well, at least as relaxed as he could get. I would come to learn that Frank was never *really* relaxed.

I flashed him a shy smile or two as we all politely chatted. I stayed for a brief time before heading back to my friend at a table far away. Again, I thought that was the end of it.

The next day, I got an unexpected phone call. I had just moved into my little house on Hutton Drive in the affluent but still affordable Benedict Canyon neighborhood of Beverly Hills. The phone rang and I tripped over boxes and cords trying to find it. When I answered, I was stunned to hear my old friend Nicky Blair's voice on the other end. Nicky and I had been friends back when he was an actor, and he actually drove me around for a while before I knew how to drive. Nicky had given all that up and switched to the restaurant business. He had opened up an Italian restaurant with his name that quickly became a local hot spot with the Hollywood elite.

"So, Francis wants to have dinner with you here tonight at 7:30," he said. "He's having his special table arranged for you."

"Francis who?" I asked, innocently.

"Sinatra," my friend replied, a little stunned that he even had to say the surname. "He'll pick you up at seven. Be ready; he's very punctual."

Nicky hung up before I could say anything else.

I didn't really know what to expect. Frank was ahead of his time because not many men like him dated Asian women then. Of course, I figured he loved the way I looked but maybe he saw something different in me. No matter what I felt, on the exterior I always appeared calm, cool, and perhaps even a little aloof. I didn't seem to be phased by anything and that was unique to a big-time celebrity like Frank. It was something I found out later that attracted him to me. I also found a balance of being ferociously independent, a lot of fun as if I was just "one of the guys," and still sweet and very feminine. I was also a bit mysterious and exotic. I found out later he wanted to learn more about me because I "wasn't like those other broads."

I went into a bit of a frenzy trying to figure out what to wear on a first date with a super famous jaguar that I didn't really know. I decided to go shopping for a while to see what I could find. But it was useless because I didn't have any idea how I should dress or what I should look like. I started to think back to what I was wearing on the two occasions he saw me. I had on a long sleeve navy jersey shirt and medium brown suede vest over slacks at the club. It was classy and conservative. Is that what he liked on me? But shouldn't I wear a dress? I mean, we are going to a fancy dinner, so that would be most appropriate, right? I must have gotten in and out of every single thing I owned. I finally settled on a classy but sexy black dress. Then came the decision of belt or no belt, or maybe a scarf or maybe not. I practiced walking in front of the mirror. This took all afternoon.

"Oh my god, this is worse than any audition I've ever had to go to," I said to the mirror. "We haven't even gone out yet and I'm already exhausted."

Then, at 6:55, the phone rang. It was Frank.

"Hey baby." Two words and not only was his voice as smooth as silk, the instant familiarity of calling me "baby" made me melt. Sure, he called every gal "baby" but when he did it to you, he somehow still made it sound special. He spoke clearly and calmly, right to the point. Just hearing his voice sent my heart racing. "I don't know if you've heard, but my divorce from Mia hit the papers and the paparazzi are all over in front of my house and they're following me."

Frank and Mia—actress Mia Farrow—had a brief marriage. Frank was fifty when he married Mia, who was twenty-one. Frank had wanted Mia to give up her acting, something that should have sent up some red flags for me once we started dating. Mia had initially agreed but got bored, so she signed on to star in *Rosemary's Baby*. After that shoot had run past its schedule, Mia had to drop a role she was going to do in a movie with Frank. That had essentially led to the end of their marriage, though the two had remained friends. Their story was all over the papers and in Hollywood, despite how regularly they occur, a celebrity divorce is always big news.

"I'm in my car heading out to the desert," he said. He had a phone in his car and, of course, no one else did then. "I want you to meet me at my place this weekend. I'll call you when I get there."

He hung up. At first, I didn't really hear the part about the desert. I only got that we would not be having dinner at Nicky's. I drew a long breath and let out a big sigh. I kicked off my black heels, wriggled out of my dress, and fell down backwards onto my very low Japanese bed. With somewhat of a free fall, I hit the bed with a thud, releasing all the stress that had been building up inside.

"Whew, I think I'll call for a pizza and I may even have a glass of wine if there's any in the kitchen."

It wasn't until a couple hours later that I started thinking about the weekend and the desert and the jaguar in the desert. It began to sink in that Frank Sinatra had just invited me to stay with him at his house in Palm Springs!

I called Fred. Whenever I was in distress, I knew I could call Fred. It was always good to hear his calm, soothing voice.

"Do you like him?" Fred asked after I told him what had happened.

"Yes, I think so," I replied. "But…"

"He's just like any other man, remember that," Fred said. "If you like him and you're interested, go and just have a good time," he added, trying hard to make me feel like this wasn't that big of a deal. "And if it'll make you feel better, I'll get you a plane ticket back. If you want to leave, you always can, and I will be there to pick you up at the airport. Okay?"

Fred always had a way to make me feel better. I was comfortable enough to take part in the adventure that was to come.

CHAPTER 14

THE NEXT DAY, I was picked up by Sarge, a tall, old school, Arnold Palmer-type of guy who was in charge of transportation for Frank. True to his boss, Sarge was there at the designated time on Friday afternoon. I would see a lot of Sarge in the months to come. He was a special courier of sorts for Frank, especially when Frank was in Palm Springs. Sarge would pick up anything Frank needed, including cans of films from the studios for Frank to privately screen in the desert.

He would also pick up people, bringing them to the Burbank Airport to board Frank's private jet, named "Christina II" after his youngest daughter. While small and less luxurious compared to today's standards, Frank's jet was pretty wild and impressive for someone like me who had never been in a private jet. It was a Learjet 23, which had just enough room for about eight passengers. Because the plane belonged to Frank Sinatra, it also had a pullout card table and a liquor cabinet that was always stocked. Frank often used it to shuttle him and his Rat Pack pals between L.A., Vegas, and Palm Springs. He also lent it out to other celebs like Elvis and Marlon Brando.

To my complete surprise, when the plane landed, there was Frank waiting for me himself.

"Hey baby," he said as I stepped off the plane.

"Hello," I replied with a sheepish smile, and we lingered for a second. Ever the gentleman, he opened my door for me and put his hand on my back as he helped me into his car, which he was driving himself. I again thanked him with a slightly mischievous, but sweet smile.

We didn't talk much on the ride, which itself wasn't very long and soon we pulled into his compound in Cathedral City, on what is now called Frank Sinatra Drive. Two streets over was the famed businessman and philanthropist Walter Annenberg's mega compound.

Comparatively, Frank's abode was a nondescript, single-story California ranch-style compound with quite a few adjacent buildings of the same style. I was told Frank had them built and added on for the anticipation of receiving the Kennedy family, with whom Frank had a friendship at one point. At the last minute, they had a change of plans and didn't come out. The rumor was it was because of Frank's alleged Mafia ties and the concern over that association. The whole complex had an orange and beige color scheme, which was popular at the time. It was very clean, very simple, yet very comfortable. One thing I remember was there were always bowls brimming with candy and nuts everywhere, which I always enjoyed in my time there. There was a beautiful pool with lots of lounge chairs and umbrellas, as well as a tennis court that I never once stepped foot on. It felt like a resort and it was easy to see why Frank, who was always in the public eye, would want to spend so much time here; it truly was a getaway.

After we walked in the house, he put his arm around my waist and pulled me toward him, giving me a kiss on the cheek. I liked the way he smelled; the scent of his aftershave was very light and very clean, yet sensual. Scent of a man is really important to me and I liked clean. I also liked how he pulled me to him, gently but with just enough force. We were somehow very casual and very comfortable with each other instantaneously.

Right from the start, we had this relaxed yet intense energy going on between us, which was nothing short of magical. It's like we could have jumped right into bed and ripped each other's clothes off, devouring each other... but we didn't. He was too much of a gentleman. Also, he was a jaguar who wanted to hunt his prey for a while. I played along, enjoying the energy that was building between us. I didn't anticipate anything and didn't even try to be sexy or coy. We just went about as host and guest at the start. It was going to be a long, romantic, mystery, comedy movie with the tension building. As he showed me around, his hand on my back, he pointed out a small room next to his master bedroom.

"This is your room," he said. "Mia had it painted pink, but you can paint it any color you want."

"It's very nice," I said. I couldn't believe that he was talking to me as if I was moving in. "Thank you... Francis."

He smiled and I could see him even relax a bit. I would soon always call him Francis and he liked it that way. He either called me Baby, or

Madam or Madam Mao. From that point forward, we had a very special connection, which grew from that comfort we had with each other and from my ability to let go of any prior fears and allow myself to enjoy the ride.

That was one of the things Frank, or Francis, liked most about me. He also liked that I was naïve and in many ways unspoiled, but still had a bit of ancient wisdom and Eastern mystery about me. Also, I made him laugh. Sometimes intentionally and sometimes, not as much.

When we were dating, I would bring my own tea to his house.

"Baby, you don't have to do that. We have everything here and we can get you any kind of tea. What kind of tea do you drink?"

I replied, "Constant Comment," which was my favorite tea at that time. One of the reasons I loved it was because it was very affordable and easily available. Francis laughed and laughed, and I realized that it's the simple things that the boy from Hoboken found joy in.

While Francis loved my simplicity, and would often tease me about it, he was never disrespectful. He treated me well and I knew always that I was his girl. In fact, I was pretty much his *only* steady girl during our two years together because we were almost always with each other. I think he saw Ava Gardner once or twice. He remained her friend and helped her in her down years. He let me live my life, doing what I wanted to do, even if he didn't always understand it. That was especially true when it came to work. I was also working and had to be away from him from time to time.

"What's with you broads? Juliet and Mia with their careers and now you too?" he asked one night, a little irritated that I had to go shoot on location for a spell.

"But I like to work," was all I could say. "It's fun and it makes me feel useful."

He just shook his head and gave me a kiss, sending me on my way.

Sometimes though, he would go out of his way to show his support. Once, I had a set call at Paramount and Francis drove me up to L.A. When we drove through the gate and stopped, I was mumbling to the guard, telling him my name and asking where I was supposed to go. Then he looked over and saw Francis at the wheel. The guard looked like he just saw Jesus. He laughed and started talking about all the people from Jersey, trying to find people they knew in common. People always did that to him. Once they found someone (who knows if it was true?), the security guard came out to shake his hand. I then reminded the guard I still needed to know where I was going.

Another time, we were spending the night at Bennett and Phyllis Cerf's to watch the moon landing. My Chevron Island commercial would come on during every station break. The theme song would start and there I would be on TV, undulating to the rhythm of the music. Francis would applaud and make me get up to take a bow around the room. He was grinning and looked truly proud of me, or at least entertained. That was a most happy memory for me.

Being a part of Frank's life was a constant adjustment. There was the time Hubert Humphrey called and I took a message, which I forgot to give to Frank, as if it were just some random guy. There was the time when New York Mayor John Lindsay came by for drinks and supper at the Waldorf Astoria and like an idiot I didn't think of calling downstairs for some flower arrangements that Frank asked me to take care of. Instead I had the driver take me all over Midtown to buy fresh flowers. I then made a mess trying to make my own flower arrangements, which he walked in on. Francis got more of a kick out of these types of incidents rather than staying mad at me.

I never thought for a moment about marrying him. He was just too different than I was at that time. After all, I *was* a hippie vegetarian who was still pursuing a career and a spiritual life. I knew I could never really live his kind of life for the long haul. Everything would come too easy. Especially the material things. You want a car, you get a car. Jewelry, you get jewelry. A house… he practically twisted my arm to find a house! He even offered me a part in a movie, *The Ballad of Dingus McGee,* as an Indian maiden, but it never got made. While that might sound great for some women, for me, it was too easy and too restrictive. Plus, there was the thirty-plus year difference between us. This was never going to be a permanent relationship.

That being said, I did let him treat me from time to time. I brought a V-neck little black dress from Jax in L.A. and wanted to wear it one night. He liked the dress but said, "You need a necklace. Go downstairs and pick one out from the jewelry store."

I went downstairs and was surprised to see that they were waiting for me. I picked out a very contemporary choker of little diamonds and amethyst. Some months later, he asked me what my favorite stones were. I said blue lapis and angel coral, two rather inexpensive gems that I liked at the time. I told my sister who loved jewelry and she said I should have told him diamonds and emeralds! But Francis had two of the most beautiful rings made for me from Van Cleef & Arpels. The stones were curved in a dome shape on both sides with tiny rows of diamonds in the crown. I enjoyed it for years until one day a theft in my house cleaned me out of most of my jewelry.

There were other thoughtful and extravagant gifts, including a beige alligator bag with a double gold chain. I made my old friend Broni go with me to the Gucci store on Rodeo Drive so I wouldn't be so intimidated. I wanted to exchange it for something more youthful and sporty. I actually thought it was too grown up looking for me. The sales lady took the bag to the back. Minutes later she came back and smiled at me.

"Now young lady, you really wouldn't want to exchange this bag. It was a special edition. As you can see, the chain is solid 18k gold. Someone very special must have given it to you, Miss. You ought to keep it."

Broni looked at the bag, looked at me and shook his head. "Let me take you to lunch," he said. "I need a drink!"

I learned that in the Sinatra household, giving gifts was a big affair and Francis took it very seriously. There was a great deal of planning that had to be done, especially because there were so many friends, their spouses, and all the staff. What to give Francis was even harder. I did luck out once with a train set from Japan that I picked up after filming in Hong Kong. Francis loved it and we spent hours setting it up and playing with it. I would also get him robotic toys. His bright blue eyes would light up like a child, and I would savor the moment, knowing I had made him truly happy.

We built a life together for a while, both in Palm Springs and L.A. and sometimes New York. Francis always preferred the desert and if I was being honest, so did I. The desert was a sanctuary for Francis where he could be alone or with selected friends to collect his thoughts, to regenerate and rejuvenate. Having so much celebrity was not as easy for him as he made it seem. He would say the kids—or young entertainers—just didn't know how to handle their success. Taking a break and getting away was important for keeping things together. I was happy to just laze about the compound and ride a bike to the juice bar, pretending to look for houses. I also enjoyed the constant company, getting to meet Francis' rich and famous friends. He was always more comfortable as a host than a guest, so he surrounded himself with people. I met Gregory and Veronique Peck, Kirk and Ann Douglas, Danny Schwartz and his Jersey wife Natalie, who told me Danny insisted that she get coached in current and important historic events so she would come off more knowledgeable at parties.

When we went to L.A. every couple of weeks to take care of business, Francis was usually met by Mickey Rudin, his attorney. They'd be whisked away to handle his many business affairs, from his recordings and work engagements to his entrepreneurial endeavors… as well as the endless investigations into his supposed Mafia ties to his philanthropic work. Frank was a very serious man and enjoyed the business aspect of his life as well.

Our evenings in L.A. were spent dining out at Nicky's, Matteo's, or Chasen's, very often with the Romanoffs—the fabled or fake Russian prince Michael and his very entrepreneurial wife Gloria. She would come up to Beaumont Drive once in a while to have a little sex with Frank. He did it as kind of a favor for an old friend. Michael, the rogue, was offered a part in *Caprice*, and he played Edward Mulhare's butler. He loved it!

One night at Frank's place in L.A., I saw a couple of black limos come up the driveway and stay for a little while. I was already in bed, but I looked out the window and saw that they seemed to be very official looking cars. I personally think they could have brought Jacqueline Kennedy Onassis. They didn't stay long. I heard the slam of the doors and they disappeared into the darkness of the night. I never found out for sure.

One summer in New York, Frank decided that we should take a little cruise on the Hudson, sailing around Manhattan on the yacht, which was a one hundred and twenty-foot remodeled naval ship. It had a number of staterooms below and of course a fairly lavish upper deck for viewing, dining, and entertaining. I remembered as we were nearing the Jersey side of the Hudson just above Inglewood Cliffs, he excitedly pointed out this science academy that he was accepted into. He said he would have loved to attend but his career started taking off. He was beaming with pride as he told us. The guests looked a bit dumbfounded and just nodded and mumbled something, thinking that Francis sometimes forgot the special gift that he was given. But I knew that sometimes he just craved a little normalcy.

A day or two later we took a trip to Nantucket. The weather was gorgeous, though I found the fabled Martha's Vineyard kind of dull. It was like a giant sand dune with not much vegetation, let alone beautiful fauna and landscape. Still, this was where all the East Coast and literary elites gathered. John Hersey, Lillian Gish, James Baldwin, George Plimpton, and many others had their summer homes there, or came to gather and visit friends out of the glare of the big city. We would have lunch with those famous non-Hollywood types and talk about recent books and politics and in-jokes that always went over the top of my head. I was always next to Plimpton's young wife who only ate giant portions of beef. I took small bites of food as I was not eating meat then and pretended to understand the conversation. The literati greats took turns holding court mostly on their latest bestseller or other books. I don't think Francis enjoyed it as much as he pretended to. It wasn't my favorite place to be.

On one trip, he found us an excuse to leave.

"Baby, I want to take you by Mia's to say a quick hello. She rented a bungalow nearby."

Though I told him I would love to, it was still a little strange to be visiting his ex with him.

Mia came to greet us at the door and gave Francis a warm hug and a sweet smile. She had a cheek hug for me. She looked like a beautiful hippie in her long, flowing caftan type of robe. I liked her right away. She leaned by the fireplace almost the entire time. I noticed how fragile she looked. She was quite thin and had poor posture with her shoulders hunched forward. She also spoke in a quiet, self-deprecating manner. She asked Francis for some sort of advice on something she was involved in and he advised her best he could. It was kind, loving, and almost fatherly. Francis was our protector. Francis was a lot of things to a lot of people.

Whether it was after a trip to New York, L.A., Vegas, or wherever, Francis and I were always happy to retreat back to the desert. Sometimes I stayed a few more days if I had to work on something or to see friends. I don't even know if I had any friends left because they'd say they never saw me anymore, and we couldn't exactly double date!

A couple we spent quite a bit of time with was the Cerfs. Bennett became my dinner partner from the very first time we met. We were introduced and he rather nonchalantly turned to ask me, "Now that you are amongst the wealthy and famous, how are you going to act?" It was a rather surprising and daunting question, but I didn't have much time to think. I smiled a quick smile and said, "I guess I'll just have to be myself." He loved it and laughed. He asked Francis to sit me next to him at every dinner party. There were endless parties and dinners and fascinating conversations, an insight into the minds and lives of the elite.

When we were alone, Francis would do endless amounts of crossword puzzles while I read scripts and spiritual books and did needlepoint. He said he developed the habit of crossword puzzles because he was a chronic insomniac. We would also go into town and shop for stuff like sundries, snacks, art, and anything orange. Francis loved the color orange. I tried to steer him away sometimes to avoid turning the whole living room orange, without much success. We would have breakfast together and the first call he made every morning was to Nancy. He loved her so much. He would call Tina through an intermediary once in a while, but he never really called Frank Jr. Sometimes we would drive into town to eat dinner at Ruby's Dunes, whose owner was an old friend of his.

Friendship was very important to Francis. He was deeply loyal to his friends and extremely generous with them. The same was true of people in need and causes he believed in, whether political or charitable. I think he was influenced by his mother, who had a social conscience and would bake cookies and bring them to civil leaders. People would come to Francis for help for their friends that he barely knew, and he would listen and give.

He was also often like a kid, which he couldn't let others see. I loved that he felt close enough to me to let me see it. There were so many things I loved about him.

And yes, Frank Sinatra was also an incredible lover. I have always been complimented on my skin. People say it's like satin or velvet. Make-up people I worked with on sets would say I had no pores, and they liked me because I never needed a touch up even after hours on set. Next to me, Francis had the softest and smoothest skin. He had the body of a very young man. It was a "natural" young man's body, before men became obsessed with excessive sports, pumping iron, workouts of every sort, and body-building protein drinks. Francis had a lot of natural gifts as a lover, gifts as glorious as his voice.

When it came to our physical relationship, Francis didn't need a lot of pomp and circumstance. He had his brown satin pajamas that he would wear, and he didn't care what I wore to bed. He just wanted me for me. I was never into sexy fancy nightgowns or negligee and didn't own any. I was strictly a comfy t-shirt type of gal. I don't remember Francis ever asking me about negligées, nor did he ever buy me one. He would complain if I dallied too long in the bathroom, fixing my hair or something.

"Hey baby, you've already hit the home run, why the hell are you hanging out in left field? Get into bed."

Francis would always use baseball terms that I only half understood.

But of all the things I experienced in my time with the Chairman of the Board, perhaps my favorite was seeing his pre-show ritual and watching him on stage. Before performing in Vegas, he would go "on the wagon" as he called it, for five days to a week. He would then have the famous composer Jimmy Van Heusen come down from the San Bernardino Mountains, where he had a place with Inger Stevens, to rehearse a few afternoons. Then a bunch of his cronies and I would all get on a chartered plane to Vegas. Let me just say, Vegas is quite different when you are with Frank Sinatra.

The first time I saw Francis on stage was at Caesar's Palace and it was quite an experience. I was seated at stage right a few tables back. I was nervous, and I crossed and uncrossed my legs, occasionally sipping my drink in front of me. Then the lights went down, and the crowd started clapping and howling. The announcer waited respectfully for a few moments before his voice came up.

"Ladies and gentleman, Francis Albert Sinatra!"

Francis walked onto the stage with mic in hand, smoothly checking out this night's audience, exuding the confidence and effortlessness as if the stage and the entire room was truly his domain. And it was. Simply and quietly he started his song, opening with "The Lady is a Tramp." He moved from song to song making hardly any dance moves. In fact, he hardly moved at all except for one or two rather awkward steps to emphasize a beat or two. He simply told the story from his groin through his heart to his face, which was always expressive. Even more than a master of his magical voice, Francis was a wonderful actor. He would take you through an emotional journey and capture your heart through his music. For each and every person there, he was yours for the night… with some left to take home.

At one point during that first show, out of nowhere, he turned right to me. Of course, he knew exactly where I was sitting and out comes, "I've got you under my skin… I've got you deep in the heart of me… so deep…"

Those electric blue eyes were staring right through me. That was the moment when I really discovered and understood why Francis Albert Sinatra was such an icon for a whole generation and more. It gives me the shivers thinking about it now. I will never forget that night or that man.

My time with Francis didn't end dramatically. Francis had a unique quality about staying friends with the people that came into his life. In our case, as my career got busier and he took other interests, we just started spending less and less time together. He was rumored to be with other women, and I met someone else myself. Next thing we knew, it was over. But the friendship always remained.

In fact, we were such friends that I still remember the very special wedding gift he got me. When Francis found out I was getting married, he had his secretary Lillian call me to ask what I wanted for a wedding present. He said that if I didn't respond soon, he was going to buy me a Ming vase. Upon hearing that, I panicked.

"Oh no, no Ming vase!" I told her. I'm a klutz and I knew I would break it in no time. Besides, I didn't really like Ming vases at all. I thought about it a bit and in the end, I asked for a washer and a dryer because I really needed a good set. Apparently, Francis had a good laugh over that.

"What, are you going to start your own Chinese laundry?" he asked.

Still, a washer and dryer are exactly what he got for me... with a card that said, "Congratulations, much happiness and no starch!"

That top-of-the-line washer and dryer lasted me some twenty years. My marriage only lasted seven. My memories of my time with Francis Albert Sinatra will last forever.

MOVIES & TV

Burgess Meredith (right) in costume for *The Ying and Yang of Mr. Go*.

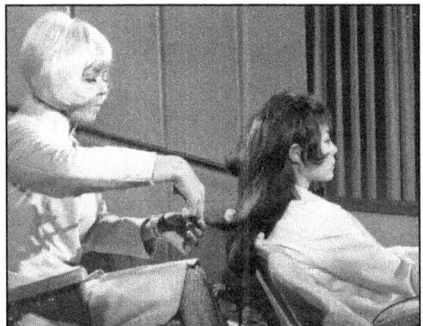

Doris Day cuts Irene's hair in a scene from *Caprice*.

Irene in a scene from *Caprice*.

92 • *A Water Color Dream*

Irene in her *Caprice* bikini.

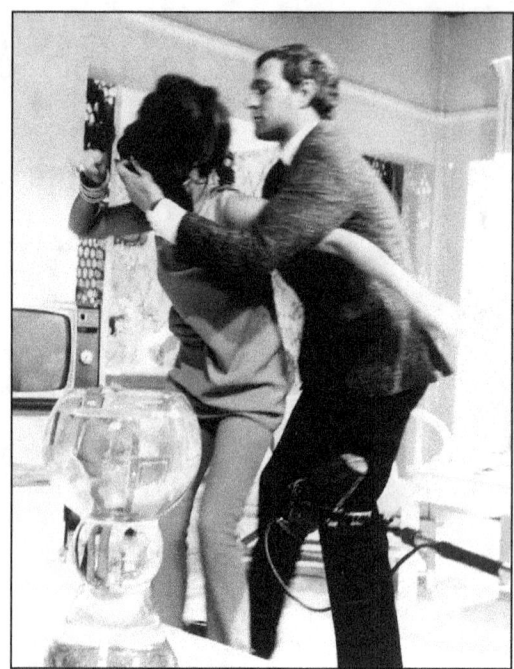

Irene with Richard Harris in *Caprice*.

Irene with Michael J. Pollard in *Caprice*.

Irene with Richard Harris in *Caprice*.

Irene appears on a billboard featuring Chevron's Hula Dollars ad campaign.

Irene with retired Army Col. Bill Olds, playing General Ti in *The Green Berets*.

With actor David Niven on the set of *Paper Tiger*.

Famed director John Ford on the set of *The Green Berets*.

Irene with Frankie Avalon in *How to Stuff a Wild Bikini*.

Marie O'Henry, Irene and Pamela Serpe with director Gordon Parks Jr. on the set of *Three the Hard Way*.

Filming *The Green Berets* in Fort Benning, GA.

With Buster Keaton in *How to Stuff a Wild Bikini*.

Irene with Robert Culp in *I Spy*.

Irene and James Mason filming *The Ying and Yang of Mr. Go*.

Irene (lower left) with Elvis Presley in *Paradise Hawaiian Style*.

With Burgess Meredith (left), Jeff Bridges (center) and James Mason (right) in *The Ying and Yang of Mr. Go*.

Irene in a scene from the 1976 film *Hot Potato* (aka *Twist the Tiger's Tail*).

Irene piggy-backs on Jimmy Stewart in 1963's *Take Her, She's Mine*.

With Jeff Bridges in *The Ying and Yang of Mr. Go*.

With Jeff Bridges in *The Ying and Yang of Mr. Go*.

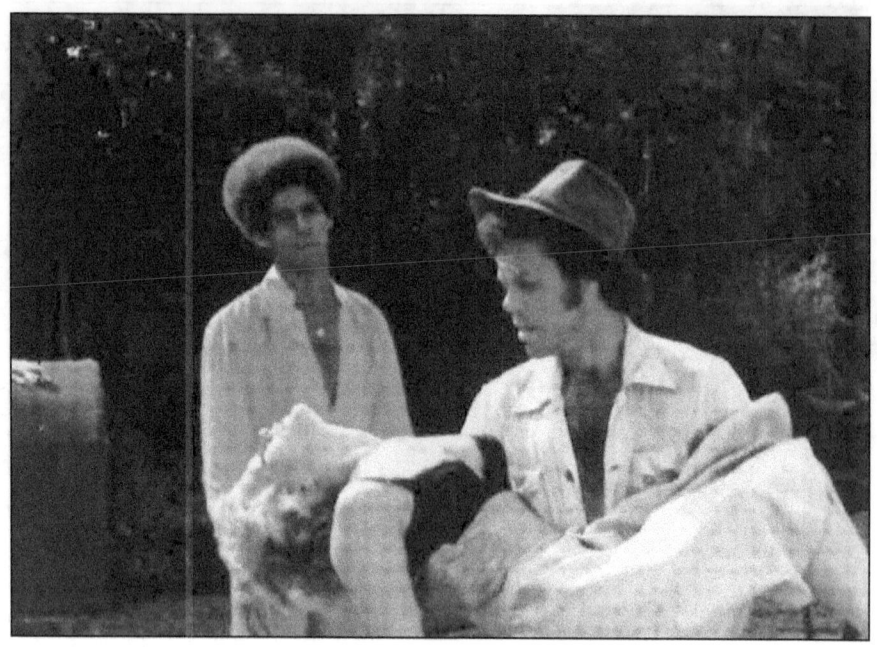

Irene with Jim Kelly in *Hot Potato* (aka *Twist the Tiger's Tail*).

With Jimmy Stewart in *Take Her, She's Mine*.

With *The Yin and Yang of Mr. Go* cinematographer John Stevens.

Irene in a scene from *The Green Berets* with Aldo Rey, Jack Soo and John Wayne.

With Little Richard (left) and Richard Dreyfuss (right) in *Down & Out in Beverly Hills*.

With Don Grady on the set of *My Three Sons*, 1966.

Irene as one of Bob Hope's girls.

Irene recording her part for the Netflix release *Over the Moon* (2020).

Irene with Elvis Presley in *Paradise Hawaiian Style* (1966).

The poster for 1965's *How To Stuff a Wild Bikini*.

With Richard Dreyfuss and Bette Midler in *Down & Out in Beverly Hills*.

Irene (left) with Robert Vaughn and David McCallum in *The Man from U.N.C.L.E.*

Irene in "Caprice" (1967).

Irene in *Paper Tiger* (1975).

SHOW BUSINESS

MOVIES
The Double Standard
The National Catholic Office for Motion Pictures, which was once called the National Legion of Decency, no longer deserves to be called an old fuddy-duddy. For more than a year now, the N.C.O.M.P. has been taking an increasingly tolerant view of sexual matters on the screen (TIME, Dec. 3, 1965). For example, both *Who's Afraid of Virginia Woolf?* and *Ulysses* were granted N.C.O.M.P. approval in the A-IV classification—"morally unobjectionable for adults, with reservations."

Still, film makers have a difficult time figuring out how far they can go without getting into trouble. Only last week, 20th Century-Fox confirmed details of a go-round over their new Doris Day epic, *Caprice*. Seems that N.C.O.M.P. wanted Fox to slice out a 3½-sec. strip of film showing Shanghai-born Starlet Irene Tsu in a bikini. Well, not exactly in. In this sequence, Irene dives into a swimming pool, and the impact dislodges the bottom half of her hikini somewhat.

With some $4 million staked on a family-market product, Fox snipped out the footage—and thanked N.C.O.M.P. for the free advertising. But the studio could not help pointing out that the British-made *Ulysses* got away with displaying the bare bottoms of Buck Mulligan (T. P. McKenna) and Blazes Boylan (Joe Lynch). Well, yes, replied the Rev. Patrick J. Sullivan, N.C.O.M.P.'s director, there is a double standard—but not the one that Fox suggests.

Ulysses got away with it (as did *Zorba the Greek* and *Georgy Girl*) because the buttocks in question were male. "A brief shot of a male derrière is not going to present a problem to a normal individual," he said. But exposure of the female rear, added Father Sullivan, is "pruriently" stimulating.

TELEVISION
Here's Johnny
After nine days off the air and on the lam, Johnny Carson came home to NBC. All was forgiven. Johnny was for givin' NBC the benefit of his presence if NBC was for givin' him the present of their benefits—that is, a lot more cash and a little more say-so over who runs the Johnny Carson show *Tonight*.

The contractual spat was abuilding before the AFTRA strike confused Carson's position (TIME, April 14). While it was true that he objected to NBC's re-running of his old tapes during the strike, Carson's chief concern was his own future. Some time earlier, he had hired Show Biz Attorney Arnold Grant, to whom he referred on the air half-facetiously as "Louie the Shyster." He used to be prosecuting attorney in the Mafia's kangaroo court." In the demand for a new contract, Grant and Lawyer Louis Nizer reportedly asked for a base salary jump from $15,000 to $30,000 a week, plus a hefty cut of the *Tonight* earnings, which run to about $20 million in advertising billings a year. Sure enough, Carson won a "substantial" (if not 100%) increase and the authority to make some personnel changes. As a result, Producer Art Stark, who ran the program for 4½ years, will get a new assignment. However, Carson's brother Dick will stay on as director.

Apart from good lawyers and proven

REAGAN & BISHOP
One four-year contract, anyway.

box-office appeal, Carson had some borrowed leverage working for him—the threat of new competition from the ABC network. Theoretically, ABC's *Joey Bishop Show*, which started last week opposite *Tonight*, was bound to chip away at Carson's audience. After a week's run, it looks as if neither NBC nor Carson has anything serious to worry about.

Introducing Idols. Bishop, himself a first-rate stand-up comic and successful pinch hitter for Carson in the past, could not seem to find his way. Using roughly the same format as *Tonight*, Bishop provided little more than late-hour tedium for viewers. His guests included Buddy Greco and Sonny and Cher. Debbie Reynolds talked about Girl Scouts; Danny Thomas kidded around to little effect. Everybody plugged everybody's newest picture, recording or TV show. Bishop introduced his rabbi and a priest, and kept referring to his jitters, which needed no introduction. Dragging his microphone into the studio audience, he introduced "one of my idols. I promised him that I would not embarrass him by taking a microphone and talking to him, etc., but I know you would never forgive me if I did not acknowledge the presence of one of the great, great stars of all time, Mr. Edward G. Robinson, with his lovely wife."

Earlier, in stilted fashion that hopefully will not become habit-forming, Bishop announced: "It's with a great deal of pleasure that I'm afforded the privilege of having as my first guest, Governor Ronald Reagan." The Governor got off one good line, noting that "I've still got a four-year contract where I am." Bishop responded, poignantly and perhaps prophetically: "You're lucky; I've got only 39 weeks."

The Homelies
FADE IN ON CLOSEUP of worried executive.
Announcer's Voice Off-Screen: Problems? Wondering how to present your product to the consumer? (*Executive nods sadly.*) Let me introduce you to TV's newest and most popular pitchmen: the Homelies. They come in all misshapes and off-sizes. (CUT TO rapid

TSU IN "CAPRICE"
She's a problem—he isn't.

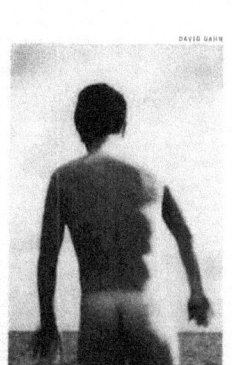

McKENNA IN "ULYSSES"

An April 1967 *Time* magazine article mentions Irene in *Caprice*.

Irene is profiled in a 1968 *TV Guide* article.

The Many Lives of Irene Tsu • 111

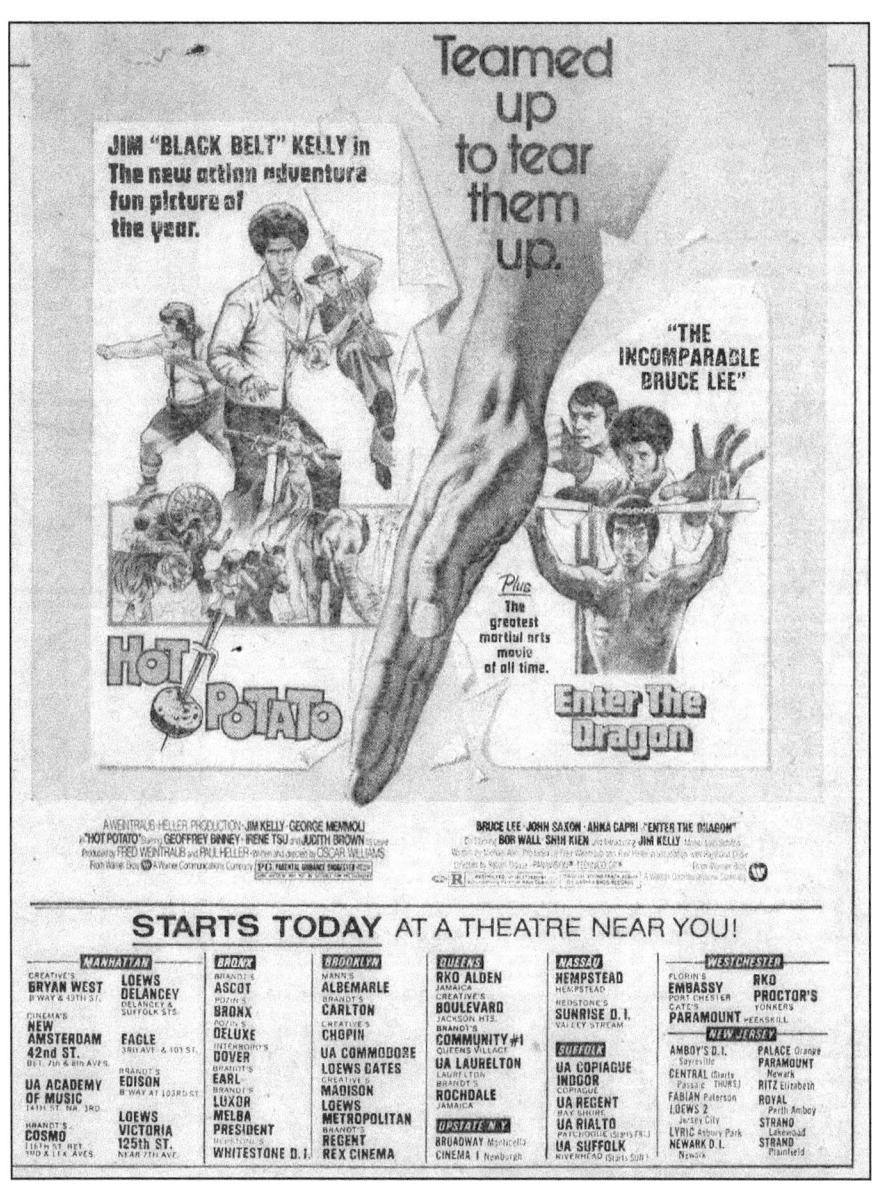

1967 newspaper ad for *Hot Potato*.

Irene and Jim Kelly in *Hot Potato* (aka *Twist the Tiger's Tail*).

Irene and Jim Kelly in *Hot Potato* (aka *Twist the Tiger's Tail*).

Irene and Jim Kelly in *Hot Potato*.

Irene's wardrobe test for *The Green Berets*.

With Wayne Brady of *The Wayne Brady Show*.

Irene in *Women of the Prehistoric Planet* (1966).

FRIENDS & FAMILY

Irene strikes a '70s pose.

Irene and Robert Whitney with director Alexander Payne.

With documentarian-writer Arthur Dong and actor D.B. Wang.

Aunt Junda, who turned 100 in September 2019.

Auntie's wedding. Irene & Florence are at lower right.

Irene's big family includes numerous aunts, uncles and cousins. Irene is at bottom left.

With Barbara Luna at a Hollywood Autograph Show.

With actor Bradley Cooper.

Irene and retired Army Col. Bill Olds in El Paso (center).

Irene and retired Army Col. Bill Olds in El Paso (far left).

Practicing yoga with Yasmine.

Lunching with Sylvester Stallone to celebrate the release of *Creed*.

Dad & mom at grandma's 96th birthday.

Dad on vacation in the U.S.

Florence with Irene & Ivan at their wedding.

Florence reads Irene's palm.

At Florence's wedding: Cousin Sophia, Alice, groom Pat Phillips, Florence and Irene.

Florence, mom and Irene.

Florence, mom, Irene & dad.

Francis Albert Sinatra rehearsing for his film *Dirty Dingus McGee*.

Hong Kong friends John Yu, Michael McCrary, Shigeta, France Nuyen.

Irene and Florence dancing at a Cuban restaurant.

Irene and retired Army Col. Bill Olds in El Paso.

Irene and Ivan ice skating in Sun Valley.

Irene & Ivan in Wakiki Beach, Honolulu, HI.

Irene with actor Jonah Hill.

Irene with artist, composer and musician Tom Hormel in Honolulu, HI.

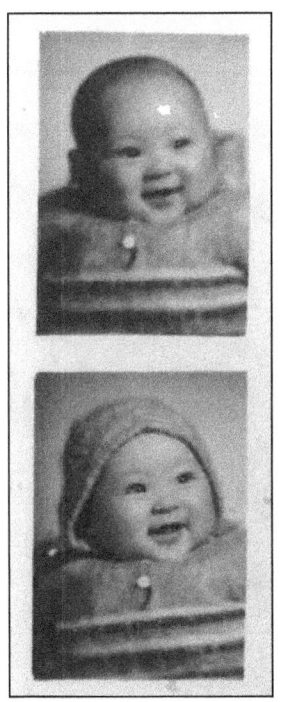
Irene's baby photos.

With actor Robert Wagner at an autograph show.

Irene with Yasmine and actress Nancy Kwan.

Irene, mom and Aunt Junda.

The Many Lives of Irene Tsu • 127

Irene, mom and Florence.

Irene with longtime New York friend Lanie Miyazaki.

Ivan & I wedding day at Bronilaw Kaper patio.

Ivan & Irene at the Smithsonian, Washington, D.C.

Ivan ice skating in Sun Valley.

Ivan at the Ellsworth Kelly National Gallery of Art, Washington, D.C.

Ivan at the Jasper Johns Pavilion, Washington D.C.

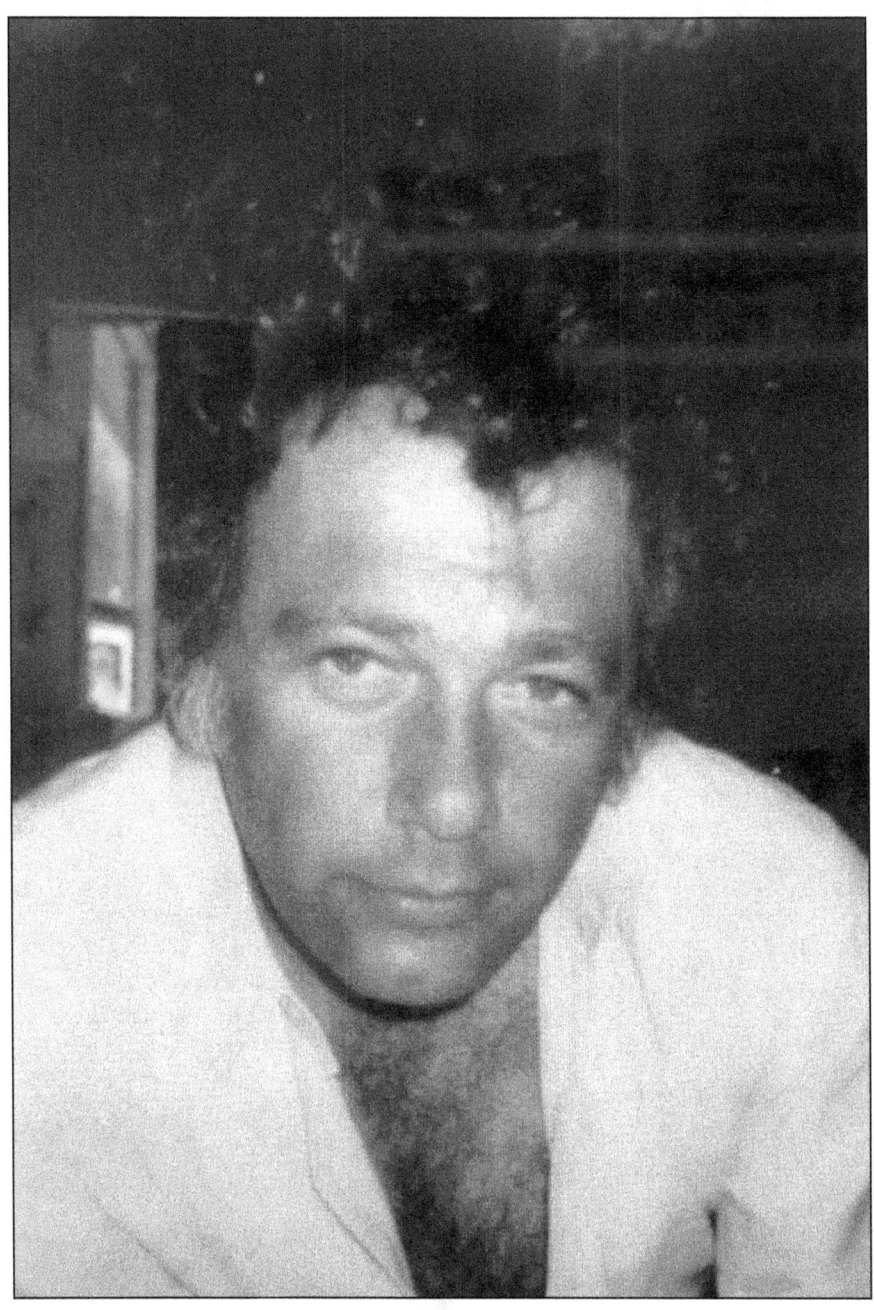

Irene's ex-husband, Ivan Nagy.

With actor-singer James Shigeta in Hong Kong.

Screen test for Marvel's *Captain America: The Winter Soldier*.

Irene's mother wears a swimsuit in Lai Chi Kok.

Irene and Ivan at their wedding with Irene's sister Florence.

Irene's wedding shower with Caro Jones, Miiko, Claudia, Elvina, Helen and Carol Nystrom.

Peter Mayer, publisher of *The Satanic Verses* (Random House).

Peter Mayer also published *The Green Berets*.

Pat Phillips, Florence and baby Roddy.

The six Lin sisters: Lida, Wuda, Linda, Luoda, Junda and mom Yuda.

With Martin at Sybil & Herbert Kretzmer's wedding.

Uncle Li Lin, later ambassador to Rome, and Irene's father on a ship to the United States.

Yasmine's graduation from Beverly Hills High School.

FASHION

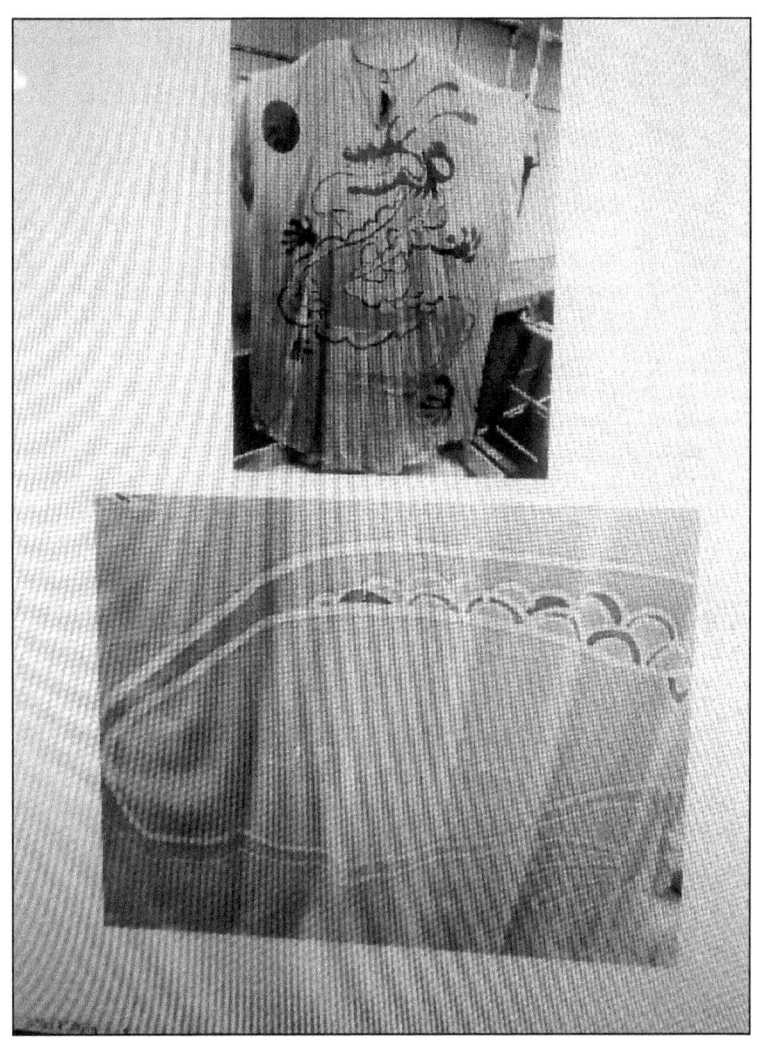

Batik Silk Dragon.

Bergdorf Christmas Catalog (Irene Signature). Featuring super model Cheryl Tiegs.

Bullocks Spring Ad.

Bullocks Wilshire Windows.

Bullocks Wilshire Windows.

Bullocks Wilshire Windows.

Bullocks Wilshire Windows.

Bullocks Wilshire Windows.

Bullocks Wilshire Windows.

Demi Moore and model (The IT Company).

MAGAZINE ARTICLES

Down & Out in Beverly Hills poster.

Cast

Jerry Baskin	NICK NOLTE
Barbara Whiteman	BETTE MIDLER
Dave Whiteman	RICHARD DREYFUSS
Orvis Goodnight	LITTLE RICHARD
Jenny Whiteman	TRACY NELSON
Carmen	ELIZABETH PEÑA
Max Whiteman	EVAN RICHARDS
Matisse	MIKE
Dr. Von Zimmer	DONALD F. MUHICH
Sidney Waxman	PAUL MAZURSKY
Pearl Waxman	VALERIE CURTIN
Mel Whiteman	JACK BRUSKOFF
Sadie Whiteman	GERALDINE DREYFUSS
Lou Waltzberg	BARRY PRIMUS
Sheila Waltzberg	IRENE TSU
Nagamichi	MICHAEL YAMA
Ranbir	RANBIR BHAI
Al	FELTON PERRY
Tom Tom	ELOY CASADOS
Ed	MICHAEL GREENE
Patrick	KEN KOCH
Dorothy	DOROTHY TRISTAN
Yamato	RAYMOND LEE
Girl Feeding Kerouac	CAROLYN ALLPORT
Roxanne	SUE KIEL
Iranian Neighbor	REZA BASHAR
Iranian Boy	JOSEPH MAKKAR
Lance	JASON WILLIAMS
Geraldo	DARRYL HENRIQUES
Nigel	NICK ULLETT
Cop	MICHAEL BLUE
Caterer	ALLAN MALAMUD
Caterer's Assistant	SALVATORE ESPINOZA
Maurice	MICHAEL VOLETTI
Stylish Jogger	BETSY MAZURSKY
Security Guards	DONALD V. ALLEN
	NEIL CUNNINGHAM
Security Alarm Dispatcher	BOBBY GOOD
Barry	SANDY IGNON
Sandra Goodnight	MARGRIT RAMME
Translator	PEARL HUANG
Minister Chan	YUNG SUN
Chinese Delegation	EUGENE CHOY
	MAE KOH-RUDEN
	GEORGE SUN
	LELAND SUN
Party Guest	ANDRE PHILIPPE
Paramedic	LEW HOPSON
Water Man	CARLTON CUSE
Helicopter Pilot	BILL CROSS
Dr. Toni Grant	HERSELF

Technical Credits

Directed and Produced by	PAUL MAZURSKY
Screenplay by	PAUL MAZURSKY & LEON CAPETANOS
(Based upon the play "Boudu Sauvé des Eaux" by René Fauchois)	
Co-Produced by	PATO GUZMAN
Director of Photography	DONALD McALPINE, A.S.C.
Production Designed by	PATO GUZMAN
Edited by	RICHARD HALSEY, A.C.E.
Associate Producer	GEOFFREY TAYLOR
Costume Designer	ALBERT WOLSKY
Casting by	ELLEN CHENOWETH
Music by	ANDY SUMMERS
Production Manager	JOHN BRODERICK
First Assistant Director	PETER BOGART
Second Assistant Directors	ERIC JEWETT
	JODI EHRLICH
Art Director	TODD HALLOWELL
Set Decorator	JANE BOGART
Camera Operator	JAMIE ANDERSON
Production Sound	JIM WEBB, C.A.S.
	CREW CHAMBERLAIN
Script Supervisor	LILLIAN MAC NEILL
Assistant to Mr. Mazursky	ELIZABETH SAYRE
Production Coordinator	KOOL LUSBY
Production Accountant	VINCE HEILESON
Assistant Production Accountant	ALLEN E. TAYLOR
Executive Assistants	DEBRA CASTELLANO
	TIM CONWAY
Supervising Sound Editor	WILLIAM STEVENSON
Sound Editor	CARL MAHAKIAN
Music Editors	ROBERT RANDLES, S.M.E.
	EMILIE ROBERTSON
Owner and Trainer of Mike	CLINT ROWE
Animal Trainer	JIM COLOVIN
Unit Publicist	NANCY WILLEN
Still Photographer	ELLIOTT MARKS
Hair Stylist	RENATE LEUSCHNER-PLESS
Men's Costumes	BRUCE ERICKSEN
Women's Costumes	PAM WISE
Make-up Artist	BOB MILLS
Additional Make-up	EDOUARD F. HENRIQUES III
Lead Man	DONALD KRAFFT
Key Set Designer	MICHAEL CORENBLITH
Property Master	M.C. AYERS
Location Manager	DOW GRIFFITH
1st Assistant Camera	DANA CHRISTIAANSEN
2nd Assistant Camera	PETER A. SANTORO
Gaffer	NORM GLASSER
Best Boy	ED (BIG ED) COOPER
Key Grip	BOBBY ROSE
Best Boy	CARL R. GIBSON, JR.
Dolly Grip	SANDY WILLIAMS
Assistant Film Editor	FRANK E. JIMENEZ
Apprentice Film Editor	COLLEEN DUNLAP
Production Assistant	RON SOUTH
Assistant to Andy Summers	TONY HUMECKE
Re-recording Mixers	DAVE DOCKENDORF
	PAUL WELLS
	KEVIN F. CLEARY
Assistant Property Master	DOMINIC BELMONTE
Construction Coordinator	PHIL READ
Greensman	PHILIP C. HURST
Supervising Painter	KIRK D. HANSEN
Scenic Artist	AL GAYNOR
Max's Videos by	GEOFFREY TAYLOR
	MICHAEL HERZMARK
Video Assist	COGSWELL VIDEO SERVICES
Casting Assistant	LISA CLARKSON
Extra Casting	CENTRAL CASTING
Special Effects	KEN SPEED
Choreographer	BOB BANAS
Transportation Coordinator	GARY L. LITTLEFIELD
Transportation Captains	DARWIN JOSTON
	DALE L. CLARK
Production Assistants	PAUL HARGRAVE
	JILL MAZURSKY
	TIM WICK
Paintings	MINO ARGENTO
Paintings & Sculptures	NORMAN SUNSHINE
Sculptures	SALVATORE ORLANDO
	NORMAN GROCHOWSKI
Kinetic Sculpture	EVERETT GREENBAUM
Custom Furniture	VERMILLION
Portrait of the Whitemans	TRACY BOGART
Color Timer	DICK RITCHIE
Negative Cutter	LEON BRIGGS
Opticals	PACIFIC TITLE
Title Design	WAYNE FITZGERALD

TOUCHSTONE FILMS presents in association with SILVER SCREEN PARTNERS II A PAUL MAZURSKY FILM Starring NICK NOLTE BETTE MIDLER RICHARD DREYFUSS "DOWN AND OUT IN BEVERLY HILLS" Co-Produced by PATO GUZMAN Based upon the play "BOUDU SAUVÉ DES EAUX" by RENÉ FAUCHOIS Screenplay by PAUL MAZURSKY & LEON CAPETANOS Produced and Directed by PAUL MAZURSKY

R RESTRICTED — UNDER 17 REQUIRES ACCOMPANYING PARENT OR ADULT GUARDIAN   LENSES AND PANAFLEX® CAMERA BY PANAVISION®   Prints by DE LUXE   Distributed by BUENA VISTA DISTRIBUTION CO., INC.   Color by TECHNICOLOR®   DOLBY STEREO® IN SELECTED THEATRES   ©1986 TOUCHSTONE FILMS

Original Motion Picture Soundtrack Album on MCA Records and Cassettes.

Down & Out in Beverly Hills credits poster.

SHANGHAI-IMPORT FÜR HOLLYWOOD

Irene Tsu spielt an der Seite von John Wayne

Unser mandeläugiges Titelmädchen ist eine waschechte Chinesin. Zum Glück für die Talente- und Typensucher aus Hollywood floh ihr Vater vor Jahren von Shanghai nach Formosa, wo er ökonomischer Berater der Nationalchinesischen Regierung wurde. Von Formosa war es nicht weit bis Hongkong. Dort lernte die wohlgeformte Wei Ho Tsu Englisch und Französisch, was ihre Sprachenkenntnisse, die sich bisher auf chinesische Dialekte beschränkt hatten, auf erfreulich internationale Weise abrundete.

Die Familie Tsu wanderte folgerichtig nach Amerika aus, und Wei Ho erhielt einen westlich-ansprechenden neuen Vornamen: Irene. In New York City vollzog sich die vollständige Verwandlung der kleinen Chinesin in ein typisches, amerikanisches Girl — wenigstens was ihre Lebensweise betraf. Sie absolvierte eine angesehene High School und studierte daneben klassischen und modernen Tanz.

Die exotische Schönheit des neuen Sternchens am Balletthimmel blieb nicht lange unentdeckt. Irene Tsu wurde als Reserve-«Gwenny» im Broadway-Stück «Die Welt der Suzie Wong» verpflichtet und ging später mit dem Ensemble während 9 Monaten auf Tournee. Damit hatte das junge Talent den entscheidenden Sprung vollbracht. Tanz-Parts und kleinere Rollen wurden ihr in verschiedenen Filmen, zum Beispiel in «Caprice», angeboten — immer, wenn ein Hauch von Exotik den Gang der Ereignisse zu begleiten hatte. Ihre asiatischen Gesichtszüge sind der grosse Trumpf, den Irene Tsu aufzuweisen hat, aber auch das grosse Handicap: «Ich werde immer nur orientalische Rollen bekommen», meint sie besorgt, «ich bleibe an einem Typ hängen. Zwar ist die Konkurrenz dafür nicht so gross, aber ich fürchte, ich werde niemals davon loskommen.»

Sie scheint nicht unrecht zu haben. In ihrem neuesten und für sie wichtigsten Film verkörpert sie wieder eine attraktive Asiatin. In John Waynes ausserordentlich fragwürdigem aber monumentalem Filmwerk «The Green Berets», einer Verherrlichung des amerikanischen Krieges in Vietnam, spielt sie das verführerische Mädchen Lin. Sie lockt den feindlichen Vietcong-General in eine Falle und verhilft damit John Wayne und seinen Männern zu einem überwältigenden (mountanen) Sieg.

Mit ihrer Rolle in John Waynes Film «The Green Berets» hat Irene Tsu den entscheidenden Sprung nach Hollywood geschafft.

Ausgerechnet nach Vietnam hat sich diesmal der Kriegsheld John Wayne (Mitte) gewagt. Irene Tsu soll den Vietcong in die Falle locken.

The Green Berets German magazine article.

Interview with Jeff Bridges and James Mason in Hong Kong.

Irene in cashmere sweatshirt for The IT Company.

Irene in the Italian magazine *OGGI*.

Irene's romance with Sinatra romance in the *China Mail* tabloid.

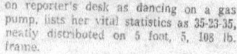

Chevron Island magazine articles.

Irene featured in the Italian magazine *L'Europeo*.

Continua l'inchiesta
sui canoni della bellezza
della donna moderna:
dopo la svedese, l'italiana,
la francese, la tedesca, ecco

LA CINESE

Da Confucio a Mao Tse-tung, la donna cinese, che noi conosciamo come ardente, remissiva, sottomessa e sfruttata, è il bersaglio millenario di una lotta moralizzatrice a ogni costo

LUIGI COMPAGNONE

SECONDO il Leopardi, tutte «le cinesi si storpiano per farsi il piede piccolo, riputando bellezza, quello ch'è contro natura»; altrove, più apodittico, egli sancisce: «Le cinesi si restringono il piede»; e, ci ripensa, e stabilisce un rapporto di relatività: «La piccolezza dei piede delle cinesi a noi parrebbe sproporzionata».

Il signor Gabriel Lafond, capitano di nave nonché membro della Società geografica di Parigi, sbarca nel 1840 a Wampoa e s'imbatte in due dame, e dalla picciolezza de' piedi, e dallo stentato camminare, conoscemmo esser elleno di una classe distinta» (cito da una sciagurata traduzione italiana del 1842).

Lafond si scaglia contro la «barbarica usanza» e spiega che «fin dall'infanzia le dita de' piedi loro vengono piegate e compresse con strette fasciature e con iscarpe di piombo usate per impedirne lo sviluppo». Sospira infine imbattendosi in piedi normali, e si sente più sollevato nel morale, finché non appura che le proprietarie di quei piedi non sono cinesi che a metà: esse discendono infatti dai tartari, stirpe decisamente avversa alla pianificazione dei piedi femminili.

«Una società che impone tali mutilazioni dee necessariamente cessare», decreta il buon Lafond, indignato anche dal fatto che «un cinese, sia di qual rango si voglia, prende quasi sempre una moglie con piccoli piedi. Essa è la moglie vera, e siccome al cinese è permessa la poligamia, ha anche parecchie altre donne co' piedi grandi però rimangono in uno stato d'inferiorità, anzi può dirsi di servitù», e sono soggette alla volontà della prima». Da perfetto gentiluomo occidentale, Lafond vorrebbe scagliarsi contro «un impero celeste di nome, non di fatto, nel quale le donne sono vendute come il bestiame, i padri e le madri mercanteggiano le figlie, e data l'eccessiva popolazione, vi è una legge che autorizza i genitori ad annegarle».

Ma forse quest'ultima congiuntura lo indigna un po' meno del «rimpiccioliimento de' piedi»; infatti egli esclama: «Mai più vorrò vedere piedi di tal fatta», e fa vela verso le isole della Sonda, minacciando col pugno le coste della Cina.

* * *

ALCUNI studiosi di cose cinesi attribuiscono a Confucio la responsabilità dell'usanza di fasciare i piedi femminili. Mi si consenta di essere d'accordo. Confucio era tutto spirito, e, come tale, decisamente sessuofobo. Una donna impacciatissima nel camminare, egli opinava, diviene tutta dedita alla casa, non pensa che ai figli, la sua carica erotica finisce per essere condizionata dalla sua pessima deambulazione.

Nei nostri velleitarismi erotici, noi, viri italici, non abbiamo mai assegnato e concesso speciali prerogative alla bellezza e al temperamento della donna cinese. In questo siamo confuciani; nel senso che, nel nostro ideale *Dizionario delle idee correnti*, ci siamo limitati a pensare di lei: donna dai piedi microscopici. Il nostro repertorio di luoghi comuni erotici è generalmente più ricco per quel che concerne donne di altri paesi. Così la spagnola è bruna, ardente, e porta il coltello nella giarrettiera; la francese è la potenziale eroina di un «roman cochon»; la scandinava, longilinea e biondissima, è dedita al Libero Amore.

La cinese è quasi sempre rimasta al di fuori delle nostre brame mentali. Geograficamente troppo lontana. Qualche aggettivo generico, al più. Piccola. Impiume. Remissiva. Sottomessa. In un celebre libro di Malraux è del resto proprio un cinese decrepito e dalla testa di mandarino, che dice: «È bene che esista la sottomissione assoluta della donna... La donna è sottomessa all'uomo come l'uomo è sottomesso allo Stato».

Sempre secondo il nostro repertorio: cinese=concubina; cinese=cortigiana; e, manco a farlo apposta, è sempre quel cinese decrepito che decreta: «È bene che esista l'istituzione della cortigiana». Dunque cubinaggio; è bene che esista l'istituzione della cortigiana». Dunque: cinese, remissione e sottomissione, a casa come al lavoro. Ma in quel libro di Malraux si parla anche di una strana bandiera apparsa una mattina nelle strade di Sciangai. Su quella bandiera è scritto: «Alle operaie il diritto di lavorar sedute».

Sempre in quel libro, si parla anche dell'infanzia e dell'adolescenza d'una fanciulla cinese. Vi si racconta che era stata venduta per dieci dollari; abbandonata poi dal compratore, un occidentale, da ogni occidentale si aspettava le prove della malvagità degli europei, di cui le avevano sempre parlato.

Una «vittima», dunque, la cinese. Una vittima del padre, della madre, del marito, dei connazionali, degli occidentali. Una vittima tenace, da giardino dei supplizi. Allora: anche una masochista? Una sen-

Irene featured in the Italian magazine *L'Europeo*.

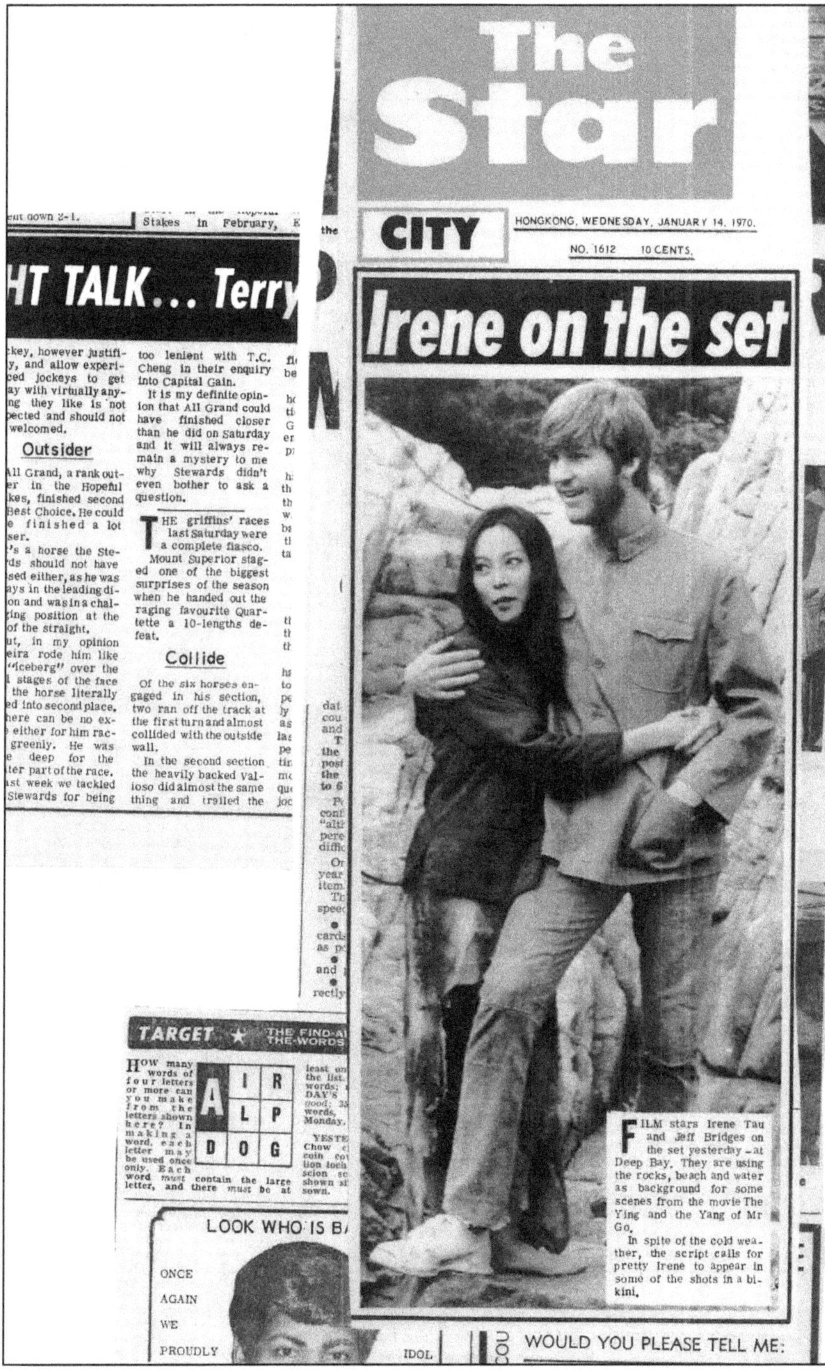

The Star

CITY

HONGKONG, WEDNESDAY, JANUARY 14, 1970.

NO. 1612 10 CENTS.

Irene on the set

FILM stars Irene Tau and Jeff Bridges on the set yesterday – at Deep Bay. They are using the rocks, beach and water as background for some scenes from the movie The Ying and the Yang of Mr Go.

In spite of the cold weather, the script calls for pretty Irene to appear in some of the shots in a bikini.

WOULD YOU PLEASE TELL ME:

Stakes in February,

HT TALK... Terry

key, however justifi-y, and allow experi-ced jockeys to get ay with virtually any-ng they like is not pected and should not welcomed.

Outsider

All Grand, a rank out-er in the Hopeful kes, finished second Best Choice. He could e finished a lot ser.

's a horse the Ste-ds should not have sed either, as he was ays in the leading di-on and was in a chal-ging position at the of the straight.

ut, in my opinion eira rode him like "Iceberg" over the l stages of the race the horse literally ed into second place. here can be no ex-either for him rac-greenly. He was e deep for the ter part of the race. ast week we tackled Stewards for being too lenient with T.C. Cheng in their enquiry into Capital Gain.

It is my definite opinion that All Grand could have finished closer than he did on Saturday and it will always remain a mystery to me why Stewards didn't even bother to ask a question.

THE griffins' races last Saturday were a complete fiasco.

Mount Superior staged one of the biggest surprises of the season when he handed out the raging favourite Quartette a 10-lengths defeat.

Collide

Of the six horses engaged in his section, two ran off the track at the first turn and almost collided with the outside wall.

In the second section the heavily backed Valioso did almost the same thing and trailed the

TARGET ★ THE FIND-A THE-WORDS

HOW many words of four letters or more can you make from the letters shown here? In making a word, each letter may be used once only. Each word must contain the large letter, and there must be at

	I	R
A	L	P
D	O	G

LOOK WHO IS B

ONCE AGAIN WE PROUDLY

IDOL

Irene and Jeff Bridges, filming *The Yin & Yang of Mr. Go*, are featured in the *Hong Kong Star* newspaper.

Irene featured in *Caprice* and *Women of Prehistoric Planet*.

Irene on the cover of a German magazine.

Irene featured in a 1969 issue of the *China Mail*.

Irene appears in the Italian magazine *L'Europeo*, 1967.

156 • *A Water Color Dream*

Irene appears in an Italian magazine.

Alla «varietà delle gioie» si opposero pur sempre i confuciani.

Travolti dall'imperativo categorico: «Moralizzare la vita pubblica», proposero alla meditazione delle fanciulle vite di spose esemplari, peraltro inascoltate. Sulle favolette morali di Liu Hang sbadigliò infatti un'intera generazione di fanciulle, spose, concubine, cortigiane. Altra fonte di sbadigli fu una *Guida all'armonia familiare*. Fu un codice di maniera, puritano, grazie al quale la donna regredì più che mai a semplice oggetto. L'*ars amandi* dei *Manuali* divenuta un ricordo, tutto divenne codificazione e organizzazione; anche la prostituzione.

A Pechino, scrive Marco Polo, «vi sono femmine da partito a venticinquemila, computate quelle della città nuova e quelle de' borghi della vecchia, le quali servono de' suoi corpi agli uomini per denari. E hanno un capitano generale, e per ciascun centenaro a ciascun migliaio vi è un capo, e tutti rispondono al generale. E la causa perché queste femmine hanno un capitano è perché ogni volta che vengono ambasciatori al Gran Khan questo capitano è obbligato di dare ogni notte a detti ambasciatori e a ciascuno della loro famiglia una femmina da partito: e ogni notte si cambiano e non hanno alcun prezzo perché questo è il tributo che pagano al Gran Khan».

Confucio e Mao

NELLA sua *Storia generale della prostituzione*, F. Henriques scrive che Mao ha fatto della Cina un «paradiso di ascetismo». Scrive, che, eliminando il concubinaggio, la schiavitù infantile e la prostituzione, il comunismo cinese ha distrutto in pochi anni un sistema secolare di sfruttamento della donna.

Un viaggiatore napoletano in Cina, Carlo Bernari, racconta che appena ieri nascere una tale sventura, la storia dei piedi fasciati era un simbolo di quella sventura. Aggiunge che è bastato liberare la donna dalla sua condizione servile per vedere sparire anche l'usanza della fasciatura, contro l'abolizione della quale avevano combattuto non solo i feudalisti fascisti, ma gli stessi contadini oppressi, talvolta già entrati a far parte dell'Armata rossa o del Partito comunista, non ancora convinti dell'origine feudale di quel costume a cui erano attaccati certo solo per forza di tradizione.

Dunque Confucio è andato legittimamente in soffitta. Ma, a questo punto, un interrogativo: nella stessa soffitta non l'hanno forse seguito i suoi avversari, i taoisti? In altre parole: cosa è avvenuto, nella Cina d'oggi, dell'antica *ars amandi*? Poiché ogni grande rivoluzione è in qualche modo pur sempre sessuofobica, Mao non si sarebbe sostituito a Confucio? Il marxista-leninista, ossia il materialista storico, allo spiritualista? Forse è lecito chiedersi se si tratti soltanto di una «boutade», o di qualcosa di più. Sembra infatti che i giovani cinesi abbiano tempo per tutto, tranne che per l'amore. Sembra che l'organizzazione non favorisca granché i rapporti amorosi.

Mao ha detto: «Per edificare una grande società socialista è della massima importanza spronare le donne a partecipare all'attività produttiva».

Ha detto: «È necessario spronare le vaste masse delle donne, che in passato non hanno partecipato al lavoro nei campi, a prendere posto sul fronte del lavoro».

Ha soggiunto: «Le donne cinesi sono una grande miniera di materiale umano. Bisogna sfruttare questa miniera...».

Ha precisato: «Fare in modo che tutta la mano d'opera femminile prenda posto sul fronte del lavoro».

Ogni giorno vediamo sui giornali fotografie di ragazze cinesi. Indossano gli shorts. Hanno facce chiare, un po' squadrate, decise. Affollano le brigate di lavoro. Sono studentesse, operaie, chimiche, dottoresse, fisiche, eccetera. Si esprimono con parole concrete, usano alla perfezione termini del linguaggio politico e tecnologico. A un'assemblea per la rivoluzione culturale dei lavoratori della letteratura e dell'arte ha parlato recentemente la compagna Chiang Ching. Le cronache ci informano che è stata salutata da fragorosi applausi quando è apparsa in tribuna.

Ella ha detto fra l'altro: «Vorrei chiedere: non è forse necessario fare una rivoluzione e apportare mutamenti se la vecchia letteratura e la vecchia arte non corrispondono alla base economica socialista e le forme artistiche non si adeguano completamente ai contenuti ideologici socialisti».

Ancora: «Ci sono alcune cose che inondano veramente il mercato, come il rock-and-roll, il jazz, lo strip-tease, l'impressionismo, il simbolismo, il fauvismo, il modernismo (non si finisce veramente mai) tutte opere che hanno lo scopo di avvelenare e di paralizzare la coscienza del popolo. In una parola si utilizza ciò che è decadente ed osceno per avvelenare e paralizzare la coscienza dei popoli».

Si vorrebbe poter domandare alla signora Chiang Ching se, tra le cose «decadenti e oscene», ella include anche gli antichi *Manuali dell'amore*; se include anche gli antichissimi versi:

Se tu m'ami, amore mio bello,
m'alzo la gonna e attraverso il ru-
   [scello...

Luigi Compagnone

La causa fondamentale della trasformazione della donna cinese è il suo inserimento nel mondo del lavoro e dell'attività produttiva.

Irene's appearances in *Caprice* and *The Green Berets* are featured in the L.A. Times.

158 • A Water Color Dream

Irene Tsu, who looks the way every man thinks every oriental girl should look (see pics), made the Green Berets look slightly shell shocked in the film of the same name (see above with John Wayne). Sailors throughout the world were astounded that anyone wearing any kind of hat would send something like "that" flying into the arms of the enemy. Irene, who likes black lace and brief bikinis, once posed for a salad dressing ad.

Irene's performance in *Caprice* is featured in *Parade Magazine*.

IRENE TSU:
Can An Oriental Girl Become A Full-Fledged Screen Star?

by LLOYD SHEARER

lovely, to play the second lead. Irene is so good in the film as a free-swinging Americanized secretary who lives a triple life that the studio wants her for other roles. "She is the sexiest, most photogenic Oriental girl we've had on this lot," declares publicity director Jim Denton, "in at least ten years."

This brings us to a pair of vital and ticklish questions: Can an Oriental—or a Negro, for that matter—play a part which the author has not particularized as a Negro or Oriental role? Has Hollywood reached the point where it is now willing to cast Negro and Oriental actresses as leading ladies?

In *Caprice*, the second feminine lead was originally written for a Caucasian actress, but when Irene Tsu entered the picture with her stimulating, provocative figure—5 feet 5, 114 pounds, 36-23-35—the producers quickly let loose with a wolf whistle, and the secretary in the film was immediately transformed into an Americanized Oriental.

Irene was born in Shanghai, the daughter of a textile designer, Dulcie Lynn Tsu; and a banker, Z.M. Tsu. In 1948, when the Communists took over, she and her parents fled to Taiwan, where Chiang Kai-shek appointed her father to a

PEOPLE AREN'T READY

Irene Tsu says hopefully, "I think I can be the first Oriental girl to develop into a full-fledged screen star. I think the time is ripe for that development."

Her agent, Fred Ishimoto, echoes her sentiments: "Irene is so hot right now that I'm asking and getting $2500 and up for her a week. Tony Curtis wants her to go to Rome to play opposite him in *The Secret Key*. It's a comedy concerning a chastity belt. M.G.M. wants Irene for a top role as a Hawaiian college coed in *The Anthropologist*. Universal wants her to play a Turkish princess. I think her chances of becoming a star are very great."

One veteran Hollywood executive believes Irene and her agent are kidding themselves. "The public is not yet ready," he states, "to accept minority actresses as leading ladies except where a script calls for it, and these are few and far between. Irene can become a well-known feature player but not a star.

"There are still antimiscegenation laws in this country," he points out. "In practically all scripts the hero ends up winning the girl. What the hell do you think would happen if we had John Wayne winding up with Lena Horne instead of Julie Andrews? They'd rip the seats out of the theater."

Irene Tsu claims, however, that she has never experienced any prejudice in America. "People have been wonderful to me, and I don't see why my luck can't hold in Hol-

government post in Taipei. Irene's mother didn't like Taipei, soon took her two daughters and headed for Hong Kong, where the trio spent seven years waiting for permission to enter the United States.

In Hong Kong, Irene attended school, learned English, majored in ballet, was offered a scholarship to the Royal Ballet in London, when word arrived that the U.S. would grant entry. The Tsu ladies sailed for New York, settled in Larchmont, N.Y., with Irene's aunt. Irene attended Mamaroneck High School, then George Washington High, determined to become a ballerina.

In the summer of 1959, when she was 15, the Chinese girl auditioned for a dancing job on Broadway in *Flower Drum Song*. A lookout from producer David Merrick's office caught the tryout, auditioned her for *The World of Suzie Wong*, signed her on the spot. Irene played Broadway for four months, spent nine months on the road with *Suzie*, then returned to New York to finish high school.

Choreographer Hermes Pan then brought her out to Hollywood as a dancer in the film version of *Flower Drum Song*. Struck by her beauty and her unOriental figure, other producers offered film and TV work: *Perry Mason*, *I Spy*, *Take Her, She's Mine*, *How to Stuff a Wild Bikini*. In Hollywood casting offices Irene Tsu became known as "the Chinese sexpot."

GOOD FOR HER

Says Irene: "It was good for me. It gave me a chance to get speaking parts instead of dancing roles. I proved I could act. Now I'm considered an actress instead of a dancer."

Never having been in love, Irene at this point is more interested in her career than marriage. "I have a nice apartment here," she says. "I drive a Corvair. I have enough money to live on. My social life is as extensive as I want it to be. Most of the men I date are Caucasian.

"Eventually I'd like to marry and have kids and enjoy the whole domestic bit. But not now. Careerwise, things for me are 'coming up roses.'"

A spicy dish of chow mein, this Irene Tsu. The producers keep reordering.

Irene's performance in *Caprice* is featured in *Parade Magazine*.

Irene appears in L.A. Times West magazine.

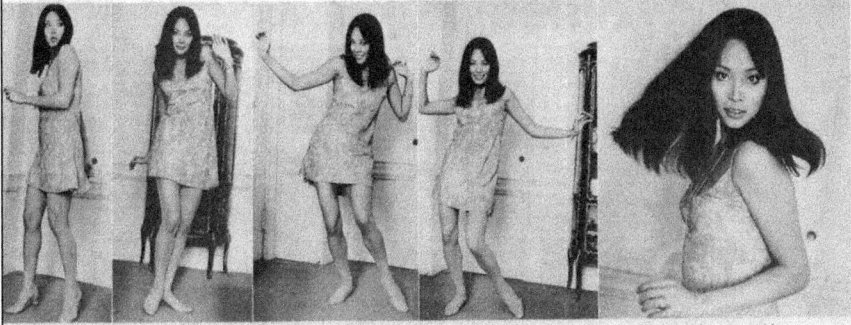

Irene is featured in *Stars & Stripes* magazine.

WEST

LOS ANGELES TIMES

with American folkways—including how to pose for pictures.

After a small role in *The World of Suzie Wong* on Broadway, the Miss Chinatown title in 1960 and parts as a dancer and actress in several films and television shows, Irene has gained her first big break in a feature role as Ray Walston's secretary and girl friend in *Caprice*, a Doris Day comedy to be released in March. Since her costume during much of the picture is a brief bikini, Miss Tsu will have a good chance to establish herself as a sexy international star. As a further indication of her growing reputation as a sultry beauty, Miss Tsu has turned down offers to be a *Playboy* magazine playmate.

But Miss Tsu doesn't have to worry—if the market for sexy Oriental girls is slow next year, there's always *Terry and the Pirates*.

Irene is showcased in the *L.A. Times West* magazine.

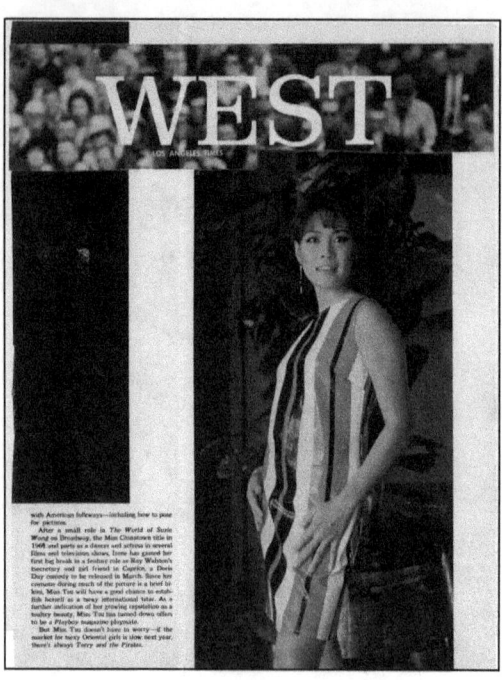

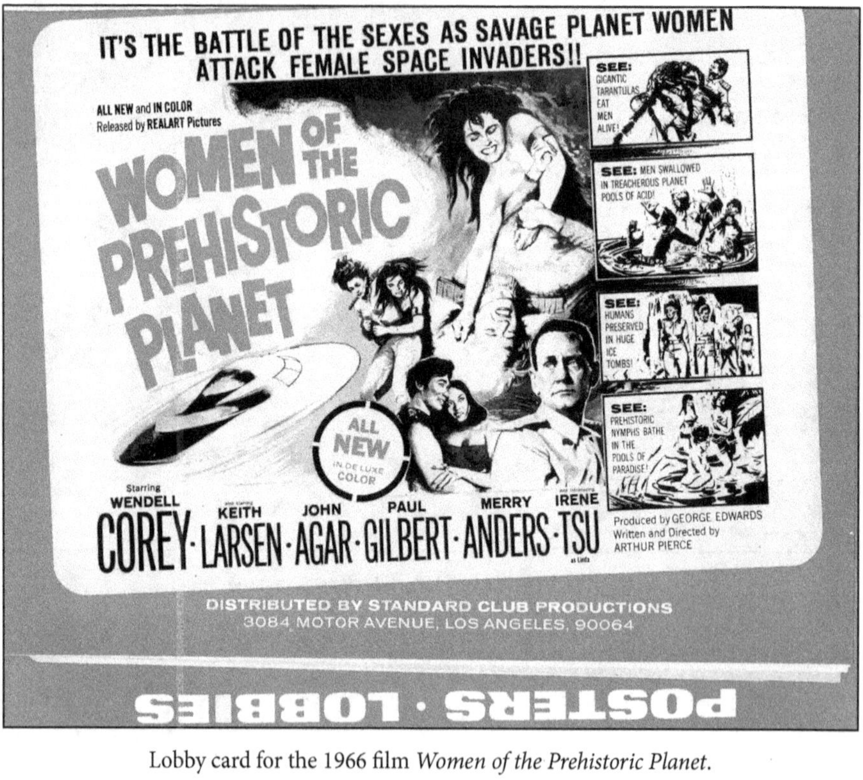

Lobby card for the 1966 film *Women of the Prehistoric Planet*.

The Many Lives of Irene Tsu • 163

'Caprice' Brings A Sweet Sue Here

By JOHN NEVILLE

It's a long way from Shanghai to Hollywood — especially when you swing through Formosa, Hong Kong, Mamaroneck, Long Island, New York City, Canada and Rome on the way.

That's the way Irene Tsu (pronounced Sue) did it, though. And it was well worth the trouble for she's had her big film break—second feminine lead in "Caprice," the kookie 20th Century-Fox film which will open May 31 at Cinema I SouthPark.

Starring in the suspense comedy are Doris Day and Richard Harris. Also in the cast are Ray Walton (television's "Favorite Martian"), Edward Mulhare, Jack Krushen (who received an Oscar nomination, for "The Apartment") and Lilia Skala (cited, for her work in "Lilies of the Field"). So, Miss Tsu is in exceedingly good company.

THE SHAPELY, Shanghai-born, mini-dress clad actress blew through Dallas Monday on a promotional trip for the picture. And, if it looks as good as she did—Fox has nothing to worry about.

In the film, Miss Tsu plays the part of a secretary for a cosmetics firm—just an ordinary All-American secretary," she said, "who lives in a bush pad (the boss keeps her), has a hippie boy friend, and takes dope."

Sounds intriguing, doesn't it? Also intriguing is the "Caprice" plot line—industrial espionage, two big beauty aids outfits trying to steal each other's secrets. There's an angle that even 007 hasn't used yet. Credit Frank Tashlin, who also directed, for the original screenplay.

According to Miss Tsu, the film will go a long way to fracture the Doris Day's perennial girl-next-door image.

This is one label that will never be placed on the oriental charmer who started as a dancer, landed an acting part in "The World of Susie Wong," appeared in the film version of "Flower Drum Song," represented New York City in a "Miss Chinatown" contest and won, and appeared as a dancer in "Cleopatra."

THE "CLEOPATRA" BIT must have been fantastic. "There were thousands of people on the payroll, no one knew what some of them did. They just turned up on Wednesdays to pick up their checks. I've never been able to find myself in the picture, but I worked in Rome on it for four months," she recollected.

Oddly, Miss Tsu's role in "Caprice" does not call for any particular type, just a "kicky" girl. She got the part because the director met her and thought "why not you?" So, she tested, and first was that. Earlier she tested for "Sand Pebbles," (the part eventually awarded to Marayat Andriane), so that wasn't that.

However, that is water over the dam. Miss Tsu is happy with "Caprice," and 20th Century-Fox believes she is of star quality. And, perhaps just as important-for one must eat- as she put it, "I'm making a good living doing what I like to do it or not—TV series are what does the future hold? Well, there is the possibility of a television series, an outdoor adventure thing for Ivan Tors. "I don't know whether I want to do it or not—tv series are such hard work and most of it will be filmed on location and that's rough," the actress admitted candidly.

SHE HAS NO DEFINITE movie commitments at the moment, but will break her tour in a week or so to do a guest shot on the Jack Carson Show, "then, there are always TV commercials."

Another thing Miss Tsu wants to do is go back to college and study language. "I speak three dialects of Chinese, but am forgetting how to write it. When I put something down it doesn't look right. It's not a matter of learning how to spell, you have to remember all the different characters. So, I think I'll start studying again."

Unfortunately, one of Miss Tsu's big scenes in "Caprice" will never make the movie house circuit. In a swimming pool sequence, she lost half of her bikini. Naturally, the cameras kept running, but the footage was snipped out. Incidentally, it wasn't her face that was left on the cutting-room floor.

Irene Tsu . . . A rising star from the East featured in new Doris Day-Richard Harris film "Caprice."

East meets West in Irene Tsu

By IAN BLACK

IRENE Tsu would appear to be the perfect argument against Kipling's statement that East and West would never meet.

On the telephone, her huskily sexy voice sounds no different to those of thousands of other healthy young American women, and it comes as a jolt to meet her, and realize that she is Chinese. And a beauty, too.

Miss Tsu is 25, and she is in the Colony to film Burgess Meredith's The Ying and the Yang of Mr Go with James Mason, Jeff Bridges and Jack McGowran.

It is her first visit to Hongkong for eight years, the last one being in 1961, the year she won the "Miss Chinatown U.S.A." title.

"It's been very strange being back here again. For the first week or so I was terrified of the crowds in the streets, much more than anything else. You never see so many people on foot in Los Angeles."

Irene smiled as she recalled: "And it was amazing to look around and see so many young girls looking almost exactly the same as me!"

In the United States, Irene Tsu's face is almost as well known as that of the President — she appears on network television 20 times a day in a Standard Oil commercial.

"I'm the 'Chevron Girl' — and it's fantastic exposure. It means when I walk down to the supermarket, or a cop stops me and gives me a ticket, a kind of instant recognition that I've never had from the movies," she said.

Irene has been seen regularly with Sinatra over the past 12 months — a fact

Irene Tsu . . . terrified of the crowds

which had the Hollywood gossip columnists clamouring for interviews with her on the subject.

But she refuses to be drawn, other than to say: "I met Frank in Miami."

Florida, last year, when I was doing the oil commercial, and he was making Tony Rome.

Irene Tsu began her career on the stage as a dancer, and at the age of 13 in Hongkong she was the only girl from Southeast Asia to be awarded a scholarship to Britain's Royal Academy of Dancing in London.

"I began dancing professionally when I was 15 and still at high school in New York. It was only a summer job, but it led in my playing Fifi in The World of Susie Wong on Broadway, and my interest in acting began."

Later Irene studied drama under Uta Haagen in New York, and then in 1961 she went to Hollywood for the film, Flower Drum Song.

"I was a dancer in the film, but I also played a cameo role," she said. "And then I went to Hongkong again as Miss Chinatown, and shortly after this I went to Rome to appear as one of the handmaidens in Cleopatra.

"I was supposed to be there for five weeks, but I ended up staying four months.

"It was chaos. Everything was being re-written and re-shot at the last minute. I was only a handmaiden in the film but to give you an idea of the kind of money they were throwing around, my gown must have cost around U.S.$1,300 alone. It was incredible."

In the past few years, Miss Tsu has appeared in numerous American television programmes, and she regards her current role opposite James Mason in The Ying and the Yang of Mr Go as a fortunate break.

"I can't tell you how excited I am to be here with Mr Mason and Mr Meredith. They're both very much my seniors in experience in this business, and I just know I'm going to learn a lot from working with them."

day, December 13, 1969

ACTOR James Mason and actress Irene Tsu arrived in Hongkong last night to star in the film "The Ying and Yang of Mr Go" produced by the Run Film Productions, Ltd. USA. The film will make use of local backgrounds. They are staying in the Hilton was made a Press conference to announce details of the film will be held at the hotel today.

These articles detail Irene's work in *Caprice* and *The Yin and Yang of Mr. Go.*

Los Angeles Times article about war films, including *The Green Berets*.

Los Angeles Times article about the filming of *The Green Berets*.

Los Angeles Times article about 1986's *Down & Out In Beverly Hills*.

Irene films the 1975 film *Paper Tiger* with acclaimed actor David Niven.

Paper Tiger newspaper advertisement.

Paper Tiger premiere invitation.

Filming *Paper Tiger* in 1975 with David Niven and Toshiro Mifune.

Newspaper articles about the filming of 1966's *Paradise Hawaiian Style* with Irene and Elvis Presley.

Irene, Jimmy Stewart and Sandra Dee, *Take Her, She's Mine* advertisement.

Ad for an early version of The Ying and Yang of Mr. Go.

Irene, Jeff Bridges and James Mason interview for The Ying and Yang of Mr. Go."

SINATRA LETTERS

Frank Sinatra's Valentine's Day card to Irene.

Irene and Frank Sinatra at Caesar's Palace, Las Vegas.

A night out in L.A. with Irene, Frank Sinatra and Michael & Gloria Romanoff.

Irene, Frank Sinatra and friends at the Palm Springs restaurant Ruby Dunes.

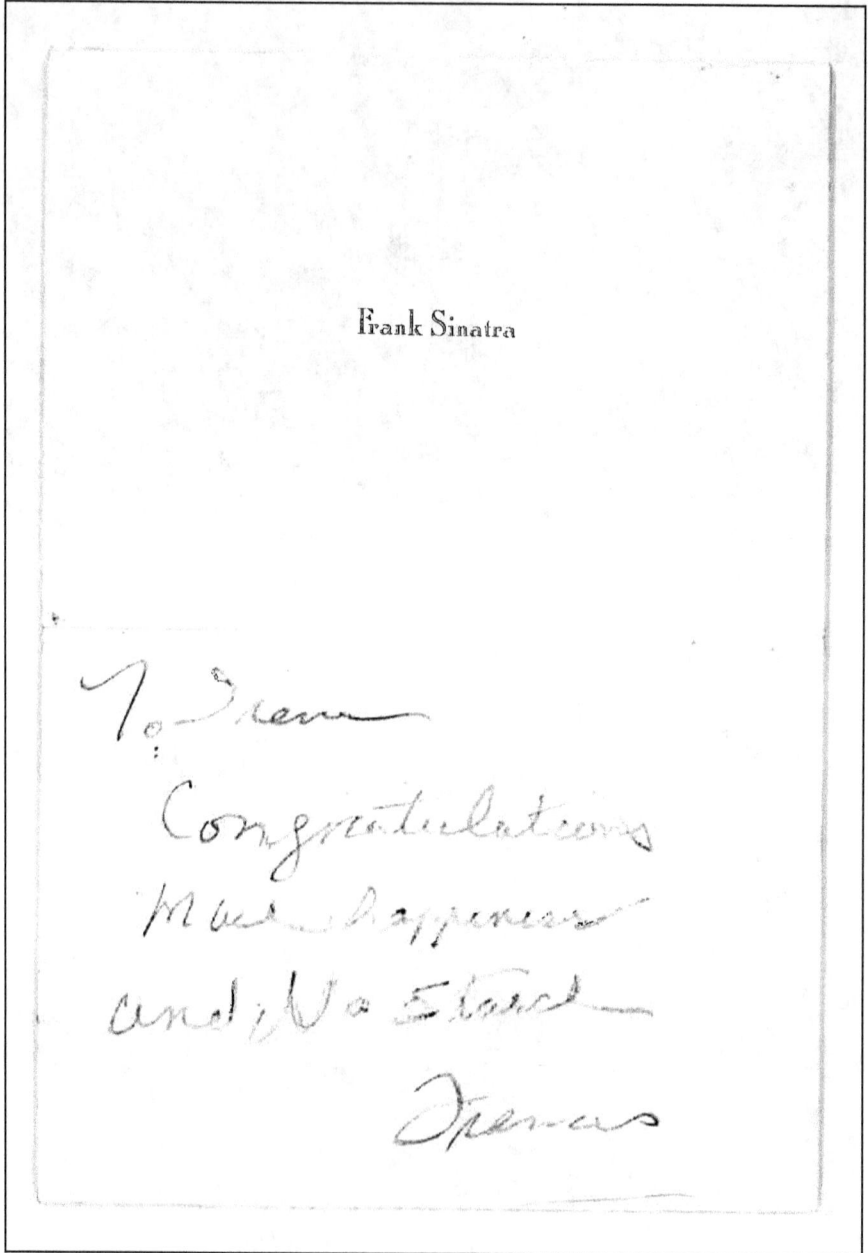

Sinatra's note that accompanied his wedding gift to Irene.

I've rejected the Japan date. Will tell you why when you return.
So, there it is, not very much — But dull!
Stay well, work fast, and hurry home. I miss you and your silly face.
I send you love, hugs and xxxxxxxxx's.

Your round eyed American fliend — Francis

Frank Sinatra's letters to Irene.

mon——
the 19th

Greetings Oh almond eyed Beauty!

Hope your virus is wiped out, and you are all whole again. I'm well and continuing my battle and maybe, just maybe, we may be gaining ground. We should know soon.

The weather here has been absolutely too much. Temp. 85 and very sunny.

Every one is well, and they ask about you constantly.

I will be here till the film starts which should be about the 23rd. By the way I've decided to play Vegas on April 3rd for 2 and ½ weeks. Then on to N.Y. and England.

Frank Sinatra's letters to Irene.

Frank Sinatra's "Secret Admirer" card to Irene.

Sinatra's self-painted Christmas card to Irene.

CHAPTER 15

I'D BEEN COZY WITH FRANCIS for over two years when out of the blue I was approached for a film to be directed by Burgess Meredith called *The Yin and the Yang of Mr. Go*. It was to be filmed in Hong Kong. Not only was I excited about the film—as I had lived in Hong Kong when I was a child—I took it as a sign that going to Hong Kong meant that I would be one step closer to possibly meeting my spiritual guru in person at the Dera in India. I had been obsessed about seeing him for many months leading up to the film opportunity.

The film was to star James Mason, Burgess Meredith, Jack MacGowran, Broderick Crawford, Peter Lind Hayes, and an impressive international cast. After I was cast to co-star in the film, I spent several months doing film promotion with Meredith while they were readying the financing. He was also looking for the young male lead to play Nero Finnegan, an AWOL American writer hiding out with my young Hong Kong prostitute character, Tah-Ling. He eventually found his lead in a very young and rising star named Jeff Bridges, who was just coming off of *The Last Picture Show*.

I remember we gathered at LAX, bound for Hong Kong on a Pan Am flight. Lloyd and Dorothy Bridges came to see Jeff off and I thought it was adorable that his mom had brought a box of homemade butter cookies for Jeff's upcoming birthday. He was turning twenty-one in a month.

We settled into the first class cabin and started to let the journey embrace us. We were served champagne, which got us talking and getting to know each other more. Eventually we graduated to guava juice and vodka. Beyond how delicious the taste was, the color was so sexy that later in life, I designed my fashion collections in guava, watermelon, and sea foam palates. I meditated on the adventure ahead: Hong Kong, the movie and any opportunity I might have to find my way to India.

At one point, Jeff got up to go to the bathroom, and when he came back, he had that charming and disarming smile that would help make him a Hollywood star. He looked like he just swallowed the last piece of the most incredible chocolate in the world. He sat down and very discreetly put something into the palm of my hand. I opened up my palm to reveal it was an old sock. I looked up at him with a puzzled expression and he motioned with his head toward the bathroom. I closed my fist around the sock and headed that way. I shouldn't have been surprised to see a little brick of dark and sticky hashish. As soon as I took it from its package, the smell permeated the room. Panicking, I quickly chewed a bit of it and swallowed hard. I had never done that before. In fact, I had only smoked hashish a couple times, but I was trapped in this confined space with the smell quickly filling the room. Someone could figure it out anytime, so what could I do?

I walked back to my seat and we smiled, ate, fell asleep, and dreamed our dreams. He later would tell me how he was undecided about pursuing an acting career because his heart was in music. But his dad took him to legendary agent Jack Gilardi, who signed him up. Jeff had no idea how lucky he was; a big agent like Gilardi was unreachable to an Asian outsider like me.

What I remember most about Jeff is that he's such a talented, good-natured, and decent human being who's full of youthful enthusiasm. You'd never think of him as a "movie star," even now. The Bridges are such decent and sweet people, you wished they were your neighbors or classmates. And sure enough, I later had Jeff's brother Beau Bridges as my neighbor in Benedict Canyon for a long time. He too was inconspicuous, shy, equally humble, and a damn good actor.

Our plane landed in Hong Kong, the fragrant harbor, some twelve hours later. I think we were greeted by the press and shuttled to the Hilton hotel on the Victoria side of the island. Jeff later told me that a British columnist stationed in Hong Kong who hung with us a bit had warned him of the dire consequence of being caught with a substance like hashish there. It would be a serious offense, and caning would just be the frosting on that piece of punishment cake. I'm pretty sure Jeff ditched his stash.

The problems with the picture started as soon as we landed. We had weeks of rehearsals in between lots of social and public relations affairs. It was apparent very soon that Burgess did not have a script breakdown or even a real shooting script. Though he was a marvelous actor of stage and screen, Burgess really didn't grasp the complexities of directing a film, especially one so far away from Hollywood, which added to the difficulties. In fact, we were the first film to shoot on location in Hong Kong since the 1960 film *The World of Suzie Wong* and 1955's *Love is a Many-Splendored Thing*, both of which starred William Holden. The first cinematographer was fired within weeks, and another was flown in.

Jeff and I rehearsed random, disjointed scenes, not really knowing what exactly we were doing or even our dialogue. Burgess had Jeff rehearse his soliloquy as Nero Finnegan like something out of *Finnegan's Wake*. Jeff went along in his youthful enthusiasm. I had no rehearsal with James Mason, who incidentally wore eyelids and buck teeth to play a half-Chinese person. Burgess would ask to see my "dance number." I was given a tape of some song by a female vocalist to rehearse and no other real direction. I can dance to practically anything, but that song was truly uninspiring and there was no beat, so to speak. I made up a burlesque-type of number and Burgess would mumble something. I guess it was approval because he said, "Just keep doing what you are doing." There was no clue as to when or where we were to film it.

By the third week Mason and Burgess were not sitting at the same table for dinner. In fact, they were on opposite sides of the room. Then there was the night that Burgess got arrested for pissing in Tsim Sha Tsui, the equivalent of Times Square. The shoot was too overwhelming for Burgess given his age and being so far from the familiarity of Hollywood.

As a funny, random side note, Francis would call me and in those days the hotel operator would have to patch the call in. Sure enough, the next day it would be all over the Hong Kong newspaper: "Frank Sinatra in love with local girl!" Such bullshit, I was from L.A.!

Jeff and I stayed close during the shoot. Burgess got us adjoining rooms so we could get closer, but that was not to be. We were close friends and respected each other's privacy. Jeff explored Hong Kong as a young American would. He spent his time seeking out the Chinese emporiums where you could shop for Mao jackets and mainland products, and hunting through alleys and hidden places in the steep steps of Victoria for antiquities or what he thought were opium dens and whore houses in Wan Chai. He was gone a whole night once and I was ready to have production call the police when he appeared in the morning and knocked on my door. With that mischievous grin, smiling from cheek to cheek, he looked like he'd just swallowed a canary! He couldn't wait to relate his experience at one of those houses. I waited with bated breath to hear his tale. He chose (or was given) a working girl and they went up to the room. But instead of the normal things that happen there, Jeff had different ideas.

"I wanted to pay her to talk to me."

It turns out they talked the whole night and actually formed a relationship that lasted through filming. She attached herself to Jeff and even threw him a party at a disco before we left.

After a long and chaotic three months, the film wrapped. Or more appropriately, we ran out of money. The hotel was ready to throw us out during the last couple of weeks. I only got paid because my Uncle Shen was the chairman of the HKSB, who underwrote the film's financing. He had one of the clerks call me whenever the funds hit the bank and I would run across the street to collect my pay.

Communication in 1970 was basically static-filled long distance phone calls patched in by operators or letter writing. Interestingly enough, I recently found letters from my dad advising me to keep my pay in Hong Kong and to come back to L.A. via Europe, to stop in Switzerland to open an unnumbered account. I folded the letter back and never thought about Swiss bank accounts or his advice to buy blue chips stocks, which he was already buying for me. I never thanked him, never even responded to his letter. I was twenty-two and was in my own universe. Still, looking back on those letters, I see that he was more involved in my life than I thought at the time.

The movie didn't get completed and released until years later. The Hong Kong crew would say that the movie was "jinxed" because we shot at the graveyard on Chinese New Year's Eve with a minimal crew. Jeff even said it was spooky as hell. The film definitely did not help to propel me on the star meter. I should have been really crushed. However, looking back, it did pave my path to one of the most important and amazing experiences of my life, the chance to finally meet my spiritual master.

CHAPTER 16

IN THE LATE SIXTIES—with the combination of the hippies, the love-ins, mind-altering drugs, yoga, meditation, and the rise of Eastern philosophy—there was a spiritual renaissance happening in California. People, even celebrities, were going on quests to find something greater and more meaningful in this existence. The Beatles, some members of the Beach Boys, and Mia Farrow went on a now infamous trip to seek enlightenment from the Maharishi Mahesh Yogi in India and it opened up the world's eyes to a deeper quest to *find* love and to *be* loved. The movement was causing young people to seek self-realization and they were finding it!

I too was looking for something greater.

I wanted that deep peace and joy within. The cycle of looking for the next job, and quickly working oneself out of a job, wasn't enough. Life could not just go from sound stage to sound stage. Sometimes I felt all my pores smelled of the musty sound stages and my life was just going from shoot to shoot. The only change I had was playing the beautiful companion to Francis, which was wonderful, but I was seeking something deeper.

I have always been a spiritual person, even if it did take me a while to find my true path. I was raised Christian by a deeply devout mother and grandmother. We followed the Christian traditions, including church on Sunday. Easter was special and Christmas was always spent caroling as my mom would dress as Santa while she put out the gifts at night. As I grew up and then moved to Hollywood, it was my faith, my closeness to Jesus that gave me the fortitude, support, and comfort I so needed while forging my way. Truly it was Jesus and Fred Ishimoto, my manager, that were my two pillars of support. But I was always open and receptive to even more spiritual guidance.

All through the late sixties, when I was hopping from movie to TV show to commercial all over the country, I was also attending various "satsang" meetings in L.A., mostly with my cousin Allen, who was a set designer on *Star Trek* (among other shows). He would take me to some meditation meetings, including some in celebrity homes like Leigh Taylor-Young, Barbara Rush, and Terry Moore. They were wonderful gatherings with people who really seemed blissful, as if they were in tune with something higher.

Allen was a devotee of an Indian guru they referred to as the Master who lived at the Dera, an ashram in northern India in the district of Amritsar. Allen was one of the few people in L.A. that actually went to the Dera and spent time with the Master. Very few people had even *heard* of him in America. There were only a few books available at the iconic Bodi Tree bookstore on Melrose. Devotees sometimes had them shipped from the Dera. Not many people really understood the books but what was such a turn-on was seeing the people who returned from the Dera. They were elevated, touched by that "something greater." When they spoke, you listened. There was something so powerful in the way they talked about what they experienced in meeting the Master. They literally glowed with bliss and love. The more you listened, the more fixated you became.

As they would tell me... you don't choose the path, it chooses you. It got to a point where all I could think of was getting to the Dera myself. Like Shirley MacLaine's book, *You Can Get There from Here,* that's all I focused on. But how? The devotees would tell me to write a letter because you have to be invited to go. I was given an address, not knowing whether it would even get there. But I sent it anyway with several stamps and marked the envelope "AIRMAIL." Several months went by and I did not hear from the Dera. Month by month I was getting more anxious and thinking of some way to get there. Then, out of the blue, came the Hong Kong film shoot. Having lived there as a kid, and it being at least halfway to India, I thought it was a good omen. The water color had once again taken on a new stroke and I was willing it to end up at the feet of the Master.

While the shoot was an adventure in itself, it was all merely the play for me on the outside. On the inside, I had one goal. I happened to find out from satsang friends that the managers of the Hong Kong Hilton where I was staying were devout followers of the Master. I got their room number and worked up the courage to knock on their door one day. There was no answer. I think someone was in but he or she did not want to respond to the knock. Disheartened, I left but didn't give up hope.

As filming fell apart, everyone was getting ready to leave Hong Kong and I was frustrated because I still hadn't heard a word, let alone gotten an invitation to the Dera. I had met the beautiful actress Yvette Mimieux and her boyfriend Stewart, whose father was the proprietor of Jungleland USA. They were working as the monkey trainer for important scenes in the film. They invited me to come along to Bangkok, then on to India to visit the tiger reserves, and eventually on to either Nepal or Tibet. I could trade in my first class ticket and make it to India with enough money to fly back to L.A.

We landed in Bangkok and spent several days seeing the sights and enjoying the Oriental, a famous five-star hotel on the inland waterway. Yvette and Stewart encouraged me to come along to some millionaire's yacht in Phuket as a side trip, but my heart was yearning for the Dera. I was getting more frustrated. Invitation or not, some of my friends were supposed to already be there. That's where I wanted to be and where I was *going* to be!

Funny enough, when the time came, I almost missed my chance to get there.

One night after dinner, as we sat around the fabulous veranda having tea and enjoying the light breeze, a hotel clerk came running over toward us and called out my name.

"Pam Am on the line to confirm your flight to New Delhi," he said.

"Oh, really?" I replied, rather confused. "For when?"

"At 14:05 tomorrow."

"WHAT?!" I exclaimed. I ran to the phone and sure enough the woman with the melodic Indian accent repeated the confirmation, which gave me hardly any time to pack and say my goodbyes. I didn't even remember making the reservation and I had lost track of time there. It's easy to do when you soak up the sights of the emerald and ruby Buddha and dine on delicious Thai cuisine washed down with ice cold Singha beer.

I was mortified and agreed to whatever she said on the phone which gave me about two hours to gather up my belongings and get to the airport. I rushed back to my friends and explained my predicament. I was still considering their side adventure. After some discussion, I announced that I had to go up to my room and meditate for a few moments on what I was going to do. I asked Stewart to come up to my room in about twenty minutes. I meditated and felt the force so strongly pulling me to the Dera; it was as if I was in some super magnet and I was helpless to veer from its course.

I gathered up my stuff in a fast-paced daze. I packed a tiny cheap suitcase that I wasn't even aware I had with one pair of pants, one pair of shorts, two sundresses, three or four t-shirts and pajamas. I replaced my good watch with a Timex (which I also didn't remember owning), put the rest of my belongings into my big suitcase, and laid out all the money and cards I owned on the dresser. When Stewart knocked on my door, I told him I was ready to go. I instructed him to ship my big suitcase back to L.A., and asked him to take all my money except for two hundred dollars. After the Beatles' visit a few years prior, there had been quite an array of hippies from the U.S. loitering in the India and the Nepal region and the government demanded that they post a bond of two hundred dollars if they got arrested for refusing to leave the country. I wanted to make sure I had at least that on me, but not much else. I wanted to take as little as possible. Stewart talked me into keeping my credit card in case of emergency. I told him I would try to contact him in a few days if I could, but he wouldn't have a location for me. I planned to return to L.A. in two weeks or so. We gathered my stuff and went down to the lobby. Stewart took care of my checkout. I hugged Yvette goodbye and grabbed a taxi to the airport to truly start my spiritual adventure!

It was after 10 p.m. and the Bangkok streets were still streaming with people, vehicles, and little boys running up to my cab selling flower leis of fragrant pikake. I was delighted as they are my favorite fragrance in the whole world. I gave them all the change I had, and they gave me all their pikake. Soon the taxi sped through the city with me laden with all those fragrant leis like a princess. I've never felt so elated. I floated on air and drifted through the airport procedures without remembering much. I was ushered onto the plane to find it entirely empty. They asked if I wanted to be seated in first class. I responded no and I remained in my meditation state, oblivious yet keenly aware of my surroundings. I felt the smell of the airplane and heard the hum of the engine, and soon the plane was ready for takeoff. Relieved that I had made it and made this decision, I must have slept most of the way as I only opened my eyes when they announced we were landing.

Upon arriving, I found myself in a very empty airport lounge space that looked more like Des Moines then Delhi. It must have been around 5 a.m. local time, and I found out my connecting flight to Amritsar was not until 8:40, so I had some time to kill. I found three empty seats in a row and managed to get some more rest with the suitcase strapped to my wrist.

I awoke to people talking and the shuffling of bags. I gathered myself to prepare for my flight to Amritsar. It was a small prop plane with very uncomfortable seats that made at least three or four stops before Amritsar. If it weren't for my obsession with getting to the Dera and my emersion in meditation, the plane trip would have been quite intolerable. Aside from the constant up and down movement of the flight, it seemed that every time it made a stop, hundreds of flies would come inside the plane and stubbornly refuse to move from your face or wherever they landed. They refused to budge even after you swatted them. They were also mammoth and intimidating. It was not my favorite flying experience, especially compared to the first class I had taken to get to that side of the world.

At last we arrived at Amritsar, the last stop. I got off the plane and wandered about through the small, dusty boarding lounge area. The people that wandered in and out wore strange garbs and looked and sounded foreign, but I paid no attention and no one paid any attention to me. I was very much in my meditative state, focusing on my path. I had no idea how much time had passed until someone walked over to me.

"Miss, you cannot stay here," said an airport employee. "We are trying to clean up."

"Where can I go?" I asked, suddenly realizing I didn't really have a plan.

"Go down the street to the airline office. You cannot wait here!"

I walked down a dusty, unpaved road for maybe a quarter of a mile, oblivious to the strange vehicles, paddy cabs, buses, bicycles, and maybe even an oxen cart. I was starting to wonder what I was going to do. Then I saw on the right-hand side a small store front with a faded travel poster and some faded pictures. Thinking this must be the airport office or at least some kind of store, I walked in. There was no one there and it was basically empty, with only some old magazines and more flies. By now I was fairly used to them.

Still, I was calm. I wasn't hungry or thirsty or tired. In fact, I had actually felt better in general since leaving the Oriental in Bangkok. I could describe this feeling as euphoric... or I was losing my mind! It felt like I was still being pulled by that magnetic compass and no matter how hard I tried I couldn't adjust or get out of its pull. I would relate this story from time to time to other devotees or friends and every time I told it I would fall right back under its spell.

After some time, a man came out and looked at me like I was some creature from another planet... and indeed I was! He also told me I couldn't wait there. I explained to him that I had come all the way from America to go to the Dera and that they were waiting for me there. I asked how I could get there.

"Oh, it's not that far, maybe four or five miles," he said. "You can walk or take a bus or an oxen cart…"

He apparently didn't realize that I was from L.A. and being the spoiled city girl that I was, I had probably never walked a mile. The other two alternatives were quite unimaginable to me as well.

"Wait, you want to go to the Dera, did you say?" he asked, suddenly remembering something.

"Yes… yes!"

"There is a car that just pulled up from the Dera."

"Oh my God, really?!" I nearly jumped I was so excited. Surely this was a sign. I walked outside, still with my suitcase chained to my wrist, and greeted the two ladies that stepped out of the black limousine that the man had pointed out.

"Hi, how are you?" I asked politely. "Did you come from the Dera to pick me up?"

Not sure what to make of me, they looked at each other with dismay.

"Who are you?" they asked, though without any malice. "We did not come to pick up anyone. We are here to pick up Maharaji's airline ticket for his upcoming trip in three weeks."

I introduced myself and said that I was from Los Angeles. The ladies were from Johannesburg, South Africa. One lady thought I must be from Singapore, but the other was excited that I was from L.A.

"My daughter lives in Los Angeles and she is also an actress and dancer," she said. "Her name is Juliet Prowse. Have you heard of her?"

"Oh my God, of course! Of course I know her!" I exclaimed. Actually, I did not know her well then, but we had been in the same dance and yoga classes and of course we had Francis in common, so I *felt* like I knew her. Much later we both attended yoga class for years and years and became quite close until she passed at the early age of fifty-nine.

"Well, I guess we'll have to take you to the Dera then. But we do have to pick up a couple of things in town."

I was definitely in a dream, and once again I knew this was all happening for a reason. I was being called.

The short trip around town was quite an eye opener. I saw that people lived on the streets; they cooked there, ate there, bathed there, defecated there, and most probably died there. There were a few storefronts and eateries, and the ladies picked up some supplies like rubbing alcohol and aspirin. I had trouble focusing too much on my surroundings. I was too excited.

It was a short ride and soon we were inside the gates of the Dera.

I had made it!

As for what the Dera looked like, it was a well-organized compound of large and small buildings done in the traditional Indian style with clean, swept dirt roads and lush, tall trees. While it certainly wasn't anything like the fancy five-star Indian hotels, it certainly wasn't dirty and shabby. It was charming and orderly with an overwhelming peace that engulfed the place. To be completely honest, the brick and mortar and the layout of the Dera mattered very little. It was the Master's presence there that was awe-inspiring and difficult to put into words.

It also wasn't so much what one did at the Dera, but the overwhelming peace and bliss one felt in doing the most ordinary chores. Even having breakfast, doing our wash, preparing food, going to the library, and walking about the village carried that feeling. Of course there was meditation time, we had question-and-answer periods for foreigners, and we attended large satsang meetings presided by the Master, always preceded by the most hypnotic Indian chants. I suppose it was reminiscent of the canters in an Orthodox Jewish temple. As for the people who lived there, they performed their daily chores in utter contentment, no matter how mundane. They greeted you and one another with "Radha Soami," which means "Lord of my Soul." One really cannot imagine a place like this actually existed in such a ruthless world, and from the moment I arrived, it became the center of my world. In some ways it always will be.

The Master was all I had hoped for and more. He is pure love and everyone there seemed to be dipped in that pure love and complete obeisance. I was granted an audience with the Master not long after arriving. I tried to think of all the questions to ask him and questions that other L.A. satsang friends begged me to ask if my trip was successful and I got the chance to meet him. I had trouble sleeping the night before as I was so excited. The next day, I was ushered into the main house of the Dera compound. Through an entrance hall I was led into a courtyard of stone pavers and potted plants with jasmine and bougainvillea. It looked, smelled, and felt heavenly. There, about fifteen feet away from me, behind a desk, sat the Master.

He wore a white kurta and a sparkling white turban that framed his beautiful and kind face. He was a very handsome man by any standard.

He wore reading glasses on this occasion and had the greatest smile I've ever seen, as if he were in tune with a fountain of pure bliss. We looked at each other and I could hardly move.

"Please come forward," he asked gently. "May I look at your camera?" I moved forward not even aware that I had a camera around my neck. When I got to his desk, I removed my camera and told him that I had gotten it in Hong Kong where I was doing a film, but I hadn't yet learned to use it. Talking nervously, I also told him that I was not initiated and that I had come from Los Angeles where I had attended a few satsangs where we had read some chapters of books that we had. I felt like I was talking nonstop.

He said he was fond of cameras and with photography. He handled my camera with care and even adjusted some settings, telling me which would be the best for the light at the Dera. He asked if I had any questions for him.

I utterly forgot all the questions I had diligently prepared. I went completely blank. After all this time, I couldn't think of anything. I willed my brain to please start working again. Luckily, something clicked. I finally uttered a question someone had given me to ask.

"Why is it that I was told you have to sit within a certain distance from the Master to receive his darshan?" Darshans were blessings.

"Do you want to be near to someone you love?" he replied simply and softly.

"Yes."

"They love me, therefore they want to sit near me," he said. And then he smiled. "There are no particular spiritual benefits whether near or far."

I walked away from my brief encounter dipped in pure bliss for his was the most beautiful face that I have ever seen. I realized that when you come face to face with a true living saint, one with God, you will have no more questions. I had made it to the Dera and I had met the Master. I was fulfilled. I truly didn't care what was going to happen next in my career, my relationships, my life. All of it would be taken care of, indeed.

After twelve days, I departed the Dera and flew back home. My cousin Allen greeted me at the airport with another satsang devotee. They said they always try to meet people coming from the Dera because they want to inhale that special glow that emanated from them. I must have floated off the plane. I don't recall my feet ever touching the ground. It was an amazing experience.

Weeks went by, and I attended to duties at home and at work. I drove to the desert to tell Francis about my adventures in Hong Kong. I did not go into my India trip to visit my spiritual Master as that would have been too weird for him. He was already less than amused that I had followed the Beatles and Mia Farrow to India and had missed the film he was preparing with a part for me. The film never really got off the ground, but he was still upset that I had disobeyed. In order for it to make a tiny bit of sense to Francis, I had to divulge my lifelong fascination and devotion to Eastern philosophy. I wouldn't know how to begin and couldn't possibly expect him—or any red-blooded American—to have the slightest interest or comprehension. Instead, we dove into the elaborate train set I got for him as a gift. We sat on the floor, ate popcorn, and made a mess of the den. Francis had to go to New York, and for once I declined to go with him, saying I had a job coming up. But truly my heart was back at the Dera listening to the hypnotic sounds of the birds. My attention was inward bound.

That experience would stay with me for the rest of my life. I would talk of it sparingly to those who didn't believe or hadn't experienced it. It was a special journey, a deeply personal one. Lately I have begun to reveal more of my inner life and of that experience to my close friends. I am not as afraid to speak out as much about that trip and my beliefs. I feel that I need to close this duality within me; to live *in* this world and not *of* it. Maybe true yoga "union" will be mine one day and I will be whole. If so, I can look back at the teachings of the Master and my trip to the Dera as a key point on this path. My karma lays in the unknown mighty strokes of the water color. Whence it shall come to rest God only knows.

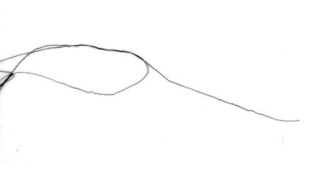

CHAPTER 17

NOT LONG AFTER MY RELATIONSHIP with Frank came one of the more fascinating, exciting, and tumultuous relationships of my life with the man who would eventually become my husband: the talented Hungarian photographer and director Ivan Nagy.

Ivan was an enigma in an Eastern European 007 kind of way. He was earthy, sexy, charming, and unfettered by social conventions. He was either loved or hated. There was no middle ground. Ivan was an extremely intelligent and clever man who did what his heart or mind dictated, no matter what. He could be kind and generous, and yet in the same moment, crafty. Ivan had a thousand-megawatt smile that completely disarmed you. You never really knew what he was thinking or even feeling, even whether he was agreeing with or opposing you. Most of my friends and relatives didn't like him as they saw him as arrogant or bombastic. He was not cut from the homogenized American male prototype. In fact, he was the antithesis of what we consider normal or culturally appropriate. He didn't care about being politically correct. Like Francis's song, Ivan's motto could have been "I did it my way." He was a natural man and, also like Francis, he played by his own rules. In that way, he was a true Aquarian; an intelligent, free-spirited, and unconventional man with a zip code in the wild blue yonder.

The first time I was supposed to meet Ivan was when *TV Guide* was doing a story on me when my commercials were running. The article was titled "The Hot Oriental on TV," and Ivan was assigned to shoot the layout. He never showed up and instead I got Michele Matte, a smelly little Frenchman. We struggled through the shoot. Years later Ivan told me that he did not want to do the job because it was only an inside cover shoot.

Nancy Reagan was being featured on the cover. I guess it wasn't a big enough shoot for him.

Months after the shoot, I got a call from Chase Mellon and his wife Ronnie, inviting me to dinner to meet a film director they were working with. I asked who.

"Ivan Nagy, he is Hungarian and a lot of fun. You are going to love him."

To which I replied. "No! He was the photographer who stood me up for my *TV Guide* shoot!"

They insisted and asked me why I never went out. I didn't have an answer because at the time I was dating Francis, and in truth no one really dared to ask me on a date. Instead I busied myself with acting and dance classes and college courses. Eventually I said yes to their urging and we made a double date at a fairly popular restaurant in Westwood.

It was pouring rain when Ivan picked me up, and I immediately felt it was a terrible mistake. We chitchatted through dinner and I couldn't wait to get home. He rubbed me the wrong way and we definitely didn't have a connection. However, they insisted that I return to Chase's house to watch some footage they had just shot. The evening dragged on. When it ended, I was relieved to go home only to find out Ivan's Lincoln was stuck in seven inches of water. Determined, I yanked the door open and got in. When he dropped me off at home he leaned in for a kiss. I pushed him away, hoping to never see him again.

But Ivan was a persistent man, calling me every day and insisting on coming by on his way from his boat in the Marina. I begrudgingly acquiesced to receive him in my kitchen. He always smelt like an old boat in his sheepskin coat. However, he did have that disarming smile and the twinkle in his eyes.

"What do you have to drink, little girl?"

My eyes opened wide and I responded with Harveys Bristol Cream some friend had given me. I am always the prey. I wouldn't really know how to go after a man but if a man comes at me persistently enough, I cave in. Maybe just to get it over with. Somehow, despite our first interactions, that was the case with Ivan.

One time he invited me to his townhome on Kings Road and I was quite impressed with the contents of his swinging pad. He had good furniture and beautiful and unusual artwork. He also had a well-stocked bar which I found mesmerizing as I did not know much about liquor. I appreciated the various shapes, sizes, and labels of the bottles. I saw all the bottles at Frank's home, but I never dared to pick them up and study them. He also had an incredible collection of LPs, lots of both classical and modern pop. Interestingly, I realized Ivan had some culture, and that he was an artist beneath his gruff exterior.

Once I realized he had such good taste, I started to get at least a little more interested.

A couple months later, he invited me to the Grammy Awards at the Palladium when he and his art director Robert Logan were nominated for Best Album Cover for B.B. King's "Indianola Mississippi Seeds." It went on for a long time, as most of these award shows do. Ivan and Robert were growing restless and they got up to get a drink or just to walk outside for some air. I was in the seats all alone when their names were called by Henry Mancini, who was giving out the awards. I panicked and stood up to look in the back when Mancini made the announcement again. I didn't know what to say or do. Just then. I saw them running from the back of the room toward the stage, jump up, and collect the awards.

Wow, that was a rush!

They came back to their seats and Ivan laughed till he cried. I loved that about him. He was so full of life! To think that several months prior Robert would be passed out on the floor of my living room and Ivan asleep in bed with all his clothes on trying to make that album cover deadline!

What drew me closest to Ivan was that we were both from countries that turned to communism. Our families suffered from that oppressive atmosphere and we both appreciated the freedom and freshness in America, especially in the motion picture industry. He told me that he had wanted to be a film director since he saw his first film at age twelve, and that any chance he had he would go to the cinema when he was growing up in Budapest. He escaped from Hungary with his Olympic ice hockey teammate's brother George. They hid on a train going to Austria. When it was nearing the checkpoint with the armed guards at the Austrian border late in the night, they hopped off and ran across to the Austrian side. As he told the story, it wasn't so easy because they couldn't be sure if it was the Austrian side or if they were still in Hungary until they heard some fraulein yelling at the top of her lungs at her husband. He was probably coming home late drunk. They looked at each other and exclaimed, "That's the Austrian side!" Tears would be running down his face as he laughed his hearty laugh sharing that story. He was one man who actually always laughed until he cried.

He would also tell stories of how the family had to hide in the basement of their villa in Buda during the Nazi occupation. His mom scraped together what she could find and made him a birthday cake when he was maybe five years old. He was spoiled rotten (as best as could be) because his mom had him when she was already in her forties. He told me he would cry because there was no icing on the cake. His father escaped to Austria or somewhere first and his mom and Ivan stayed while the Russians overran Hungary. They often starved and Ivan remembered how his mom once ran up a hill to give the Russian soldiers a watch she took off her wrist for a loaf of bread.

Ivan continued to experience those starving times when he and his buddy got rescued in Austria by the Red Cross and brought to America. They were dropped off at the Monterey Army Language School where they drilled foreigners in English eight hours a day. They starved when they first got to Hollywood, still knowing barely any English. They were busboys in a restaurant so they could eat. Their favorite food was bread and lard! He loved food, and ate and drank ferociously all his life, not the least bit concerned about calories or cholesterol. By being deprived of it for so long, he had an appreciation for it. It was refreshing for me as I was starving myself for perfection to be in front of the camera most of my young life.

Opposites attract!

The turning point of our relationship came when he told me he was going to visit his parents in Europe for a couple of weeks. I wasn't working on anything particular, so I said I would meet him in Europe. He thought I was kidding. I was young and had money and I had friends in London, so of course I meant it. Besides, I'd never been to Austria or Hungary.

I got off the airport in Wien and realized that he might not have remembered what flight I was taking from London as it was hard to get through long distance in those days. I tried calling his home from a public phone at the airport and his mother answered. She couldn't understand English, so she just hung up. That went on at least three times and I begged any passerby for change like a crazy woman. Of course, I was ignored… I was a bad beggar! I finally had to call an international operator to generate a collect call from L.A. to Ivan's mother's home. She refused and prepared to hang up again. Then Ivan came to the phone and said "Halloo" in that strong, calming voice. After I explained, he said, "Stay there. I'm coming to get you as fast as I can."

I collected my emotions and waited with calm and beauty like a seasoned actress. I looked across the rather plain open space of the terminal and eventually saw a man in a long dark cashmere top coat and a Borsalino hat coming toward me. He looked like a European industrialist, not a Hollywood photographer bum. I fell in love then and there.

He had gotten us a room at the best hotel in Vienna, the Hotel Sacher, famous for its chocolate torte, and we spent the next ten days touring Budapest and the Adriatic coast, ending up in Dubrovnik. I thought if I could stand being with this man for ten days straight then I was going to marry him. My little sister had already gotten married a few years before and I thought it was time.

After that trip, I waited for him to pop the question… which he wasn't doing fast enough. I'm an impatient person, so at my twenty-third birthday I decided to force the issue. My dear friend Tom Hormel—yes, the company that makes Spam—offered to throw me a party, which was quite the event. I had met Tom through either Broni or Henry Miller, I can't remember who. He promised to give me a birthday party at his studio on Pico Boulevard. It was truly a place where you could create anything your heart desired. Music, paintings, sculptures, pottery, and there was a Jacuzzi with black lights in a cave. Tom took a lot of great pictures of me that I will treasure forever. I wished I had more time to spend there but, alas, as a working actress I had little time to simply hang out.

I was thrilled and honored that the party was attended by Henry Mancini, David Rose, and other well-regarded musicians. I invited my sister and her hubby and, of course, I invited Ivan. But I also gave him the ultimatum that he would propose that very day or I never wanted to see him again. Oh my heavens! I read or saw in films that this is how it had to be done. But still, it was a bold move. I said, "Please only show up at Tom's if you're sincere." Then I drove off to drown myself in merrymaking.

I went to Tom's, drank champagne, and maybe got a bit high, playing conga drums, which I didn't really think I could play. But there I was, along with professional musicians. I remember my sister looked up, amazed to find me on the conga.

"I never knew you can play conga."

"Neither did I! But I did hang out with a conga player while in San Francisco as a teenager and I just mimic all his moves and remember all the beats for some reason." I shrugged.

Then, from out of the corner of my eye, I see Ivan slumping in the door looking like a sad dog.

Oh my God, did he get rolled by street gangs or beaten up by hoodlums?

He looked so sad. I ran to him to give him a big kiss and hug. Very soon, like a true trooper, he smiled his thousand-megawatt smile and joined in the merriment, like the party animal he was.

When we finally made it to my Benedict Canyon home, I put my hands on his face and said, "Please honey, you don't have to marry me. You look so sad. I can't bear to look at you like this." We hugged and tears were running down his face, and then we both laughed.

We married nine months later on August 15th, my dad's birthday.

As a side note, Tom Hormel passed during the writing of this book and I attended his memorial, which was an elaborate affair beautifully orchestrated by his wife Marisa. She flew us all to Miami and created an impeccable memorial service and reception with a sit down dinner for a hundred and fifty people and the sixty-piece Henry Mancini Institute Orchestra performance at the University of Miami. Tom was such a gifted composer, pianist, dancer, artist, sculptor, and photographer. He once said if he died, he would want to come back as Tom Hormel! Well, yes indeed. One of the things about my life is that I kept meeting colorful people. In that, I feel very blessed.

The ceremony for our wedding was at Bronislaw's home on Bedford Drive. Broni gave me away. Sadly, my parents made up some excuse and never showed. They did not show for my sister's wedding a couple of years before, either. I never understood what that was all about.

Until Ivan, I believed perhaps in this lifetime, I would be loved by a few men but was never *to* love, which was a very sad thought. I contemplated on what would be my wish if I had the choice. It would be tough, but to love perhaps would be my choice. Although we don't get to choose at all if water color is your medium; you just let it happen for better or worse.

Ivan believed in me one hundred and fifty percent. Ivan was controversial. He taught me a lot about American modern art like the works of Jasper Johns, Rauschenberg, Claes Oldenburg, Frank Stella, and more. I was terrified when he made me agree to buy some of their limited edition lithographs at what I thought was an abhorrent amount of money in the seventies. Of course, most of them went up in value fifty times over the years. He loved living life, enjoying life. He would be drinking a bottle of Chateau wine at the kitchen table when I came home and I would ask, "What's the occasion, homby?"

"Oh, I'm just celebrating life, hommy."

He couldn't ever say "honey" right and those became our nicknames for each other.

What can I say...he was right! He smiled his bright smile as his eyes twinkled. Ivan was optimistic about just about everything. It was contagious to live with someone like that. We lived like a king and queen on an actually modest income and twenty thousand dollars as a gift from his parents. We lived in my Benedict Canyon home that I bought for forty-four thousand dollars, barely enough for an automobile today. He also went to Europe and brought back a beautiful Maserati for a few thousand dollars.

We always found a way to get what we wanted.

Ivan told me about a film once that he was passionate about. It was a film written and directed by Roberto Rossellini, *Il Generale Della Rovere*. A common criminal named Grimaldi, played by Vittorio De Sica, is captured by the Nazis. They make him pretend to be a general of the resistance so they can get information that would benefit the Gestapo. Grimaldi initially goes along with scheme but later has a change of heart and embraces a more selfless perspective. The common thief is sentenced to go before a firing squad and he never does reveal his true identity. He'd rather go to his death as an important somebody then be released as a nobody. In the last scene, you see Grimaldi walking proudly through the crowd of fellow prisoners and onlookers as they cheer the much feared and admired Generale della Rovere. Tears streaming down his face in joy of a death far better than the non-existent, meaningless life he lived.

That was Ivan. He saw life as a stage.

CHAPTER 18

SOMETIMES ALONG THE INTERESTING PATHS of my life, I also have the occasional experience that gives me pause and opens my eyes up to fate, timing, and my own mortality. One of those moments occurred when I reflected back on having dinner with the famous hairstylist Jay Sebring a few days before he was murdered, along with Sharon Tate, by members of the Charles Manson family.

I had met Sharon through Roman Polanski, who was friends with Broni. I didn't care much for Roman. I remember once I visited them at their rented beach house and Roman was really mean to me, constantly trying to pick me up and throw me into the pool. It was a cold night. I spent some time with Sharon, who was always busy fussing with her makeup.

Around that time, I also met Jay, who was a close friend of Sharon's, and he asked me out to dinner. I remember going to his house, which was a very strange place. It had apparently been Jean Harlow's love nest back in the day. It was very dark and I didn't really like it. I also had some issues with Jay. He wasn't the least bit ready for me and I had to wait for him. We didn't get out of his house until 9:30 p.m. I was pissed as I was starving. When we finally did get to dinner, we had an okay time. I couldn't tell if he was into me, but I knew he was into himself. Honestly, I thought I probably wouldn't go out with him again.

I later heard about his death from a girlfriend who was close to Sharon. I somehow hadn't seen it on the news. At first, I couldn't wrap my head around it. It was such a horrible and bizarre thing to have happened only a few days after my dinner with Jay. It made me really scared. After all, I was in the same Benedict Canyon neighborhood. I would be fearful for quite some time of any noise I heard on my rooftop. It was the story in Hollywood for quite a while and to be honest, everyone was on edge…

As the decade turned and throughout the seventies, my career was still moving along at a rather busy pace. I shot a number of big movies like *Airport 1975,* produced by Ross Hunter who gave me my first film job on *Flower Drum Song.* I once again found myself costumed by the legendary Edith Head. Unfortunately, she was rather limited in what she could do with us in this production as we were fitted with gabardine pants and a simple top.

"Darling," she said, "I'm sorry I couldn't get you anything more glamorous. But maybe we could just do this point a little differently..."

That was an exciting film shoot because the movie featured so many stars, like Charlton Heston, Karen Black, Linda Blair, Sid Caesar, and the iconic Gloria Swanson.

Of course, I knew who Gloria Swanson was, but had never seen her in the flesh. I played a stewardess on the ill-fated flight and reported every day of shooting to a mock plane interior they had set up on a sound stage at the Universal Studios lot. One day word got around, echoing through the cast and crew, that Gloria Swanson was going to be on set. Everyone was very excited. Finally, I saw this very small woman in a white turban come up the ramp and take her seat next to the window on our fake plane set. Everyone around her simply observed. She had hair and makeup personnel on standby around her as she prepared herself. At one point, she asked for a hand mirror and studied herself, tilting her head up and down and from side to side and making sure her makeup was to her liking. She was checking to see what her best angle was for filming. She settled on a three-quarter profile with her chin up, and then she was ready to shoot her close-up!

Then, just like that, she was gone.

Gloria wasn't the only actor on that set with magnetism. Karen Black, with whom I worked very closely on the film, was amazing in that she could pull you into a scene immediately. She was such a strong actress that you couldn't help but feel like you were present in the scene the moment you started with her. Charlton Heston also had an energy of his own. He was also very kind to me during the shoot and after. In fact, later on, he was one of my sponsors for becoming a member of the Academy of Motion Picture Arts and Sciences. While we were filming, we had time for a little chitchat here and there, but I honestly spent most of the time thinking about how he looked in *Ben-Hur*!

During this time, I also worked as a guest star in just about every big TV series, loading up on my acting credits. There are quite a few of these, with which I share some fond and fascinating memories.

I got to work with Jack Lord and a young Erik Estrada on *Hawaii Five-O*. It was always a great treat to get to do *Hawaii Five-O* because guest stars flew first class to Honolulu and then got put up at the Kahala Hilton, a true five-star venue. The building was situated with the beach on one side and lagoon and pools on the other, with water shooting up from the lagoons. It was a visual feast! The interior was well-planned open spaces with fine furnishing and quality art on the walls. The rooms really made you feel like you ought to be on a honeymoon or with a lover. Chocolates and orchids adorned your pillow every night and the sheets were so sensuous and scrumptious that you never wanted to get up.

The thing that really stood out in my mind was when I met Erik, a rather conceited macho Puerto Rican straight out of Spanish Harlem, New York. He had just done the Don Murray film *The Cross and Switchblade*. He was more intense then handsome. One of the first things out of his mouth after we were introduced was, "I'm going to make it. I have to make it. If you know where I came from, there is no going back."

Then he paused and asked, "Is that her?"

"Who?"

Looking at the direction he was staring, I saw a young blondish girl of around twenty. "Her mother is the casting director, right?"

"I think so. She was given a small part so she hangs around the set most days," I replied.

"Great, I'm going over to introduce myself."

"Oh, okay."

"Watch, you'll learn something," he said as he swaggered toward his prey. Later he told me that his plan was to get close to the casting director mom "because she does a lot of shows."

He was right. In no time, the young lady was smitten with Erik and the mom was obligatorily friendly toward our Latin lover. He did indeed climb up the Hollywood ladder rather quickly and he was a capable actor brimming with machismo, a good thing on screen. Was this the reverse of the famed "casting couch" in Hollywood? I have not seen or spoken to him in so many years but if I ever do, I would ask him and he'd probably say, "Bullshiiiiit… they are always all over me, you know?" Then he'd smile his big crooked smile and wink. Damn, he was charming!

Then there was Mr. Lord, who, though he stayed pretty much to himself, was cool and aloof. He had what seemed like a pound and a half of deep tan pancake on his face. His hair was a sculpture in black lacquer, but he looked great. Whenever we rehearsed on the beach, he would have the teamsters set down planks and move the truck in to block the trade wind from his perfectly sculpted hair. I once asked the makeup lady Jack's age. She whispered that he was a lot older than he looked. He was in his sixties at the time. I thought he looked more like he was in his forties or *maybe* just over fifty. Good for him!

Working on *Ironside* with the brilliant actor Raymond Burr had special challenges as I found out that he had a gift of reading his lines from cue cards instead of memorizing them as other actors do. So there would be cue cards all around you: the right of your head, your left ear, your shoulder, your waist, even the top of your head when they were doing his close-ups. You were to do your lines without breathing in fear that you would disturb those meticulously mounted cards on wire stands. On screen you would never know it as he delivered his long speeches without any effort. That is indeed brilliant!

It was a wonderful show and I was signed to do three episodes. Unfortunately, I broke my left ankle in a bobsledding accident in Austria with Ivan and came home with a World War II-era plaster cast. This was much to the dismay of U.S. doctors who, for the last twenty-five years, had been using the ultra-lightweight fiberglass casts. Sadly, my stint on that show was cut short.

I was grateful to shoot an episode of *The Rockford Files*, a beloved show that starred the handsome and talented James Garner and was produced by Stephen J. Cannell and Meta Rosenberg. And just my luck, my episode was slated to be directed by James Coburn, another idol of mine.

I was excited as I had a good part as a research assistant to Garner's character, Jim Rockford. The two James were obvious friends and laughed and patted each other on the backs during the shoot… at first. However, by the third day they were avoiding one another and were barely speaking to each other. It was a dilemma as I sometimes had questions to ask about the scene I was in. I wasn't sure what was happening. I asked Meta and she basically said to let her talk to James Garner, and then she would tell me what to do. That's how it went for the remainder of the shoot, though I did reach out to James G. at times when we were in the same scene.

Later, through mutual friends, I was invited to the Coburn home with his new wife, and it resembled a mini-Moroccan palace fitted with Moroccan tiles, mirrors, rugs, exotic bells, and wind chimes, with the fragrance of incense filling the air. It was downright intoxicating. I cannot be positive if they were vegetarians, but it would be hard to imagine that an exponent of the glory of beef would somehow be a kindred spirit to the esoteric Coburn.

I shot an episode of *Wonder Woman* with Lynda Carter, which was by far the most casual and disrespectful sets I've ever been on. Some of the crew members would be playing cards and listening to the radio so loud that actors could barely hear the dialogue. No one seemed to care, including "Wondie." She was dropped off on the set by her then producer boyfriend in his green Bentley some fifteen feet from the camera set up. I had forgotten about the show until recently when a fan posted on Instagram and Facebook a clip of the fight scene I did with Lynda. In this scene, Wonder Woman was without her "Wonder" outfit, rendering her powerless. We did a knock-down-drag-out fight scene. I did amazing martial arts! I punched, kicked, flipped, got knocked down, crawled back up, knocked down again, and jumped over Wonder Woman as we both landed on our butts. As it turned out, our characters learned we both worked for different branches of the same organization. The show also featured Roddy McDowall and Joan Collins when I looked at the credits.

I was also in a couple of interesting films, including *Three the Hard Way*. I really don't know how I got into this Blaxploitation film of the early seventies except that Ivan thought I should go into casting with glittery argyle knee socks, roller skates, and corn rows. So I did, and ended up as one of three girls—one white, one black and one other, I can't remember which—riding motorcycles and baring our breasts when we unzipped our motorcycle jackets. The director was the soft-spoken Gordon Parks Jr., and the stars were Jim Brown—often mentioned as the greatest NFL player in history—and Fred Williamson, another star football player of the Kansas City Chiefs and Oakland Raiders. I don't remember much of the filming except the continuous throng of girls going to Jim and Fred's trailers, as my dressing room was just a few trailers away from theirs. So much testosterone, I was speechless!

Also involved in the project was Jim Kelly, famed martial arts star of *Enter the Dragon*, who I would work with again in *Hot Potato* in Thailand after Bruce Lee's untimely death. I bring him up as it reminds me of Bruce Lee and my brief interactions with him… as well as the story of when Ivan blew perhaps one of the biggest opportunities for both of us.

I got a call from Bruce once asking about my experience of shooting in Hong Kong. I don't know how he knew of me or how to get a hold of me, but that's something that was just always possible and happening in Hollywood; people found each other. He had been invited to be in a movie there. While he had worked in *The Green Hornet,* he was not yet the big international superstar. I told him it was wonderful over there but also had been difficult. Though I thought it would be different for him. His father, after all, was rather well known.

A few months passed and Ivan got a call from an old friend, Andrew Vajna, who made his name as a hairdresser and designer and was now working as a producer. He told Ivan about this guy named Bruce Lee, who was about to blow up and become a major star… but that he had a short window to make a movie with him if Ivan could come up with something.

Ivan was completely taken by surprise, but we immediately hopped on the next flight to Hong Kong to take a meeting, even though we didn't even have a script. I remember going through paperback novels at the airport to see if we could come up with a story. Because Ivan's English was so bad, he couldn't read them fast enough. "Ivan, can't we just come up with something simple?" I said.

When we got there, Andy had arranged a dinner for us with Bruce and Raymond Chow, the head of Golden Harvest, which would soon become known for launching martial arts movies onto the international stage. Ivan was completely grumpy all throughout the dinner. Complaining about the Chinese food, he ordered a steak, which, of course, looked like a piece of greenish shoe leather. He was also irritated because Bruce showed up about forty-five minutes late, as he had been doing his training, which he always did before his meals. Bruce would soon be known for his rigorous and disciplined training. Upon meeting Bruce, I noticed he was a rather small guy, but he had big energy about him. It was as if all this energy was compacted in his small frame. He also spoke English very well. I could see that he had something special about him.

The dinner went on and nothing really happened. However, later, Ivan blew it. He had a discussion session with Andy and he said he couldn't shoot Bruce.

"Why not?" asked Andy.

"Because both sides of his face are different."

What the hell?

Andy was also flabbergasted, but that was that. He had this one small chance, this window before Bruce blew up to international superstar status and we missed it. It was the dumbest thing Ivan ever did. His ego got in the way!

But, we moved on…

While in Hong Kong, I also called up Sir Run Run Shaw, the movie mogul of Shaw Brothers. He was like Louis B. Mayer and was knighted in the eighties. He also lived till he was one hundred and six! Somewhere along the way, I met him (perhaps while I was filming *Yin & Yang*). I'd been to his studio in Clear Water Bay where I saw Chinese film productions shooting round the clock—they didn't have the Screen Actors Guild or Ronald Reagan to fend for them. I watched a lead actress running into a scene, sliding on her belly and hands and knees, scraping her chin, and fully prostrating herself on the dirt ground before they yelled cut. I was appalled that there was no stunt coordinator, stunt doubles, nor pads on the ground or much of anything. It was very different than in Hollywood!

Ivan and I got invited to Shaw's home in Deep Water Bay where the Hong Kong billionaires have their estates. It must have been a forty-person sit down dinner. Quite a few Hollywood celebs and ranking world sports figures were amongst the guests. We were seated next to Carol Channing, who I'd never met before. I thought, "Oh boy, here we go with Ivan and Chinese food again!" But Shaw was brilliant. He had every course served in individual silver bowls with a lid. So whatever looked unappetizing, you could just stir it a bit, close the lid, and it would be swiftly taken away. After a couple courses we noticed that the silver tureens were all numbered and we made up a poker game to play. Food and game; there would never be a dinner like this! Ms. Channing brought her own thermoses of food. I think she said they were pureed carrots, or spinach, or beets, or lamb? She traveled with her thermoses and never touched her lips to anything else. She had a large head, big eyes, big lashes, and a huge mouth for her robust laughter. She was a larger than life sort of femme.

A TV movie I was in called *Judge Dee and the Monastery Murders* took place in Seventh Century China and was about a magistrate traveling the countryside with his three wives and how they had to spend a night in a haunted monastery. I just watched it after so many years and it was indeed bizarre, almost Fellini-esque, like a fantasy. Talented director Jeremy Kagan took liberties to create a Seventh Century China of his imagination with strange ancient practices and costumes. I had fun playing the naughty second wife with operatic makeup of red and yellow. The makeup photographed beautifully, though I do remember once after a long day's shoot I pulled into a gas station to fill up and scared the living daylights out of everyone.

All the top Asian actors in town such as Mako, James Hong, and Soon-Tek Oh were cast in the film. The lead, Khigh Dhiegh, was actually an African-American, and he was great. I spoke to Jeremy and he said he was so happy that I agreed to be in the movie as I added intelligence, insight, power, and beauty to this character. Wow, I was really thrilled hearing that from someone like Jeremy.

I had the chance to meet Don Murray on *Deadly Hero*, a film Ivan was directing in New York. I had a tiny part in the film, but I'd always admired Murray, who received an Oscar nomination for Best Supporting Actor in *Bus Stop* with Marilyn Monroe. He was one of the most versatile, underrated actors in our industry. Both sexy and wholesome, like a cross between Brad Pitt and Pat Boone, his hoodlum priest character left a deep impression on me as a teen.

We were in the production office of *Deadly Hero* when he walked by to tell me about the next film, *Damien's Island,* which he would be directing in Hawaii. He asked if I would read a little with him. I was so surprised as I had just come back from a fashion trip in Malaysia and Hong Kong. I was exhausted and bone thin. He must have thought I looked like an emaciated leper but yes, of course I would read for Don Murray. I meditated for a few seconds and read, and Don really liked it. He even said to Ivan that he thought I was a wonderful actress. It lit me up from the inside.

He gave me a wonderful part in the film... as the head leper! Brilliant cinematographer Andrzej Bartkowiak from *Deadly Hero* came along to film as well. Filming in Oahu on different locations was not easy. We lacked proper dressing facilities, and I remember people would visibly back away from me as the makeup of my leprosy was so realistic. Some even got off the elevator of the Ilikai Hotel in Waikiki because I forgot I had that latex leprosy makeup all over my face. I wanted to call out that I was actually the beautiful Polynesian with Elvis in *Paradise, Hawaiian Style*, but I don't think anybody would have believed me!

Even with all the shows and movies I did, there were the occasional opportunities I missed out on. One of the biggest was *Apocalypse Now,* though looking back on the well-documented chaos of the film shoot, I might have also dodged a bullet.

I don't exactly remember how I met legendary casting director and producer Fred Roos. He was this soft spoken, almost shy and attractive guy who was known as "The Godfather" of casting. He helped boost the careers of Harrison Ford, Candy Clark, Ron Howard, Mackenzie Philips, and so many more. Fred helped usher in such movie classics as *The God-

father, American Graffiti, The King of Marvin Gardens, Two-Lane Blacktop, and *Five Easy Pieces.* He won an Oscar for producing *The Godfather, Part II* with Francis Ford Coppola. An A-list producer for the past forty-plus years, he helped nurture to screen most of Francis and Sophia Coppola's films. You really wonder how he could have done so much high-profile work and remain such a Zen like sort of guy.

Back in the late sixties and seventies, we had this wonderful friendship as he was my neighbor in Benedict Canyon. I would stop by his tiny house with beautiful cabinetry made for him by Harrison Ford whenever Harrison was in between films. I would chat away about all the perils of a sometimes-successful actor. Fred liked actors, and he would just gaze at me, stroking his Siamese cat. They looked alike, Fred and his Siamese.

One day he asked if I wanted to play Marlon Brando's Montagnard (Vietnamese "mountain people") wife in a film. They were on an endless location shoot in the Philippines. I was at first very intrigued by the offer. It was a tiny part, but nonetheless it was with Francis Ford Coppola and Brando. I really was tempted but Ivan voted against it. He said the part really wasn't there, that I would be sitting around in that jungle bored out of my mind and fighting off all the other bored and drugged-out guys.

"You'd be calling me to bring you home every day. Forget it, hommy."

Actually, I already went to the Philippines a couple of times from Hong Kong to check out some embroidery and local designers for my fashion business, which comes up a bit later in my story. I'd made a few important friends who entertained me. In the Philippines you really need to know the right people to get things done. I had pretty much turned down *Apocalypse Now,* but I went back to Manila to visit and explore local fabrics and designers. Fred was there and he immediately invited me to a play the very night I arrived.

"Do I really have to go? I'd rather crash in my hotel."

"Yes, you really have to," he said. "It stars Imee Marcos, Imelda Marcos' daughter. You'll be picked up at 6:30."

We went into the theater through heavy security. The play was *The Diary of Anne Frank.* How bizarre was that?! I'm in Manila, watching Imee Marcos as Anne Frank, in Tagalog. Not long into the play I had to go to the bathroom really badly, so I got up to move toward the exit. Fred was really not pleased but nature will not relent. The doors were locked. I made some faint tapping and it finally opened a crack and I pronounced my dire plight to the armed guard, and they let me through. I asked for the ladies' room and they pointed to a direction and I ran for it without another word. They stood guard just outside and told me to stand at the door until the intermission. It was an overall bizarre experience. God only knows how Anne Frank was chosen for Imee. She was way too old for the part, but perhaps she did have a compassion for such a human tragedy.

A couple of days later, one of the assistants drove me to the location where they were shooting *Apocalypse Now*, which was about an hour away. I was going just to check it out. On the way I stopped to have the famous "boku pie" made of young coconut in a pie shell. It was delicious at first bite but made me sick after. The whole location was set-dressed as a Montagnard village. Vietnamese extras roamed freely. There was equipment everywhere, most notably Coppola's massive fancy Italian Espresso maker. The aroma mixed in with the dirt and the jungle gave you kind of a natural high, a disorientation hard to ignore.

Coppola was nowhere to be seen. I was going out of my mind—like the rest of the people there–in a hurry. I was told he was filming Brando in some cave that can only accommodate the director, actor, and cameraman. It was off limits to anyone else. I waited and waited only to find out that they had moved to a different angle of the cave. I walked about and saw Dennis Hopper screaming and laughing from the balcony of a dilapidated two-story structure. A couple of local girls were hanging about. I didn't know if it was a set, or if he actually took up residence there. With Dennis, one never knew, but he was visibly drunk or drugged out or both. He threatened to jump off the balcony into the filthy pool below. Crew and locals cheered him on. He had obviously done this before. It was nearing 3:30 when I begged the assistant to take me back to Manila.

All the time, I was thinking Ivan was right.

The film turned out to be a blockbuster nonetheless. Coppola was just too powerful!

The seventies were exciting because I was always busy working on shows and movies. But, never quite settled, my water color life was also making another stroke, and I started exploring a new career to satisfy another side of the artist within me.

CHAPTER 19

It must have been the mid-seventies. I was very happily married to Ivan, and we entertained and went out a lot, just enjoying our young, married life. My days were satisfied taking dance and different classes and courses at UCLA. Then this film project appeared.

It was *Paper Tiger* starring David Niven and Toshiro Mifune to be filmed in Malaysia. They were doing a worldwide search for the part of a Malaysian revolutionary. I was considered for the part along with some Israeli star. Ivan jumped in to help and shot a bunch of hot photos of me on a Malibu beach. They were spectacular and he got them placed in the *Los Angeles Times* and *South China Morning Post*, among others. I think it drew the attention of the producers. I got called in and landed the role.

Then came the incredible fitting. Little did I know this would be the start of something very big for me.

I was being fitted for boots. The wardrobe guy out of London phoned to make the arrangements. I never understood why it was so important that they wanted to have these special boots made for me by some really famous boot artisan in L.A. I never even knew they existed here right on 3rd Street. Molds of my feet were taken and many fittings later I got several pairs of these light tan-colored, soft leather boots. It was such a shame they had to stomp on them and beat them up to make them look like they'd been through the Malaysian jungle. The rest of the outfit was a creative effort between wardrobe, Ivan, and myself. We combed through army surplus stores and had white tanks dipped in tea for the aged, ragged look. We also put patchwork on ripped Levi's. It all worked as a collage of a chic, seventies' hippie revolutionary. It was a time of Hanoi Jane Fonda, after all. Off I went to Kuala Lumpur for three months of shooting.

Kuala Lumpur was definitely exotic. It was reminiscent of Hong Kong thirty years ago in parts; modern in the city and rather primitive in the countryside. The cast and crew stayed in two hotels within walking distance of each other. Of course, you could also take the short cut through a bit of dirt and foliage that was more than likely full of snakes. Niven, Mifune, German star Hardy Kruger, producer Euan Lloyd, and director Ken Annakin were at the Hilton as they had their families along. I was at the Holiday Inn with the rest of the crew, who were mostly English.

My room was one floor below our stunt coordinator Bob who had done three James Bond movies and was quite a stud… or at least *he* thought he was. One night I heard terrible yelling and screaming in English and some crashing noises. The next day Bob told us that he had picked up this gorgeous girl with long black hair and a slim beautiful figure at the bar. After some drinks he took her up to his room and thought he was going to show her some stunts, but it turned out that she… was a he! Upon this realization, he didn't quite know how to extricate himself out of this situation, so he picked his guest up and threw him out the window! I suppose he whooshed past my window and landed on the awning three stories down. He apparently sashayed away like a pro. From then on, I looked at every beautiful woman in the hotel with x-ray eyes. I checked out their busts, their behinds, their walks, and even their hands. People must have thought I was gay.

Niven went through his scenes so effortlessly, like a seasoned professional. He played a rogue of a tutor to Mifune's son. Off set he was a charming ladies man and often had cocktails and supper with a local model… a real "she" I'm sure. Niven taught me about drinking wine, of which he was never without. He lived in Cote d'Azur, south of France. He said no matter how much wine you consumed at dinner, as long as you drink lots of water before you go to sleep, even if you have to pee all night, the next morning you'll never wake up with a hangover.

Mifune is probably the biggest star who ever came out of Japan in that era. He starred in such memorable epics as *Yojimbo* and *Seven Samurai* by the famed director Akira Kurosawa. The first time I met him, he invited me to a tea ceremony at his suite that was attended by his girlfriend Mika Kitagawa and his interpreter Miiko Taka of *Sayonara* fame. He had a remarkable presence on and off screen. Once I saw him in a scene where he wanted to stand with his back to the camera, then turn to deliver his line into camera. He got his way. The camera rolled and his powerful back came into focus. I've never seen so much power and magnificence. I later visited him and Mika in his home outside of Tokyo and brought him his favorite whiskey. He was a majestic icon who loved his Chivas Regal!

Filming and rehearsals went slowly as we had to go to so many locations. I rehearsed with the martial arts guys from the Army who were my doubles and did the stunt work. They did a form of Tae Kwon Do and were phenomenal. I could quickly see why I had to have those specially made boots. I went to some local classes and was astounded that they practiced on cement floors and kicked into bamboo walls. I was not in good physical shape then as I had been recently diagnosed with hypothyroidism and had gone on meds just before I left for the shoot. I was barely a hundred pounds and my face broke out in endless pimples, so much so that the producer started phoning my husband for an answer.

In between the filming, we were constantly entertained by local dignitaries. There were almost always expats who looked rather bored or curious of their homeland folks and wondered to themselves if indeed they had chosen the best of both worlds. They all drank too much. The wives went on shopping sprees and usually showed off their finds, especially the beautiful colorful "batiks" they found in a store at the Hilton lobby. The urged me to go see the boutique Aran Nova Batika, so one off day I wandered over.

I fell in love with the beautiful unique colors and designs. They are neither water color nor rigid like oils. They are exotic and unfathomable! They were like nothing I had ever seen.

Soon I met the owner, Razak Samad, an elegant, tall Malaysian royalty. He took an immediate liking to me, as he said I looked like his sister. His wife Vicky was a very pretty and stylish blonde from London whose aunt was one of the curators at the Victoria and Albert Museum. She was a very good artist, and later we found that we had complete similar tastes in design. We were all about the same age. They loved the few records of American pop songs I had brought with me. We had dinner together almost every night under the banyan trees in the local style and drank Singha beer. Vicky worked on the party scenes in the film.

They explained to me the batik process and showed me the small studio where the painters and the dye master worked next to a river, washing the cloths of fine Swiss (or Chinese) cotton and hanging them on lines to dry.

"That's where those beautiful scarves and caftans and shirts came from?" I exclaimed in utter amazement.

"Yes, all of it," she said. "We have them cut and sewn by sewing ladies in town."

"Oh my heavens, my mom would love to see this," I said. "You know she's a terrific artist and I've always wanted to be an artist."

He told me how they could really use a new roof as the monsoons were coming and I told them I would try to see how I could help. That's how I ended up owning part of a batik factory in Kuala Lumpur, Malaysia. Before the film ended, they asked if perhaps I could bring some of this clothing back to L.A. and sell them to boutiques there. I hadn't thought of it, but I told them that maybe I could try. I really, really loved the stuff. I had a couple of wrap skirts and wrap tops made up, as well as caftans and scarfs and half a dozen shirts for my husband.

When Ivan came to meet me in Honolulu, I opened my suitcase and surprised him with all this newfound clothing. I thought he probably may not like them or just might humor me and say that he did. To my surprise, he loved them! He grabbed one shirt after another and tried them on immediately. He wore one that evening when we went out to dinner, and the next day another one, and the next day another one. I told him I was now part owner of this batik shack/factory, and he encouraged me to send for some samples to take to the boutiques I frequented in Beverly Hills. Ivan always had a mind for business like his mother. He was creative and always thinking outside the box.

Little did I know I had inadvertently entered what was to be the most creative period of my life.

CHAPTER 20

I DIDN'T KNOW THE PROPER BAGS to put my samples in, so I just put them into paper bags. The first place that I went to was Dorso in Beverly Hills because the owner Betty Dorso used to be an editor for *Vogue Magazine* in New York. I had met her through the local Bicentennial Committee, and I respected her very much. Plus, her store was right in the heart of Beverly Hills. I made an appointment and she greeted me with, "Hi Irene, what have you got for me?" eyeing the paper bags.

"Just some batiks from Malaysia." I pulled out the colorful pieces and laid them all over the floor. She had some lady bring over a clothing rack and hang some of them up. "Now that's better...let me see." She leaned her chin on her artistic hand and cocked her head to study them, just as she had done for years at *Vogue*.

"Nice, very nice, very special, but I really don't know what to do with them. Look around in my store, I have very expensive designer merchandise here."

I nodded. "Of course, of course they are gorgeous."

Betty then pointed to a smaller bag I had brought along. "What you got there?"

"Oh, nothing really, just some silk pieces that I'm working on."

She grabbed them out of the bag without another word and on to the clothing rack they went. They were cream (natural-colored) silk pieces of two camisoles, one short sleeve top, and a pair of drawstring pants. Vicky and Razak had showed me this creamy silk and Vicky and I decided to do a few pieces of simple separates because maybe not all Americans would like batik. I was into fabrics because Mom had been a textile designer for ages.

Betty touched them, scrunched them, and shocked them, saying, "They are scrumptious, heavenly. What do you call this kind of silk?"

"Eighteen momme habotai silk, and they are washable…I was told," I hesitantly uttered, careful not to say the wrong thing.

"Very nice indeed. No buttons, no zipper, very clean. I like them, but I do think you need another piece, three quarter or longer sleeve as a cover up to the camis. Yes, do a piece like that. I'll give you an order."

"Yes, yes of course, I'm thinking of a short kimono wrap top with a self-belt."

"Now you are talking, Irene. Five easy pieces. When can I have them?"

Oh crap!

I got the first taste of the fashion biz: its lightning speed. Things had to be fresh, new, and instantaneous. "Uhh, I guess three weeks or so…" I improvised.

"I'll give you four weeks." Her order included some batik pieces as well. She then asked me into her office to write the order while the sales girls ruffled through my pieces with *oohs* and *ahhs*. They knew Betty was not easily interested.

My very first order! I was so excited as I was making up the prices to quote her. Ivan had told me to triple the price FOB (freight on board) and we should be okay. We'd never been in the fashion business or *any* other business. He at least did have a company named Camera Five which sold photos to the news and magazines with his London partner. They were considered photojournalists. I felt like I just did a good audition and got my next job!

That's how I got started in the fashion industry.

There was a mountain of difference between the two industries. As an actor, once you get the part—which of course may take years of training and luck—everything is basically done for you, with the exception of your own preparation. The actor's job is to study the script, immerse in your character, know the lines, and work with the director to do whatever the part requires. In fashion, you must first write the script, then create the pieces from fabric to cut, design to fit, down to the button and trim. I was functioning on pure instinct and innate artistic creativity—which I credit to my mom—as well as my own good eye for fashion. All these years as an actress and in the public eye, I learned to create an impressive and unique look. I understood fashion, yet lacked the technical knowledge like people who had gone through a fashion institute or trained with notable designers. I skipped a few steps, just like in my approach to the acting profession. Mom would always say that I jumped in from the deep end. But wasn't that the way she taught me to swim in the Lai Chi Kok pool?

I was too elated to be scared and I went on to procure orders from other store owners around town. Then one day someone mentioned that I should go see Fred Segal, the trendiest boutique on Melrose. Why not? I managed to get an appointment with one of the managers, who were strangely all named Ron. There was Ron Herman, Ron Robinson, and Ron Ross, and they did all the ordering and ran the successful store. I went in with my paper bag of men's shirts and swatches, and they threw them all over the counters of other merchandise. They looked, scrunching the sheer cotton voile of wild prints, which was the rage of the seventies, and the larger collars and cuffs that incorporated six rows of stitching for stiffness. They tried them on themselves and looked pleased.

They looked at one another, and one of them spoke at last and said, "We want an initial order of twenty dozen. But since this is a substantial order from an unknown source, you need to get the go ahead from Fred. He's in Malibu trying to develop a motel property he bought to turn into a shopping mall. He's so busy, he's never here anymore. We'll call him and you just go out there tomorrow and tell him we want to order twenty dozen."

"Sure, no problem," I said. "Thank you so much."

Well this time I was beyond excited.

Twenty dozen… that's two hundred and forty pieces! How much fabric does it take? How much is it anyway?

I think I went into a phone booth and called Ivan. "Ivan, I'm going to meet Fred Segal tomorrow! If we are in Fred Segal, we are in!" At that moment, to me, Fred was bigger than any producer I knew.

The next day, I went to see Fred, who was a boyish forty-something. He was standing on a dusty pickup truck in some sort of horse corral, which stood in the middle of a falling down motel. I yelled out an introduction and he waved me over. I climbed over some bric-a-brac, careful to be both athletic and still ladylike. I made it over and he wiped his hands off on his dusty jeans to shake my hand. I blabbered on about my merchandise and carefully took a few pieces out.

"Put them away, put them away, the Ronnies told me what they wanted, it's fine, all fine with me. Tell them to write it up. I wish all is fine with this place. I'm having my sixth meeting with the Coastal Commission this Thursday and I pray to God that it'll be the last. If I get what I want, let me tell you, young lady, I'll never have to or want to set foot in my store again."

Sure enough, he did it. It stands today in Malibu as the Cross Creek shopping center of fabulous boutiques, cafes, and restaurants including the famed Nobu restaurant. Fred always was a man of vision.

With his order, my little label, The IT Company was officially launched.

CHAPTER 21

I REMEMBERED READING something on Tom Ford after his first film was released. He said that the making of the film had its difficulties, but nothing compared to the collections he had to put out season after season.

As I grew into the fashion business, I began to understand the perpetual dynamics of creating the newest style mixed with familiarity, to excite yet to soothe, from fabric to trim to details to economy. I was once again breaking ground, only this time it was in the fashion industry. Using contemporary, bold color combinations, I was the first one to introduce hand-painted silks to the fashion industry in America. And it was done with dye on wet silk. How fitting is that for a water color artist?!

I'm glad that I always had a fascination with fabrics. I learned how big-name designers got their own fabrics. They would go to textile fairs in places like Como, Italy, choose their designs, and have them printed so they would have their exclusive fabrics. I had the opportunity to accompany a dealer who represented American textile designers—including my mom's boss, the Hargittais in New York—to such a fair. There I saw Emanuel Ungaro, Gianfranco Ferrè, and even Karl Lagerfeld, international names that I'd only heard of. It was a dream being in an ice cold chateau in Como where they served piping hot pasta cooked in the humongous fireplace. I kept my gloves on the entire time and had a glimpse of haute couture in the making.

As I took the orders, I was phoning nightly to Kuala Lumpur to give them instructions, and they would tell me when they could ship the goods. The two hundred and forty shirts for Fred Segal was a bit difficult because even if they had enough fabric they were not yet contracted with a shirt-making factory, but rather relied on home-sewing ladies. As a result, the shirts were not reordered by Fred Segal because they were not uniform enough, and some came in smelling of curry.

I can only laugh about it now.

By then, the silk habotai took off and it was much easier in execution. There were no buttons, no trims, and we used bias strips to make spaghetti straps and ties for closure. The sizes were small, medium, large, and the drawstring pants were copied from my favorite pajamas. They turned out to be such a good fit that people were ordering them by the dozens. The caftans were one size. In fact, Ivan shot an ad with four people—a big guy, a regular woman, a super thin super model, and a baby—that read "One Size Fits All." It was a rage!

In L.A., we decided to form a group called Young California Designers, and together we would put on a fashion show at the Pacific Design Center that would be attended by all the bigwigs of New York. Publications like *Women's Wear Daily, Vogue, Bazaar* and merchandisers from Bloomingdales, Bendel's, Neiman's, and hip specialty stores all attended. Ivan had the chore of selecting the models. We had the beautiful, but very strung-out black super model Donyale Luna, who was discovered by Fellini. By then she was most likely a heroin addict, among other things. She would send me out for whiskey at ten in the morning. I was shocked but I went, of course… anything to get her to walk down that catwalk. Then there was the beautiful Cassandra Gava, who was not going to be outdone by Luna. There were also two teenage sisters, who were thirteen and fourteen. Their dad was a veteran actor. They were beautiful but had never walked in heels before. In desperation, I sent them down the ramp barefooted. While "Beethoven's Fifth" played over speakers, Luna and Gava went up and down the ramp making lewd gestures with the champagne bottles. It was more like a striptease act done to Beethoven than a sophisticated high-end fashion show.

Sure enough, the next day *WWD* creamed us, saying, "We didn't need IT Company's cheap theatrics… otherwise it showcased many a good, talented young California designers including Leon Max, Christine Albers, Phyllis Sues, Loren Judd and DBA by Theodore quite a few more."

The group decided to show at the Plaza Hotel in Manhattan. That's how hot we got. By then we had to get a telex machine to communicate with Kuala Lumpur. It made a lot of noise and punched out holes like a ticker tape machine. It would shake and vibrate when receiving messages. To tell the truth I was afraid of the damned thing, that it may explode at any moment and spew paper all over my work room. About then, Ivan went to the bank to arrange any line of credit. He secured a twenty thousand dollar credit line from our friendly Canadian banker. Ivan was a good schmoozer.

I arrived at the Plaza Hotel around July or August of 1976. Each company had a room on the same floor. Mine was just an average-size room but I thought the number was okay. I can't remember what the number was now, but I know I had a good feeling about it at the time. I'm particular about hotel room numbers. I'm not exactly superstitious but the number just had to feel right. Fred, my manager had arranged to have entertainer Pat Suzuki meet me there. He said she loved fashion and had nothing better to do at the moment, so she really wanted to hang with me. I'd never met Pat but she was a friend of Fred, and I really could have used some help. Pat starred in *Flower Drum Song* on Broadway. Oh my gosh, a Broadway star! Why would she want to do this?! It couldn't have been the meager money I was budgeting to pay for assistance. Regardless, she came by to help me. As it turned out, she was the best. She knew New Yorkers and she was (and is) such a creative spirit to be around. We've remained friends all these years.

People were mostly showing fall merchandise and some holiday lines at the show. I had none of it, just natural silks and some batik, but the buyers came. Some ordered a few items, but the big order would come later.

One day while we were there, at around six, I was just closing my door to start my yoga, when I heard a knock that kept persisting.

"Bergdorf Goodman."

Oh my God, it's someone from Bergdorf Goodman!

"Be right there," I said as I slipped on something, swung open the door, and greeted this smart-looking woman.

She introduced herself and began to go through my measly rack. "What else have you got?" she asked, sounding like Betty Dorso. "What's draping on that chair?"

"Oh, nothing really... it's just my batik silk caftan. It's really comfortable, much better than a robe and I can even walk around the floor in it to see my friends in other rooms."

She reached out her hand and grabbed it, and of course she gave it that scrunch, squeeze, and shake test. "Let me see it on you."

I slipped it on and modeled for her. "Of course, it's one size fits all, so it drapes a bit on me. But I don't mind it and I have a matching scarf that I can put around my waist to lift it up to a mini." I giggled and laughed as I bloused it and made it quite short.

"I like it. Yes, I do like it." As I continued to romp around the room, Pat commented in her sparkly way. "It looks good on me, too, and I'm at least twenty pounds heavier."

"I want it for our Christmas catalogue," the rep said. "Twenty dozen with matching scarves and it has to be in store no later than end of October. You can make it of course?" She smiled and seemed rather relaxed all of a sudden, thinking that making this last stop on her way out of the hotel turned out to be a jackpot.

Well it was certainly the Powerball for me!

"Call me tomorrow. You can give me the price then. Or rather, I'll give *you* the price."

"Sure, sure, thank you so much!" I think I even curtsied.

"Thank you, sweetie," she said as she handed me her card, a triumphant smile on her face as she got up and left. Patty and I jumped up and down and I fell face down in bed, smothered my face in the pillow, and screamed. Then I rolled over and said a silent prayer.

After that, it was urgent calls to Ivan asking him to telex Kuala Lumpur to deliver the news. "Guess what, we are going to be in the Bergdorf Goodman Christmas Catalogue! Oh my God! I have to come up with at least fifty designs or something. They have to be one of a kind. I have to go back there right away and work on it with Raz and Vicky. I'll call them tomorrow night to make sure she is writing the offer…"

Ivan was always the calming force. "You'll do fine, hommy. This'll put the IT Company on the map. I'm so happy for you, my little beauteous one. I love you."

I got back to L.A. to turn in my orders to my little team at my workshop, "my atelier" now located at on Huntley Drive in trendy West Hollywood. I got kicked out of my garage at home because Ivan couldn't stand tripping over bolts of fabrics and boxes that would take over part of our living room, as well as the noise and vibration all night from the telex machine. We somehow found this day care center right next to the Pacific Design Center, or "Blue Whale" as it was called after its design. We lucked out!

I remember asking fellow California designer Nancy Heller's then husband Bob Heller about setting up the ledger. I knew nothing about ledger sheets. He'd say, "Irene, remember it's not in the schmata… it's in the real estate. You'll have one great season, then two so-so seasons, and a bad season, and you are back to square one."

Boy, were those the wisest words I've ever heard. Ivan and I never had any children. Who's got time when you are doing four fashion seasons a year, and going to Asia twice a year, and New York four times a year? Designing, manufacturing, selling, going to department stores to make appearances...everything from A to Z with a constant flux of inadequate or mediocre help. It is a high speed, super-hyped, cutthroat type of business.

The part I loved was the creative part: the designing, the search for shapes and colors, the making of something from nothing to create something that was only in my mind's eye. There seemed to be this group energy, this creative oneness that designers drew from. Designers looked to the streets, to music, to films, and oftentimes to each other to come up with their version of this universal creativity. I felt a kinship to Japanese designers, especially Issey Miyake who described in his book that Asian clothing let the body dictate the shape. He said it moved with the body to form its shape rather than the European fashion which had their origin in the Victorian clothing. They corseted and molded the body into the shapes of the garment. The American designer I admired most was Halston from the seventies. He broke the rules of his time and created clothing with one seam and mostly cut "on the bias" to allow the body to move and shape the garment instead of the other way around. They were modern and sensuous and loved by celebrities.

I dashed back to Kuala Lumpur to brainstorm with Vicky who had already started some of the designs on paper. The '76 Bergdorf catalogue modeled by the super model Cheryl Tiegs had a description that read:

"A COLLECTORS ITEM - A one-of-a-kind gift, to give or to own. Glamorous, romantic....A Bergdorf-designed silk crepe de chine caftan, each individually hand-batiked in original patterns of birds, dragons, butterflies, florals or geometrics in exotic clear coloring. Each hand signed by artist Irene Tsu. One size fits all. $165.00"

Vicky and I basically divided our designs into these three categories: Winds & Dragons, Florals & Fawners, Geometrics. Each design would be done in four different colorways: bold complementary, bold contrasts, pastel complimentary, and pastel contrasts. I gave her a Pantone color chart book and we communicated the colors from numbers in the book on the telex. It worked perfect. I couldn't have found someone whose taste and design sense was so similar to mine.

I went back to L.A. thinking all was going to be terrific until I received a call from Raz who explained that we could not possibly produce the caftans in batik as the batik process uses wax which means each piece had to be dry cleaned. Dry cleaning was very expensive overseas, and we couldn't afford it as the profit margin was already slim. We either had to tell Bergdorf we had to cancel the order, raise the price, or go to Seoul, South Korea where they utilized a paste method similar to the gutta resist method they used in France.

I feel like I need to explain a little of the batik process and the other resist methods. One basically does the design with wax or paste to white out or "resist" the design. Then you dip the whole cloth into different dye vats to give the background the multi hues while the design remains white or a pale color. Then you remove the wax and paint in again and again with different colors until you get the result you desire… or whatever happens. Only the waxing of the batik process gives you that crackly look because wax cracks. Therefore, no two pieces are ever exactly alike. It never was an exact science in those days and therein lied the beauty of batik. The resist using the gutta or rice paste would not have the crackling; it would be smooth or colors might overlap. Whatever worked, worked.

It suited my water color nature just fine.

I did end up going to South Korea to set up a factory to help us with our operations dilemma… and those adventures could fill up several chapters themselves, especially when it came to how they handled women in charge. They would have me wait for two to three hours for a meeting, insisting that they need to meet with the "Boss." I explained till tea was coming out of my ears that I *was* the boss. They reluctantly obliged. I could not wait in the lobby to be picked up by my factory staff. They would hustle me away thinking I was a "working girl." I did convince Ivan to show his face once in Seoul and thereafter all was copasetic. As our fashion business grew, I would make a couple of trips there every year, and each time things did get better. New hotels were going up, and more westerners were coming.

Meanwhile, I had added a small cashmere collection out of Hong Kong with the help of talented designer/production guy for Calvin Klein and Perry Ellis. His name was Bobbi and he was like a brother to me. I did cashmere sweatshirts with pockets and zip front hoodies with leftover CK cashmeres. "Summer Silk, Winter Cash: This is IT, The IT Company!" They were a hit. Most evenings I would hole up in his room at the Sheraton in Kowloon, brain-storming design ideas and listening to all of Bobbi's latest love escapades while chomping down room service. It was pure creative decadence.

My designs were now in every important catalogue from Bullock's to Saks to Neiman's, as well as several top specialty stores in the country.

We were shipping night and day and not getting paid fast enough. Of course, the corporations would always be paying the big names first and us last.

I was shuttling from Hong Kong to Seoul to L.A. then to New York, working and arranging fashion shoots. Incidentally, I was able to hire Demi Moore as one of my models for a fashion shoot before she became famous. She had just been signed by Casablanca Modeling Agency and my hairdresser friend next door said that I could hire her for a hundred dollars a day as she was not so busy at the time. Yes, indeed! She showed up looking like she just rolled out of bed, and she was moody too. But after makeup, as soon as she got in front of the lights, she lit up like a million dollars. This unknown model would soon become a huge star.

There is no business like the magic of fashion or show business.

Still, the schedule and work of running the business was starting to take its toll. Ivan would say over dinner at Konditorei, an Austrian café that was one of his favorites, that we never talked about anything anymore but business. He was right and that would soon be a problem.

In New York, we met Ben Shaw, the major promoter and owner of many top designers. He had made the likes of Giorgio di Sant' Angelo, Halston, and many others, even Calvin Klein. When we went to dinner with him at Elaine's, the Upper East Side eatery that was the hub of top designers and film and stage industry elites, we would always be ushered in by Elaine herself to a top table. Famous designers and models would come by our table to pay homage to Ben. It was impressive. Even more so, he thought I was promotable. I was to be his next protégé. Once again, I was going to be a starlet in the making!

Ultimately, however, my fashion design business simply grew too fast, especially for a couple of artists with very little business experience. The only way we could stay relevant and continue growing was to get a lot more financing to assemble a better crew from production to sales to marketing. Honestly, the more volume we did, the more we saw our margins diminishing.

We got to a point where we needed to either scale it way back down to what it was when we started or find a big-time partner like Ben Shaw. I was practically sleeping on my cutting table and sometimes airbrushing in my backyard till I would have cramps in my fingers. I couldn't be burning my brain and body much longer even though I loved stretching every creative fiber. I knew that it had to change. When we found Ben, we thought it might have been an answer, but in the end, he didn't really deliver. Ben was an old man by then, and while he talked big, he didn't really *do* anything to help us.

Suddenly it all got to be a bit too hard.

Ivan and I were struggling, not just in the business, but also in our relationship and our personal lives. Of course, it wasn't just the rag business, it was also Ivan feeling like he couldn't have continuous success in TV or films. He turned forty and felt that he was neglecting his career. He needed to hang with his people instead of devoting so much time to my fashion business. He did not like running a business. In fact, he said he created a monster. I said I was quite happy having my little business in my garage. It was him that wanted us to triple our volume every season, but by then, it was too late, and it ruined my marriage to Ivan. It was the most horrible emotional and financial struggle. We had an ugly divorce because Ivan also fought to gain control of Irene Tsu Designs. He argued that I didn't have exclusivity to my name/label as Yves Saint Laurent or Kenzo did not own theirs. Imagine him comparing little old me to those iconic names! His belief in me, even as he fought me, was astonishing to the end.

Deep down, I knew that I became a success greatly because of it. I made a terrible mistake parting from Ivan. I was immature, impulsive, and foolish and I've lived to regret it to this day. I told Ivan when I married him that I was on loan to him for seven years, and then I was going to go back to my spiritual path. Instead, I stayed in fashion and burned for another seven years not knowing what else to do.

I did scale the business back to try and make it more manageable. The stores and boutiques still wanted my merchandise, as did some existing clients I had. I was trying to do everything out of L.A., working out of my garage with a tiny crew. I always tried to make the best of every situation because deep down I know we are just actors in this big play. But eventually, this show had to end.

Looking back, I realized my biggest mistake was trying to make my designs accessible to the masses. If I had stayed small and high end, I think it would have been a different story. Still, I can look back and celebrate the success and creativity that I enjoyed in my eleven years as a fashion designer.

But it did come at a cost. It was a harsh growing process in those three short years of business with Ivan. I sacrificed my health, my marriage, my innocence. I was an artist, an entrepreneur, and an old hag at thirty-two.

Life moved on, right or wrong, and today I believe we are just pawns being moved by some greater force than ourselves. We only have limited free will. The Chinese would call it "ming yun," your life path, your fate. One lives by one's "mien," as it's commonly called.

After things settled, Ivan and I stayed in each other's lives, even when he went through some hard times and when he found himself in a relationship with Hollywood madam Heidi Fleiss. Ivan and I had already been divorced for several years. We somehow went back to being rather good friends and co-owners of a property in West Hollywood.

I decided to give a party one night in my party friendly house in Benedict Canyon and it was going strong. I glanced over at the door and saw Ivan walking in with Heidi. I don't remember inviting them. I don't believe I'd even met her but there they were in my living room. I thought she was striking in a not-too-pretty kind of way. We greeted one another and the first thing out of Heidi's mouth was, "You two are soulmates!"

"Who? Me and Ivan?"

"Yes, you two are soulmates!" she declared again. We laughed and I didn't think about it until years later.

CHAPTER 22

During this time, I would also meet two other famous people who would play a big role in my life.

One was Bikram Choudhury of Bikram Yoga, another idolized Indian guru that fell prey to the temptation and excesses of rock stardom.

It was at a party when I first heard of Bikram Yoga. A beautiful statuesque woman was doing what looked like some kind of yoga pose. Her name was Victoria and she was going on and on about how she absolutely loved Bikram's classes. I was looking for some form of workout that I could maintain as I was getting somewhat beaten up. I had torn cartilage in my left knee and a shoulder injury from karate. Victoria and I became instant friends and I promised to check out the class the very next day.

It was in the basement of a bank building on Wilshire Boulevard in Beverly Hills. I walked down the steps to see that the class had already started. There was no one there to sign me in. Piles of shoes and random clothing were strewn about. I heard a deep, melodic voice calling out instructions, interspersed with laughter and clapping. In the small clearing, away from the filing cabinets, were about a dozen or so students sitting down Japanese-style with arms outstretched in front of them, hands in prayer, forehead on floor, and butt on the heels. Then I saw a deeply-tanned and incredibly toned body with a black headband and black speedo gyrating on the back of one the female students. He was actually surfing on her back, calling out instructions.

"Palms together, stretch, stretch, stretch like you are going to touch the wall." He hopped off her back, made a loud hand clap and laughed. "Excellent, excellent, Emmy. Turn around…lie down…Sevasna (dead man's pose)…complete relaxation…"

The room went completely silent. After class was over, I tried to pay but was told that I could leave a donation in the basket by the door. I couldn't see any basket, so I left. I loved the class. It was challenging but I thought he, Bikram Choudhury, was funny.

I didn't realize at the time that forty-plus years later I would still be practicing and teaching Bikram Yoga.

There really weren't many yoga classes or real teachers back in 1976. There would be some health clubs that offered some sort of yoga, mostly for older people to stretch and do some breathing. Most of the days at Bikram's class, you could also work out side by side with a celebrity from the movie/music industry like Quincy Jones, Candice Bergen, Louis Malle, Juliet Prowse, Raquel Welch, or star athletes like John McEnroe and John Lloyd. I'll never forget the time that Kareem Abdul-Jabbar came in with two of his teammates. One was Magic Johnson. They were such giants, it seemed they took up all the air. For about ten dollars here, you could get an incredible workout, a towel and shower, and be massively entertained by Bikram. Bikram's Beginning Yoga class was the best ticket in town in the seventies!

In our forty years of friendship and teacher-student relationship, I have to be grateful to him for giving me the health, vitality, and joy of his practice, without which my life would not have been the same. I would say most of his long-time students feel the same way. As a teacher, he is unparalleled. He can seem harsh and even insulting at times, but you soon realize that his main goal is to push your physical and mental limit to the max, beyond what you thought possible. He will cajole, tease, joke, yell, or sing you an Indian love song, just to get you to do your personal best and to show that you are loved. I believe he cares deeply about each of his students.

Coming from India by way of Tokyo at the urging of his guru Bishnu Charan Ghosh, his mission was to spread his brand of yoga to America and beyond. His guru was the brother of Paramahansa Yogananda. The young, former world-class weightlifter landed in Hollywood and almost immediately sought out Dr. Anne Marie Bennstrom, an early advocate of the health revolution in the seventies. In fact, she was the first to establish the modern-day health club/spa located on Hollywood and La Brea while she had her ashram, a cult-like fat farm where members were put on a rigorous exercise schedule and a diet of raw vegetables. Anne Marie incidentally was my role model when I was still a teenager. She told me that Bikram showed up at her health club one day and demanded to teach yoga there. Anne Marie said she'd have to see how she could fit him into her schedule when Bikram demanded, "You don't understand, I want to teach here today." She found a time slot and he taught his first class there that day.

His very early students were Shirley MacLaine, Freda Payne, and Lainie Kazan. He told us that it was Shirley who told him that he must charge because in America, if you don't charge no one respects you. By the time I signed up at his Rexford Drive location, I believe six hundred and eighteen was my number. If there is still a number system now, it probably would run into the millions.

A funny side story that shows how connected the people in my life were: Broni and I were shopping at Saks Fifth Avenue one day and I was talking to the sales lady while Broni disappeared. Minutes later he came back with a very attractive young woman who was also working there in some capacity. He introduced her as Patti Reagan. After saying hello, I asked "Reagan, like in Ronald Reagan?" She said yes, that he was her dad. Broni would take Patti to lunch and coffee a lot but he lamented that he may have been followed by the secret service. I then got Patti interested in Bikram Yoga and she started coming very often. It was there she met young Paul Grilley, who took a bus down from Montana to study with Bikram. Grilley was one of Bikram's most devoted students and became a great yoga teacher. Paul asked Bikram one day, "What should I do boss? Patti wants to marry me," to which Bikram asked if he loved her. "I don't know. I'm confused but she loves me." That was all Bikram needed to hear. "Good, marry her." So, Paul married Patti in a beautiful ceremony at the Bel Air Hotel less than a year later with the White House in attendance.

I've never seen Bikram touch alcohol, but he drinks Coca Cola and brags about American junk food (though I've never actually seen him have any of that, either). He is a small eater and mainly eats protein like steak and lobster. He also cooks Indian at home with his wife Rajashree, who is a fabulous cook. He loathes vegetarians and would tell them right in front of everyone in class, "You smell like a rotten vegetable...go and have a Big Mac."

You never know whether he's serious.

There is no boundary in his classroom. He conducts it as though you are standing around his family kitchen. After my rather painful divorce he would tell me out loud during class, "Ireeen, you are divorced, why are you still not married? You have to find a husband who drives a Mercedes or a Bentley."

Oh boy, I wanted to sink into the floor, but deep down I knew he was just being a dad. He would also bring up my relationship with Sinatra like a nosy uncle. With Bikram Yoga, we are like a big extended family... whether you like it or not. Mostly, all his core students love it, at least from what I've experienced.

He used to have elaborate parties, playing loud disco music and Bollywood soap operas with lots of Indian food. He loved to dance and had a good enough singing voice to be recorded by Quincy Jones, though it never materialized. His daughter took after him, and a few years ago she gave a party at their home for four hundred of her close friends. Like father, like daughter. Raquel Welch, Bikram's long-time student, technically bought him his home in Benedict Canyon because she published a beautiful tabletop book where she did all his yoga postures but neglected to give Bikram credit. His publisher sued her publisher and Bikram got the money to purchase the home in the early eighties. He also would brag about how he cured Richard Nixon of some neuromuscular ailment and how he could have saved Elvis. I never verified the claims. The man was and still is an enigma.

In the early days, he would do shows and pull a Mack truck with his ponytail or bury himself in the sand and breathe through a straw to demonstrate his yogic power. He drinks hot water with lemon and honey while he conducts classes and takes a steam bath almost daily. He actually does his abs workout in the steam bath. He is the first person I saw that did the "Nauli," a yogic exercise that moves your ab muscles from one side to another and squeezes them together to the middle to form a three-inch column of muscle. It's pretty amazing to watch. Bikram has extraordinarily discipline.

Even without a formal education, he's been able to dream big and succeed. When his fame grew, he understood that he needed to grow his schools. I was coerced into taking him to visit different malls for the possibility of acquiring another yoga school, or so I thought. We stood in the middle of the mall and he looked around and said to me—and to himself perhaps for the first time—"Look at that McDonald's, Starbuck, Target...this is the American way, this is the way to go."

Right then and there, he gave birth to McYoga!

We also lost the sweet, dear, harsh teacher we knew.

Another important man I met around this time was Dick Shawn.

While my nasty divorce was proceeding, I received a call from my pal Barbara, the British unit publicist from *Paper Tiger*. Barbara was in town and wanted to meet for a drink. It was a great diversion and with someone to whom I could vent my anguish and sadness. I suggested the Beverly Wilshire Hotel since I was not a drinker and did not really know any bars. We were having a dandy time, but I forgot that Barbara did not stop at one or two drinks. A couple of Perriers later, I was heading out to the ladies' room.

On my way out, I saw Dick Shawn in a booth with another fellow. My heart went thump! My heavens, he was the very person whose live hit comedy show I was trying to catch for weeks. But each time, my friends would back out at the last minute. I was afraid I would miss the performance all together. On my way back to the table I worked up enough courage to stop by and tell him in person. He was a very handsome fellow and had a charismatic voice and accent. I told him I definitely wanted to see his show and boldly left him my company card. I went back to the table and giggled and laughed with Barbara. She said I did good. It felt good and added some sparkle in my gloom-and-doom life at the time.

Dick called not long after and said he had set aside a seat for that Friday night's show and asked if I thought perhaps, he wanted to order a dress from me. He made me laugh right away. He was not a great comedian for nothing!

Friday night I saw the most fantastic show. A few days later he called to ask me to a cast party of a film he had just completed. I went and it was the beginning of another date that lasted almost eleven years.

Thus began the "matzo ball" cycle of my life!

Dick was *very* Jewish. Not that he observed the Jewish holidays or diets, but he would mostly make fun of his own Jewishness. Being Jewish was always a source of humor for him. Comics of that time and culture were very close-knit, so I got to meet a lot of funny man superstars like Milton Berle, Sid Caesar, Shecky Greene, Buddy Hackett, and many more, who were always hanging around. I never got too close to them as they were really in Dick's circle, but I would see them around and drop in from time to time on their lunches at the Friars Club.

Over the course of our time together, one of the most fascinating things was watching him prepare his act. First of all, I knew his act so well that *I* could take it on the road! He would rehearse on me constantly. In the morning, he would pick up the paper and look it over while he had his coffee and bagel. He wasn't really looking at the news; he was trying to find lines or items he could use in his act. He'd try something out and say, "Baby, what do you think about that?"

Our relationship was fun, funny, and drama free...save for the occasional uncomfortable experience.

On one of our dates, we had gone into Brambles on Beverly Boulevard and ran smack into Ivan seated at a table of ten or so people. He spotted Dick and me and proceeded to get up from the table and charge toward Dick to punch him out. Dick dodged his punch as he was also a hefty guy, a natural athlete who went to college on a baseball scholarship. Remember that Ivan was on the Hungarian Olympic ice hockey team at seventeen. Ivan's friends jumped in to wrestle him back to the table. It was not a good scene, but that was only the beginning. After we supped, we went outside to wait for our car and there was Ivan waiting as well. I was a little numb, expecting the worst. Ivan walked over to apologize to Dick and turned on his charm. He said how much he admired Dick's work and hoped someday to have the opportunity of working together. They soon started joking and laughing. Ivan was a guy's guy and so was Dick. They parted, patting each other's backs like old chums. Only in Hollywood, I suppose...

In the beginning, Dick played my therapist, even in regards to my divorce from Ivan. He was analytical and wanted to help and to understand me better. He liked to gab and apparently had years of therapy. He was interested in human nature. He would ask, "Did you guys talk and try to work out your marriage? What did you talk about? What went wrong?"

I didn't know what to tell him. "We never really talked...we had this silent understanding."

"Silent understanding? What on earth is that?"

"I don't really know. We were not into analyzing each other and loathed shrinks." We were not Americans nor Jewish inside.

Dick was on the road a lot, as was I for my fashion business. We met up all over the country when he gigged, sometimes small venues and sometimes big like Vegas and Tahoe. It was an exhausting lifestyle, but he loved it as much as I did creating designs. He was interested in design and had great taste in clothing as well. His dad was a haberdasher in Buffalo, where he grew up. We were both artists and we lived a nomadic kind of life which suited me fine. He was close to all four of his grown children and he would always buy them toy gifts...and one for me, the fifth child.

In the end, that was what ended our relationship. When we met, I was thirty-two and Dick was already in his fifties. He treated me like one of his kids at times and the age difference, while not a problem at first, caught up to us years later. It wasn't a bad break up at all; we just sort of drifted apart. I found a younger man and he found a neurotic Jewish girl who meddled in his work.

That ended up being a disaster as she stuck her nose into every aspect of his business; wanting to be on set, taking his calls, making deals on his behalf, sometimes without him even knowing. She even brought back wild animals from South America! I'll never forget when I got a call from his daughter inviting me to a play. It turned into a discussion about this new girlfriend and what a mess everything was in Dick's life. "Dad needs to have you," she said. I went to the play and for a brief time, Dick and I actually rekindled our romance, but I didn't really want to be entangled in that anymore. His daughter Wendy incidentally is married to Joey, John Travolta's brother. There is another unique, fabulously talented, and beautiful man.

Still, I remember Dick and our time together fondly, just as I do with all the people I've had the pleasure to know and to love over the course of my blessed life, one that continued with amazing experiences both personally and professionally over the course of the eighties, nineties, and even today.

CHAPTER 23

Throughout all those relationships, friendships, businesses, and new life experiences, I still continued to pursue my life as an actress. I'm still playing in this exciting, enigmatic industry and enjoying my journey, the roles I play, the people I meet, the life I get to live.

In that time, not only have there been some significant and career-defining roles, there have also been some rather amazing developments that forever altered my personal life.

In the eighties, one of my more interesting roles was in *Down and Out in Beverly Hills*. It was by far one of the best film experiences for me. I went in to see casting director Ellen Chenoweth—who has done lots of big films—for a part as a Chinese interpreter in this now classic Bette Midler, Richard Dreyfuss, Nick Nolte film by Paul Mazursky. I read with her and she kept looking at me. Finally, she said, "Can you go to the bathroom and remove your earrings and wipe off some blush and lip stick? You just look too pretty."

"Sure, okay." I came back and sat across from her again and she was still looking at me.

"You still look too glamorous or something, but wait… Paul told me that he was thinking of perhaps casting a non-Caucasian actress as the dentist's wife. I'm not exactly sure which way he wants to go but I want you to go see Paul."

The next day I waited in the reception area of the Beverly Hills office of Paul Mazursky for what I thought was an eternity. It actually worked for me because I went into a long meditative state to calm myself. When I finally went in to meet Paul, I was powerfully calm. In any acting class, an actor prepares to enter this ideal state.

I read a short scene with Paul and he was delighted. He exclaimed, "You are Sheila Waltzberg! Wonderful!" He then practically took me by my arm and led me down the hallway. "I want you to meet some people." There was his co-producer Pato Guzman and others. He would stick his head in their door and say, "Meet Sheila Waltzberg. This is Sheila Waltzberg!"

I had now crossed over to play a Jewish princess! Once again, I was cast in a non-Asian role. I valued each and every one of these experiences, especially as I got older and started to realize their importance. Even as recently as the eighties, that didn't happen for many Asian actresses.

I flew out of his office to call my agent, I was so excited. I felt bad I could no longer call Ivan since we were no longer married. However, when I started filming at Disney, Ivan called me and said he was on the lot working with some writer or producer and they mentioned that they just saw the dailies (raw footage shot that day), and that there was this knockout Asian actress who just got cast. Ivan laughed till he cried and said, "Shmuck, she's my ex-wife!"

"*You* are the schmuck!" countered the exec.

The filming was glamorous as the budget was ample for those days. Paul catered all his favorite deli food every day and being a compulsive eater, he would stuff handfuls of it in his mouth every time he walked by the catering setup. Paul gave us some of the most brilliant and enjoyable films of the last three-plus decades. He was nominated for five Oscars among other awards, a true genius from Brooklyn.

I also got to work with famous costume designer Albert Wolsky on the film. I remember that he took me shopping at Neiman Marcus for my costume. With the budget they had, I could have selected anything! He picked out a few things, and funny enough, I wasn't crazy about any of them. I wanted something funny and memorable. We settled for a dress that was a fraction of the price of the outfits he was pointing out. It was a one-shoulder, full-length black dress that had a huge, white flower the size of my head. He agreed to it and we bought multiple copies. Thank God we did! For the scene where I jump in the pool, that dress shrank up to my knees. We had to go through a few of those dresses.

We were filming that big party scene for days. Everyone was in that big setup, including Little Richard who was banging on the piano and singing. Nick Nolte was about ten feet away sipping on a big soft drink. I was so thirsty but couldn't step out because they were lighting the scene forever and they needed me there. I asked Nick's right-hand man if I could possibly have a sip of Nick's soft drink.

"You sure you want it?"

"Yes, please, anything. I'm dying of thirst." He then handed me the huge paper container and I eagerly took a substantial gulp before I realized that it was practically pure vodka with a splash of O.J. I choked, and thanked him nonetheless, giggling with a big smile. His guy told me later that Nick wanted to take off twenty-five pounds for the film in a hurry, so he was on a special "Nick Diet" of diet pills and vodka with O.J. Some days he looked awful, but when you saw him on screen he lit up and looked like a million bucks. Nick is a true film star!

In the late eighties, I also worked on the miniseries *Noble House* on location in North Carolina at the Dino De Laurentiis Studio with the gorgeous Pierce Brosnan and the amazing actor John Rhys-Davies. Most of the cast was British and they would hit the bar after the day, not getting off the stool until they were ready to fall into bed. However, they all showed up in the morning on time, bright-eyed and word perfect on their lines. That's probably a big part of their Shakespeare training.

I was taken to a department store to shop by the wardrobe lady, but I had no idea that shopping for wardrobe was a serious crisis in North Carolina. The merchandise was so different then in Los Angeles. We had to find a suitable dress that they could pad me up to be plump and matronly as the wife of a powerful tai-pan. Skinniness was definitely not in vogue nor becoming of the wealthy man's wife in those days. At last, a round necked, mid-sleeved dress with turquois colored flowers was chosen. Honestly, I thought it came right out of Walmart, but I guess it worked on film along with a short bob wig. Still, it was a great work experience in South Carolina with a British crew and every day we had the best *Italian* food in the commissary. Of course, it was Dino De Laurentiis!

Around this time, to go along with the acting, I also found another myself taking on another career, one that has brought me a lot of success and joy, and that I continue today...

I've owned my own home since I was twenty-one. After getting over the initial shock of not knowing how to turn on a sprinkler, and a little difficulty making it up the curved and rather steep driveway, I settled in to sit in every corner of the room and meditated. Then I went into ripping out the shag green carpet and taking a hammer to the wall in the living room hallway. In the middle of the night, I bashed and punched holes in that wall. Later, I was told it was a supporting wall and that a beam had to be put in to support it. I never did and it never fell down. It was a mid-century home, which is very valuable now. I sold it after two failed marriages when I needed to get out of there emotionally. It was the worst real estate mistake I've ever made. I got five hundred thousand or something for it and recently it was appraised at over two million. *Ouch!* But I did buy another, a five-bedroom with a huge pool and no driveway. I did good on that one! So, in a way, I've always been in real estate. I liked architecture, which I was not allowed to study. I liked the redesigning part of it, making something out of nothing. It was like what I could do with cloth and cut, only this time it was brick and mortar.

When the clothing business got really draining and not profitable, I met a young contractor through my best girlfriend from yoga. I learned building from him, and he said that I should get a real estate license. It never entered my mind because I never thought about selling real estate. However, I liked learning a new craft, which incidentally didn't have as much age and race discrimination. I was always a quick learner and hard worker, and I found that knowing so many people in this town was a real advantage. I was given opportunities even though I was green. Meanwhile it also gave me a chance to buy my own real estate and play architect and contractor. A career in real estate was a natural progression for me.

For years, I hid my acting career from clients because I was afraid they may perceive me to be a flake or disappear when a film job came along. As the Internet changed our world, people would look up my name and see who I was, and they seemed to like and be amused by it. It's been some twenty-five years since I got my license and I'm very thankful for the knowledge and all the people that I had the chance to meet. The last few years I have been working with quite a few clients from China and I really enjoy the chance of speaking in the Chinese dialect. It gave me an edge and I enjoyed these smart, hard-working people and being able to help them. Real estate has proven to be an exciting and fruitful challenge for me in so many ways.

In the nineties, as I was getting my real estate license, my acting work continued. I did the film *Comrades: Almost a Love Story*. It was an amazing experience; the first Chinese language film I'd ever done. It must have been 1995 or so when I first met Peter Chan in a hotel in L.A. He was in town to cast a Hong Kong film among other things. He was Thai-Chinese, a graduate of USC film school, and a highly acclaimed Hong Kong film writer/director/producer. I was very pleased to have the opportunity to meet him. I had brought with me my portfolio of photos from an array of films, magazines, and press. We were going through them and he seemed to be mesmerized. He said unfortunately he couldn't use me in this film as he had promised the role to another actress from Taiwan. However, he said he would think of me for his next film, which he was in the process of writing.

Is he kidding? His next film?

He wanted to be nice, having brought me in for nothing. It's the film industry after all.

As I've shown, I have no sense of time and I always kept myself busy. A year must have gone by. One afternoon I got a call. It was a man's voice that I did not recognize at first, but soon realized was Peter's. I greeted him in English, then Chinese, and felt an immediate kinship. He was asking me to be in his next film. He said he would FedEx me the script right away because I would have to come to Hong Kong in three weeks. I was so elated I think I crumbled to the floor, said a prayer, and knocked my head on the floor three times for Chinese "joss."

The next few days I waited for the FedEx envelope to appear at my door. It came and I ripped it open to read it. Well, surprise... it was all in Chinese! Of course it was, what was I thinking?! I even opened it from the wrong end. I can read about twenty words in Chinese and they were mostly for ordering food, though I speak rather good Cantonese as well as Mandarin and a bit of Shanghai dialect. My sister and I almost starved once in a Chinese restaurant in San Francisco where the whole menu was written in Chinese on the wall. We finally just walked around the restaurant and pointed at different dishes.

This was a Hong Kong film to be shot in Cantonese with Hong Kong star Maggie Cheung and Chinese pop star Leon Lai, as well as internationally acclaimed romantic star Tony Leung Chiu-wai. I was to play Lai's aunt Rosie, a chain-smoking, boozy character who put her nephew up under the stairwell in her boarding house in Hong Kong. She may have suffered from delusions of grandeur when she spoke about how William Holden had befriended her and had taken her to all these fancy places in Hong Kong. She kept his photos and all the souvenirs, such as knives, forks, and napkins that she had stolen from these fancy eateries. No one really believed her until after her death when they found her trove. Peter showed a lot of my real photos and magazine covers at my character's funeral scene.

It is quite a character and Peter no doubt wrote it for me. I realized that I'm a whole different person acting in my childhood tongue. I was no longer *acting* like a Chinese person. I was just myself, an actor. It was such a transcending experience. The film was a hit, and Peter won a

Golden Horse Award, which is the Chinese equivalent of an Oscar. He went on to be one of the top-grossing filmmakers in China. He put me in another of his films, *Golden Chicken*, a few years later, starring his talented wife Sandra Ng. Then, as I was a realtor, he gave me the listing to his magical home in Hollywood Hills with truly the best view of all of Los Angeles.

In the late nineties, I was on *Star Trek: Voyager*. I did two episodes as Mary Kim, the mother to Ensign Kim, played by Garrett Wang. I felt rather small and lonely during shooting as we were just filming on a small section of the very impressive high-tech set of the interior of the ship. Robert Ito played my husband. He was such a nice man and had co-starred in the popular series *Quincy, M.E.* His first film in Hollywood was *Women of the Prehistoric Planet* with me, Wendell Corey, and Keith Larsen. We played Adam and Eve!

The actual filming of the *Star Trek* scene was strange as Ito and I were in some kind of booth talking, almost yelling at Garrett because he was on the Starship and the reception was bad. But I did get in my two cents as the "tiger mom" urging him to speak to Captain Janeway for a promotion, to Garrett's dismay and utter embarrassment.

"But... Mom... Mom..."

The other episode was filmed a couple of years later. In this one, I was pregnant with Garrett. I had a big belly and walked toward the camera saying something. Then I remembered I was all alone on a mattress, huddled in practical darkness. I didn't understand what was going on, but *Star Trek* is in a time and space all of its own... the brilliant creation of Gene Roddenberry!

A funny side note and curious fact that I remember—when I worked on *Star Trek*, I had to be fitted with a certain kind of bra that was custom made. Apparently, the show's producers wanted their actresses to have pointy breasts!

Anyway, a couple years later, I picked up the phone one day and heard a familiar voice.

"Mom?" said the male voice. "Mom, can you find me a house?"

"What? Garrett... Garrett Wang?" I replied. "Oh my goodness, son, how are you? Of course I can find you a house."

As a realtor, I loved schlepping him around the Hollywood Hills looking for houses. The other realtors would be very impressed because of *Star Trek* and because Garrett was so handsome. The one-story modern home we found for him was atop of Runyon Canyon and had a fantastic view of the Hollywood Sign and a small pool. It was perfect for him. Over the years, some local realtors would call and ask if Garrett would sell his house. I kind of lost touch with him because he was always traveling for the *Star Trek* conventions all over the world. I really hope he kept it, as it would be worth a small fortune now!

I've continued to do a lot of film and TV work, including *Lost at Home, CSI: NY, Law & Order: LA* and *Cold Case*. On that show I played a mom who lost both of her sons; the older one murdered the younger one. It was a tragedy of Greek proportions! The director wanted not a stitch of makeup on me and powdered my face with some whitish powder to intensify every wrinkle and dent. I was not recognizable to any of my friends… just as well.

When I was working on *Law & Order*, I rode in a limo one day with Alfred Molina and he started chatting with me in his British accent. I finally had to ask:

"How come you have a British accent?"

He looked at me for a second and then simply said, "Because I'm British."

"I thought you were Hispanic!" I said, laughing. Who could blame me with a name like Alfred Molina?!

There truly has never been a dull moment in my life and what's best about being a water color artist is the anticipation of what's next, and embracing the mystery and the adventure.

I continue acting today, and in the process of writing and editing this book, I got to work on two wonderful projects, one of which provided me with… my first nude scene!

In 2019, I was offered a short film called *Caregiver*. It was written by Nick Hartano, based on his own mother's ordeal, and co-directed with Sam Roden, two very talented young filmmakers. It was this extremely physically challenging part as a stroke victim who is paralyzed on one side of her body. I read the script and really wasn't sure how I could handle this unfamiliar territory.

How my bread winner, head of the household character became half a vegetable and had to save herself from near drowning was quite an ordeal. However, when you are an old pro, you just do it. Your focus and your adrenaline simply take you over to cross that finishing line. Studying Olivia Colman's performance as the partially paralyzed Queen Anne in the brilliant film *The Favourite* was a true inspiration. We have so many brilliant and talented actors!

Then, right in the final stages of editing this book, I was offered a role in *Over the Moon,* a world premiere animated musical for Netflix, directed by the award-winning Glen Keane, who was an animator on several of Disney's biggest hits, including *The Little Mermaid, Aladdin,* and *Beauty & the Beast.* This film is about a little girl who builds a rocket to fly into the heavens to meet a mythical moon goddess. I play the head of the household, a strong, matriarchal grandmother who feeds everyone, especially my little granddaughter, at the Moon Festival.

I already had some experience doing voiceover before, under much more strenuous circumstances. I provided the voice of the tough, hatchet-wielding mother of a gang leader in the video game *Sleeping Dogs.* I remember when I did it, thinking "Oh my gosh, couldn't they find someone off the streets of Hong Kong for this?!" I lost my voice from all the screaming and yelling I had to do.

The *Over the Moon* session was fantastic. We recorded in a five-star recording studio in the Valley. Glen directed me on every line. Sometimes he would have me change my intention or feelings about the lines. Sometimes he would have me change the tone or style, like running sentences together. I eagerly obliged, feeling good about working on such a big project with such a great group of professionals

I'm looking forward to seeing it and to the next opportunity and adventure to come!

CHAPTER 24

OF ALL THAT I'VE SEEN AND DONE, all that I've experienced in this amazing life, there is perhaps nothing quite as unique nor any role quite as rewarding and challenging as my ultimate adventure: being a mother.

It was a brief second marriage that got me thinking about motherhood.

I thought, "Well, I guess I have done everything else!"

After a few attempts at in vitro, I decided not to go that route because then I would be tied to my soon-to-be ex-husband forever and that would indeed be an awful thought.

So I decided to adopt a child who really needed to have a better chance in life. Of course, I wasn't sure how to go about the adoption process, but my brilliant sister Florence succeeded in adopting a gorgeous boy from Bulgaria. She told me how to get started.

I sought the aid of Mr. Nui of the U.S.-China Affairs Agency, who told me that he saw a little baby girl who looked just like me. She was placed in a newly built model Social Welfare Center where they housed the very old who had no family, along with young children given up for adoption, which I think is very smart of the Chinese.

After a lot of back and forth to make the arrangements, I was sent a photo of my soon-to-be daughter that was the size of a postage stamp. I bored into the photo with laser eyes and fell in love with her instantly. I cried just looking at that tiny photo. I named her Yasmine Ananda and I knew that she was my baby. Yasmine was the name of Rita Hayworth's daughter by Prince Aly Khan. I read that she took her mother to live in New York away from the peering eyes and gossip mongers of Hollywood when Rita was in the downward spiral of Alzheimer's. She kept her peaceful and safe till her last day. I was deeply impressed. I loved the name. It wasn't American or Asian, but was just exotic. And in Sanskrit, Ananda means "bliss." She is bliss and joy. She is my gift.

After all the arrangements were made, I flew to Quan Zhou and met with about twenty primarily American families. Some of them brought their girls from a previous adoption. They were ordinary, loving people from all walks of life; from a Beverly Hills police officer to a scientist from Boston to a couple from Buffalo. The group was sent to different locations where their babies awaited, and some of them had no idea what kind of baby they were about to receive. I was with a small group of six or so and went to Jiujiang, a small town east of Shanghai, about an hour's flight from Quan Zhou. I went to wait in a hotel with the other expectant parents.

There I saw local women stepping forward to hand over a baby to an American woman whose name was called out. With tears of joy flowing down their faces the new mom reached out her arms to receive this little bundle of life. I could never forget the one instance when a Chinese peasant woman stepped forward to hand over her baby who was swathed in rags. The top of her head was sunburned, with her hair sun-bleached and reddish. She turned to speak to me in Chinese as I was the only Chinese looking foreigner standing nearby. She asked to get her baby's clothes back. I hid my astonishment as I believed that the baby did not really have clothing on, but mere rags. She, however, was quite insistent on getting those "rags" back. Perhaps to wrap them around another baby. My heart felt heavy.

My Yasmine was not amongst those babies that came from the peasant women. She was a vision, a princess who came through the red-carpeted lobby of the hotel escorted by a nicely dressed young woman in her thirties. Yasmine was dressed in a very pretty red plaid dress and wore a pair of white Mary Janes three sizes too big but with clean, white socks. She was over two years old then and had a pretty short haircut and a beautiful heart-shaped face. Of course, I'm not being prejudiced whatsoever as her mom, but she *was* perfect! My best friend Helen from Hong Kong joined me in China for physical and emotional support. She took a photo of me when I first set my eyes on my baby on the red carpet. I don't think I had and would ever look that happy again in this lifetime.

Thank you, my Yasmine Ananda!

The following week the tour leader organized sight-seeing trips and banquets for the group as a gift for the Americans who had come all this way to China. The tours posed some problems as I couldn't use a stroller… even with the help from Helen. We visited ancient temples ten stories high and I honestly was looking for an elevator! What was I thinking? It was built in the fifteenth century or something. I carried all of her twenty-four pounds up the ten stories and I believe my back has never been the same since. It was a good first lesson in motherhood.

Sleeping was difficult as baby Yasmine refused to sleep. She was probably terrified. I tried everything, even lullabies, which were not my forte. Helen and I went shopping for baby formulas as a supplement to the meals we were served. But we weren't familiar with their brands nor could I read the Chinese. We picked up baby laxatives by mistake and fed them to Yasmine. Again, another lesson about the mistakes we can make in parenting. It could have been worse, I suppose.

Much like the end of my spiritual journey to the Dera, my adventures in raising Yasmine and her development to a beautiful and beloved young woman are both personal and could fill up another book. Just know that, as it is with any parent, there have been ups and downs and a life filled with love toward my child.

I do want to share one final amazing thing that happened during this time, something that truly brings my personal story around full circle… and it all happened because of Yasmine.

To say that it was tough as a working single mother would be a gross understatement. I had no clue about finding day care that would accept a non-potty trained three-year-old who didn't speak or know any English, or finding a reliable nanny, or how to appropriately childproof my house for a toddler. I was really overwhelmed, so imagine my relief when my mother and father agreed to leave their brownstone in Riverdale, New York and come live with me.

Not only did they finally get a chance to become grandparents at eighty, I actually got to live with both of my parents consistently for the first time in my life! It was truly a joyous time as I got to be both a child and a mother.

It was at this time that I also finally formed a connection with my father, a connection I had sought after for so long. He finally showed a sense of pride in what I was doing. I'll never forget the moment he looked at me with his secret smile and said, "I give you a PhD in life." It meant the world to me. Near the end, when he got too weak to walk about, Mom would ask me to come to his room. I would sometimes hesitate, and she would urge me on. "He just wants to look at you. You are so beautiful." I would stand by his bed and jabber on about something stupid, and he would just look at me and let me hold his hand. It had taken a lifetime, but in the end, he approved of me. I felt his love.

Being a mom is the toughest and the best part I was ever called upon to play. It is by far the biggest stroke on my water color canvas. I am grateful, and after all I've experienced, all the amazing times and opportunities I've had, I still get excited about what's to come, where the water color is going next.

⇒ EPILOGUE ⇐

THE WRITING OF MY STORY came about a long time ago when I was attending Los Angeles City College. It was the spring of 1972. I was a cinema major when they didn't really have much of a cinema department but just a few trailers with a few pieces of equipment. I had this wonderful professor, Tom Stempel, who I'm proud to say is still a friend. Years later, in 2006, I went back to his class as a guest speaker. After a question-and-answer time with the film students, a couple of them raised their hand to offer to write my story. Tom echoed their suggestion. "You should write your book!"

I didn't think about it again until about ten years ago when my parents passed. I became aware of the passing of time and that I needed and wanted to write about my strange and unique life experiences. I moved down to Cardiff-by-the-Sea to be near my then boyfriend and to raise Yasmine near a male figure. I wrote down bits and pieces on different notepads and scraps of paper, but mostly it was in my head.

I filled my head with the collage of my life. Meanwhile I bought books on writing, on autobiographies, and took a course or two in local community colleges. I enlisted the help of writer Frank Chin (*Year of the Dragon*) to help me with my backstory. When I moved back to L.A. four years later, I went to see dear, sweet Tom.

"Tom, I'm having trouble. It's not coming together for me."

"Irene, in order to write your memoir, you need to look backwards. You are still looking forwards."

"Shit, I'm still working like a mad woman and raising my teenager and trying to date a little…"

I knew he was right, and what he said resonated with me. Little by little, I organized the chapters of my life. I had to go to IMDB to remember what TV shows or films I did and when. When I saw it had over eighty titles, I was surprised. Some I remembered vividly and some I did not at all. I Googled myself and saw so many photos that I tried to identify from when and where they were taken. Then, chapter by chapter, I started writing as though I were doing a painting. Fast and furious, I could not stop, it pretty much wrote itself till I collapsed.

In many ways, this book has been the most frightening thing I have ever done, especially as I continue to fall in love, run amuck, living a teenager sort of life.

I remembered how when my dad took me to see his fortune teller as a young girl, when he said I would be a "jack of all trades, master of none," and that I was "restlessly creative."

He was right!

I've had an enormously colorful life. I grew up with all the parts I played. I played the daughter, the sweet daughter, the disobedient daughter. I was a secretary, a nurse, a doctor, a judge, a business woman, a villain. In my real life, I've been a dancer, an actor, a designer, an artist, an entrepreneur, a realtor, a builder, a wife, and a mother.

A master of none, that's for sure.

I imagine that I'm the one that laid down the first stroke of my water color, when perhaps I'm just the instrument of the mighty hand of the Higher Power that governs heaven, the stars, the galaxy, the water, earth, wind, and fire, and all the creatures small and large. I wake each morning, I yawn, I wiggle my finger and toes, and as long as all seem to be in working order, I am grateful for another day of living, giving, laughing, loving, crying, and dancing till dawn… and then closing my eyes and dreaming of where the next stroke leads me.

THE END

IRENE AND ME
by Pierre Patrick

Running an agency in Beverly Hills has its share of challenges in developing, choosing, and working with clients. Some are money makers, some are special and unique, some are award winners, and some are the ones you dream of.

Irene Tsu is on the top of that list.

I discovered Irene as a kid watching my beloved Doris Day in a film call *Caprice* on television in Canada. Irene was Doris's co-star and she captured my attention. I started seeing Irene on different series and more films on television, and I noticed quickly she was very special, sexy, and so believable as an actress in everything she did.

I got the pleasure of meeting her through a longtime friend of Irene's and an actress at our agency, Bunny Gibson, who started her career on *American Bandstand* and stars in the popular series *Bubbies Know Best*. Signing Irene as a client and helping with this book was a dream come true.

My assignment was talking to her friends and interviewing some key people that helped her career. Those interviews appear here.

I discovered through so many conversations the impact that Irene has had on so many lives that she touched with so many colors. In a conversation with Yoga Master Bikram Choudhury, he shared with me that back in the early seventies he opened the first Yoga Center in Beverly Hills and Irene was one of the first stars to join in a long list of celebrities. Not only did Irene join, but she conquered yoga and became one with its movements, its concentration, and its ultimate quest for love, peace, and self-fulfillment. Irene's life became more serene and focused and her career soared as an actress.

My personal discovery of her is that she represents joy, health, happiness, and commitment. In an industry full of bad choices made by so many, she decided to take a water color path through life for people who have admired her. Her friends (and certainly me) are so glad she did and is taking us there with this book.

NANCY KWAN

Pierre: How did you meet Irene?

Nancy: Irene and I met in New York in 1959 on the first national tour of the play, *The World of Suzie Wong*.

Pierre: You and Irene became roommates during the movie "Flower Drum Song." How was that experience, considering Irene was only sixteen years old and it was her first time away from home?

Nancy: Irene and I got on well as roommates. Irene was very popular with the boys and dated a lot.

Pierre: How did your friendship grow and develop throughout the years?

Nancy: Even with our busy schedules, we managed to stay in touch with each other through the years.

Pierre: Can you recall special moments, shared stories, and anecdotes between the two of you?

Nancy: I do remember being at her wedding… both times!

Pierre: You, Irene Tsu and Miyoshi Umeki were pioneering Asian women in American cinema. Were you aware of that impact at the time?

Nancy: I do recall someone telling me that the film *Flower Drum Song* was the first film made by a major studio (Universal) with an all Asian cast. And the film was a financial success and (we were) proud of it!

Pierre: How do you feel about the progress made by Asians in American television and cinema today, like "Fresh Off the Boat" and "Crazy Rich Asians?"

Nancy: I believe the awareness of Asians in film and television has improved through the years, but we still have a long way to go! I hope the younger generation will step up and bring their own creative ideas and images to the screen. What a joyous ride I took along with Irene in working on this manuscript.

FREDA PAYNE

Pierre: So you met Irene at the yoga place, and you became friends right away?

Freda: Well, you know what, I knew a lot of ladies who went to yoga and we became friends because we knew each other from yoga. And then Irene and Bikram got to be very close and sometimes Irene would have little parties, little get togethers at her home in Beverly Hills and we became friends. And we have the same lawyer as well, Stanley Handman. We have that in common and we became girlfriends like that.

Pierre: Cool, so tell me about those parties that Irene used to have?

Freda: They were parties, were primarily like it would be on behalf of Bikram. Maybe it was his birthday or something like that. This was before he got married and a lot of people from the class would be there. Different ladies, and maybe a few gentlemen as well. It would just be a nice party with food. I think her parents were still alive then and because I think they stayed with her as well. I think she had a guest house there. She had a nice place. It was just a nice party, you know, just a nice, quiet party with good food and music and then dancing and, you know, all that.

Pierre: Tell me about your thoughts on Irene? Tell me what type of person she is, how you would describe her?

Freda: Well, I know Irene is an actress as well, but of course real estate is mainly what she does. But she is also an actress. I like Irene because she is talented; she did yoga well the last time I saw her. She is a dedicated person and she is a loyal person and I don't think she is a phony at all. She is just a real down to earth person.

Pierre: *So, basically, throughout the years you stayed in touch and invited each other to different things and that kind of a thing?*

Freda: Yeah, sure, she supports me, and I support her.

DON MURRAY

Pierre: *Tell me about Hollywood and New York when you were growing up?*

Don: Well, I was born in Hollywood, but actually grew up in Long Island. My dad had been a singer and dancer on Broadway. When movies started having sound, suddenly all of the musical and comedy performers on Broadway were very much on demand in Hollywood. I happened to be born when my dad was working in motion pictures. When I was one-year old, we moved to Long Island, just outside New York City, and that's where I was raised. I moved into New York City in 1948 and lived there until 1952. I was on Broadway performing in *The Skin of Our Teeth* and Joshua Logan happened to see me in that. He got the idea that he wanted me to be Marilyn Monroe's cowboy lover in the movie *Bus Stop*. He screen-tested me for that and chose me for the part. So began my film career in 1956. That was my biggest break as far as movies go.

Pierre: *So doing your first big film, "Bus Stop," and getting an Oscar nomination right off the bat... that's pretty amazing!*

Don: Yeah, that was pretty surprising! [Laughs] I never expected anything like that.

Pierre: *How was it working with Marilyn Monroe?*

Don: Number one is that, as reported, she was difficult to work with in the sense that she was always late and she had a hard time remembering her lines. So, we had to shoot in small pieces. Stop and go, stop and go. I was very seldom able to get a sense of flow when doing a scene. That made her difficult to work with. But she was not a mean person or anything like that. She was amazingly insecure. As a matter a fact, she was so nervous about acting that she would break out in a rash and have to be dabbed with a white cream to cover the rash.

Pierre: *In that movie you work with the great director, Joshua Logan. Tell us about that?*

Don: Absolutely. I give him the credit for my performance because he was the one that told me how to play the role. I would just listen to him.

Pierre: *Were there any other directors that had a major impact on you?*

Don: I think I learned more from Joshua Logan than anyone else. In second place would be Fred Zinnemann.

Pierre: *After working with Joshua Logan and many other great directors you became a director yourself and directed Irene Tsu in "Damien's Island."*

Don: Yeah, that's right.

Pierre: *This film combines difficult subjects—leprosy and Hawaii, which is certainly seen as paradise for so many people. What made you want to do this project?*

Don: Well, I was fascinated by the priest that went and worked with lepers and then caught leprosy himself, Father Damien.

Pierre: *How was Irene Tsu selected for this film?*

Don: I selected Irene because, well, first she was very beautiful and I wanted someone that was very physically beautiful because it added to the tragedy of the sickness growing on her. She was very gracious about being turned from this very beautiful woman into someone who was obviously dying of leprosy. It was a real acting job, a difficult one to do. She did it very, very well and allowed this physical deterioration to take hold of her.

Pierre: *So, you had seen her before, either in film or television? Or, how did you discover her?*

Don: Well, I was directed by her husband in a film called *Deadly Hero*. That's how I met her.

Pierre: *How was Irene to work with?*

Don: She was just wonderful to work with! I didn't really have to tell her how to create her emotions or anything like that. She had all of this emotional fire that was always something she was able to bring out in the film. She was just a joy to work with, really.

Pierre: *Did you ever work on anything else together?*

Don: No, but we've kept a friendship for all these years.

Pierre: *What are your overall thoughts on Irene?*

Don: I think she is just a dedicated artist which made it so nice to work with her. She was a big part of why the film turned out so good.

Pierre: *So you were happy with how the film turned out?*

Don: Yes, I was very pleased with how it turned out. We had trouble with the Catholic Church. They took exception to the scene where Father Damien is asleep and the young leper girl crawls into bed with him. He gets out of the bed because he doesn't want [the disease]. Then the girl goes out and commits suicide. That's something that upset some people. I remember we had a screening with a bunch of nuns there and as soon as the girl crawled into bed with him all of the nuns got up and left! [Laughs] So we did have that problem.

Pierre: *That's amazing! But you kept the film intact and didn't edit anything out?*

Don: I didn't change anything. We weren't doing something sensationalist, we were trying to show what actually happened with Damien.

Pierre: *That's great! Well thank you so much for your time, this will add a great new dimension to the book.*

Don: Please give my warm regards to Irene, I remember her very fondly.

DIAHN MCGRATH

Pierre: *Tell me about your first meeting with Irene?*

Diahn: It was 1969 on a Sunday afternoon. Henry Miller struck up a conversation with me, and the next thing I know, he asked me if I would like to come to dinner with him across the street. "I want you to meet my friend Irene Tsu," and I said, "Fine." That was the beginning of a wonderful friendship. I liked her right away. She is a hard person not to like.

Pierre: *Diahn, tell me a fun anecdote, something fun that happened?*

Diahn: My wedding. When I was marrying my husband, I didn't plan on having a big wedding. I invited friends, I had a dress, I had ordered a wedding cake, and I had a chef come and prepare food for thirty people. Irene came an hour before it started. We had planned on having the wedding in the garden. When Irene came in, she said, "Where's the flowers?" I said, "I don't have any flowers." Irene said, "It's a wedding, you have to have flowers." She went all over the property and picked up any wild flower she could find. She made these little bouquets, and hung them all over the top of the garden, and on the sides where the minister stood. She said, "You just can't have a wedding with no flowers at all." It was beautiful.

Pierre: *You made a film together?*

Diahn: Yes, Irene and I made the film in 1975, *Deadly Heroes*, directed by Ivan Nagy. We were very much part of the planning and the concept. I felt that the director really liked Irene. Irene played a backstage seamstress. She had a very nice little scene where she sewed one of the performers into her wardrobe. This was the only time we have ever worked together and we have never lost touch. She's like a soulmate. We both took different directions in life. My life now revolves around the law. Irene's life was always about acting, art, designing clothes, yoga, etc. Irene is now also a successful real estate agent, which shows her eye for business. My life took a different direction. I want to stretch the fact that Irene was always good at design. As a matter of fact, I still have some of her sweaters that she created for me. They are so comfortable and fashionable.

Pierre: *Can you tell me about any of Irene's performances that you liked? Or can you describe the way she is as an actress?*

Diahn: She is like a butterfly in all of her performances. One of my favorite films is *The Green Berets,* starring John Wayne.

Pierre: *Tell me about Irene as a person and a friend?*

Diahn: One thing that is very important about Irene is her great sense of humor. She makes me laugh all the time. I was very supportive of Irene's adoption. It shows great heart to do something like that. Not everyone can make that kind of commitment and put out that kind of love. You become selfless to adopt a child, and really build a life for it. Irene has always been able to be independent and do what she has wanted to do. She has been able to do this without a team of people. It takes a great amount of courage and I admire her for it. Of course, friendship is very important to her. If you're a friend of Irene, you are a friend for life. The movie that I did with Irene was the last film I made. I quickly decided to change my life around. I tried designing, I tried art, but becoming an attorney really inspired me, and kept me financially secure, happy, and it became extremely rewarding to me. Irene has always been supportive in all of my life changes, and that's why I truly consider her a great friend.

KATHY GARVER

*In a very special episode of "Family Affair" called "Eastward Ho" (written by Edmund Beloin, Henry Garson and Edmund L. Hartman), Bill Davis offers Ming Lee (Irene Tsu) to stay in their penthouse. Ming Lee is engaged in an arranged marriage to Bill's friend Eng Ho (Benson Fong). Cissy, Uncle Bill's niece (Kathy Garver), becomes her best friend her and she and her boy-

friend Gregg offer to take Ming Lee out for the evening. She meets someone and refuses to marry Eng Ho.

Pierre: *How did Benson Fong who was destined to marry Irene Tsu become an important character on "Family Affair?"*

Kathy: Well, our creator, producer, writer, Edmund Hartmann, has quite a fondness for the Asian culture. He and Benson were good friends and, as a matter of fact, Mr. Hartman's home was all done in Asian motif. He just had this wonderful connection with the culture and with Benson; and had worked with Benson a lot. Benson was also in *My Three Sons* and played Irene's grandfather in that series. That was all produced by the same company (Don Fedderson Company); he especially had this fondness in his heart for Asian culture. Such wonderful actors were Benson and Irene. She had lots of subtleties. She started on *Family Affair* as a bright young girl to becoming something very dramatic with her character. There was this whole other dimension to her and depth that was very compelling.

Pierre: *There weren't that many Asian actors working at that time and Irene broke several barriers.*

Kathy: I think she did, too. Because as you say there were not a lot of Asian actors doing things. They were standouts and very appealing.

Pierre: *In the "Eastward Ho" episode you came to the defense of Irene fighting Uncle Bill to give her the freedom to fall in love, stay in America, and marry who she would eventually choose.*

Kathy: The episode shows true love is true love and you shouldn't be forced into something because somebody wants you to do it. I think that was somewhat of a tendency of Uncle Bill because he would give me enough rope to hang myself just before the noose tightened; either I would come to the rescue or he would come to the rescue. Their freedom that was given to make decisions, and I think that was the theme from *Family Affair*, the relationships that Uncle Bill would have with the kids and this would expand with guests involve in our lives.

Pierre: *Did you ever see Irene after?*

Kathy: I had the pleasure of seeing Irene at different Hollywood events throughout the years. She was always gracious and wonderful.

FRED ROOS

I can't remember when and where I first met Irene. Was it in the sixties or seventies? She would probably remember. I just know that she was a terrific young actress who worked all the time...and she seemed to know everyone. She was always fun to talk to.

She also had a good eye for art and artists. Was it Claes Oldenberg that was a friend of hers? If I'm right, she also owned a great three-dimensional "painting" by him. If I remember right, there was a car in the work. Does she still have it? Must be worth a lot.

She also had a good sense of design and business, and I remember her fashion business...constant trips to Hong Kong and the Philippines to get the clothing made. I believe she introduced me to people in Hong Kong who were helpful to me on my trips there.

I did offer her to play the wife of Marlon Brando in *Apocalypse Now*. It was really a tiny part but I thought perhaps she would want to do it.

This is not much, but I don't have one of those memories that can remember every incident of my life. I'm sure that if Irene and I were sitting together, she would jog my memory. However, it seems like I've known her for many decades.

JEFF BRIDGES

My specific memories of my time with Irene in Hong Kong making *The Yin and Yang of Mr. Go* are a bit hazy; it all happened almost fifty years ago.

I do remember sharing with her the excitement of working with James Mason and Burgess Meredith.

I remember fondly us exploring Hong Kong together, and getting to know each other playing sweethearts in the film. My memories of our time together are ones of joy and excitement.

DORIS DAY

In a previous interview, conducted by Pierre Patrick for BearManor Media, Doris talked about working on her film "Caprice" with Irene Tsu. Here for the first time is an excerpt from that interview:

Doris Day revealed in her book, *Doris Day: Her Own Story* that she was very displeased in making *Caprice* as soon as she saw the script, which was presented to her by her husband, agent and manager, Martin Melcher. However, she was forced into it, and made the best of it. The first thing Doris did was switch the leads in the script. She became the spy who uncovers drug trafficking in cosmetics.

Pierre: *Did you know that "Caprice" is becoming a cult film? There was a major screening of it at UCLA recently.*

Doris: Oh no, *Caprice!* You know that Richard Harris and I would get on set in the morning and didn't know what was going on in the story. I loved working with the cast, Richard Harris, Ray Watson, Edward Mulhare, and lovely Irene Tsu. I got to know her a little bit because her chauffeur would drive us back and forth to Beverly Hills every day. Frank Tashlin was our director, who I had just worked with on *The Glass Bottom Boat*, and I loved him. He had an inane sense for comedy. *The Glass Bottom Boat* is one of those movies that I watched the most in Carmel, and I always laugh. Another plus was our costume designer, Ray Aghayan. He designed the coolest fashions for me and Irene, that were very mod, fitting the sixties period.

Pierre: *"Caprice" is becoming quite an intellectual film, a little bit like Quentin Tarantino's "Pulp Fiction."*

Doris: That is why Richard and I couldn't understand the movie!

www.ingramcontent.com/pod-product-compliance
Lightning Source LLC
Chambersburg PA
CBHW061936220426